Christy,
Good work in your
writing!

Fiction as Research Practice

Developing Qualitative Inquiry

Series Editor: Janice M. Morse
University of Utah

Books in the **Developing Qualitative Inquiry** series, written by leaders in qualitative inquiry, will address important topics in qualitative methods. Targeted to a broad multi-disciplinary readership, the books are intended for mid-level/advanced researchers and advanced students. The series will forward the field of qualitative inquiry by describing new methods, or developing particular aspects of established methods.

Titles in this series:

1. *Autoethnography as Method*, Heewon Chang
2. *Interpretive Description*, Sally Thorne
3. *Developing Grounded Theory: The Second Generation*, Janice M. Morse, Phyllis Noerager Stern, Juliet M. Corbin, Barbara Bowers, Kathy C. Charmaz, and Adele E. Clarke
4. *Mixed Method Design: Principles and Procedures*, Janice M. Morse and Linda Niehaus
5. *Playbuilding as Qualitative Research: A Participatory Arts-Based Approach*, Joe Norris
6. *Poetry as Method: Reporting Research through Verse*, Sandra L. Faulkner
7. *Duoethnography: Dialogic Methods for Social, Health, and Educational Research*, Joe Norris, Richard D. Sawyer, Darren E. Lund, editors
8. *Collaborative Autoethnography*, Heewon Chang, Faith Wambura Ngunjiri, and Kathy-Ann C. Hernandez
9. *Engaging in Narrative Inquiry*, D. Jean Clandinin
10. *Participatory Visual and Digital Methods*, Aline Gubrium and Krista Harper
11. *Fiction as Research Practice*, Patricia Leavy
12. *Applied Ethnography: Guidelines for Field Research*, Pertti J. Pelto

Fiction as Research Practice

Short Stories, Novellas, and Novels

Patricia Leavy

Walnut Creek, California

LEFT COAST PRESS, INC.
1630 North Main Street, #400
Walnut Creek, CA 94596
www.LCoastPress.com

ISBN 978-1-61132-153-1 hardback
ISBN 978-1-61132-154-8 paperback
ISBN 978-1-61132-707-6 consumer eBook

Library of Congress Cataloging-in-Publication Data:

Leavy, Patricia, 1975-
Fiction as research practice : short stories, novellas, and novels / Patricia Leavy.
p. cm. — (Developing Qualitative Inquiry; 11)
Includes bibliographical references and index.
ISBN 978-1-61132-153-1 (hardback : alk. paper) — ISBN 978-1-61132-154-8 (pbk. : alk. paper) — ISBN 978-1-61132-707-6 (consumer eBook)
1. Literature—Research—Methodology. 2. Qualitative research—Methodology. 3. Fiction—Social aspects. I. Title.
PN73.L43 2013
807′.2—dc23
2012050528

Printed in the United States of America

∞™ The paper used in this publication meets the minimum requirements of American National Standard for Information Sciences—Permanence of Paper for Printed Library Materials, ANSI/NISO Z39.48–1992.

Contents

Preface

> Although I live my professional life in the halls of the academy, seeking to both learn and communicate truth, or at least truths, it is in the world of the imaginary I have most closely experienced the real.
>
> —Ulrich Teucher, May 21, 2011, ICQI Conference

My sabbatical started, I suppose, in a predictable way. After quickly abandoning my long-held plans to organize my disorganized home and instead spending several days lounging about and catching up on the world of daytime television, I was ready to do *something*; something productive. My book *Method Meets Art: Arts-Based Research Practice* (2009a) had recently come out, and with my sabbatical came an opportunity to try and help promote the book; an opportunity the rigors of my normally overbooked life had never before afforded me. I put my undiagnosed OCD skills into service of my book promotion–project by searching the web for arts-based researchers, art education researchers, and even clerks of local art museum bookstores. I soon had a robust Excel file full of potential contacts. Next, I drafted several pitch letters announcing the release of my book. Soon I was cutting and pasting letters, names, and email addresses. At first I felt glad to be using my time so "productively," particularly in service of a book I deeply believed in, but soon my feeling of pride gave way to utter boredom. I couldn't spend my days merely hitting the send button. My creative juices were stirring and needed an outlet. So I took a break from self-promotion for some self-expression.

Fiction as Research Practice: Short Stories, Novellas, and Novels, by Patricia Leavy, 7–13.

Without an agenda or deadline I was free to explore, and my short-lived bout of clerical work had heightened my need for creativity. I opened a new Word document and prepared for some fun. I thought perhaps I'd write a little poem. Although I am not a skilled poet, I had written many poems before, some research-driven and others pure fancy. But no poem came; not even the seeds of a poem. In need of inspiration, I grabbed one of my manila folders filled with "notes" and "ideas" scribbled down over the years as I worked on various projects about women's identities—some "insights" jotted down on napkins or the back of business cards. I had been writing a lot of poetry based on my interviews with young women about their romantic lives, sexual identities, interactions with the men and women in their lives, body image issues, and their overall sense of self. Perhaps my notes would provide a doorway into a poem. No such luck. Although I tried to string a few lyrical words together in hopes of backdooring my way into writing a poem, it was not to be.

Not eager to return to the fairly mindless task of cutting, pasting, and hitting send, I had another idea: I would write a short story. I had wanted to do this for years but always managed to fill my calendar with other tasks that appeared to make the world of fiction a faraway vacation destination I simply could not travel to. I thought for a moment, wondering what to write about. As the writer's block filled the space between the computer screen and me, my subject matter became self-evident. I would write about a writer, but not just any writer, one who was failing. Then I remembered something an old flame had once told me about a writing group he was in. And so I typed:

> "'Casey bombed into town with her daily organizer.' It's the worst first line I've ever heard? I mean, you're left with this organizer, just sitting there, for no reason. You never mention something so irrelevant right in the beginning. It's awful. Nowadays everyone thinks they can write. There are no real writers anymore," he said, flinging the manuscript on Prilly's desk. (Leavy 2011b, 3)

At first I thought my little story was about a writer being rejected, but by the end of the first page I realized the editor rejecting the manuscript was my main character, my unconventional and at times unlikeable heroine—Prilly Greene. (A lot of readers have since asked me about Prilly's name. Actually, it is tied to the promotion emails I had been sending. I sent several emails to faculty at Leslie University—one to Dr. Sanville, whom I have never met. Her return email was signed, Prilly.)

Suddenly my folder of scattered "notes" and "ideas" about the interviews I had been conducting for years started to slip in. I kept writing.

That night my boyfriend, Mark (now my husband), asked: "What did you do today?"

"I wrote," I replied.

"What did you write?" he queried.

"Actually, I don't know. It's fiction, I think. I sat down to try and write a short story, but it's already ten single-spaced pages and I haven't even introduced all of the characters."

"Why don't you email it to me and I'll read it during my lunch break tomorrow?"

"Ok," I said.

The next morning I emailed it to him, and that afternoon he responded: "You should write a novel!!!" In that moment I knew two things: I was going to marry this man and I was going to write a novel.

This is how my novel *Low-Fat Love* began, and how I journeyed from being a proponent of arts-based research to becoming an a/r/tographical novelist or fiction-based researcher. I knew I would marry Mark at the moment he encouraged me to write the novel because his response gave me a feeling of calm certainty. Here was a person who wanted me to become the best version of myself. He showed me unconditional support and that he wanted me to grow—he was a real partner. My novel, *Low-Fat Love*, would be about just the opposite. I took everything I had learned in my personal life and through a decade of interview research and teaching about gender, self-esteem, the psychology of unhealthy relationships, how women's identities can develop in the context of male figures, and the toxicity of women's popular culture, and I wove together a story that I hoped would be accessible to women and men of all ages and backgrounds. When readers tell me how they feel frustrated reading about Prilly's insecurities and how she kept making the same mistakes, I respond that she represents all of the students, interviewees, and friends over the years who I desperately wanted to shake and say, what are you doing?

I consider the book the ultimate blurring of my artist-researcher-teacher identities because it represents all I have learned over the years through those overlapping roles, as well as many life experiences that are inseparable from how I think about and act in the world. Frankly, the book also communicates the messages I most want to impart on the young men and women I meet through teaching and research. I learned through writing the book that I was better able to get at, illuminate, and express "the real"—that which is truthful—than I had ever been able to do in any other form. Moreover, I was able to produce an accessible and hopefully enjoyable experience for diverse readers while remaining truthful. I have come to learn the deep value of fiction for being truthful, for giving shape to our research, and as a highly effective pedagogical tool.

I have also learned how pleasurable our work can be—something I believed when I began in my chosen field but perhaps lost along the way. I have never had more fun in my life than when writing *Low-Fat Love*. I enjoyed it so much that an entire day would pass with me hunched over the computer forgetting to eat or even shower. Each day I was eager to enter the worlds of the characters I had created, to see what they would do, if they would learn from their mistakes and confront their shortcomings. I also felt free of the constraints I experienced in my roles of professor and interviewer (in which there is a limit to the "life advice" you can dispense). Since we spend so much time in our lives doing our work—our work becoming integral to our lives—we should do the work we love, that which makes us feel fully alive. It is in this way that we have hope of impacting others. Here I take a cue from feminist musician Tori Amos, who said: "When you stop putting yourself on the line, and you don't touch your own heart, how do you expect to touch other people?"

Through writing the book, and later experiencing the joy of talking with some of those who have read it, I have learned a lot about the value of fiction in work and life. I hope to communicate what I have learned in the pages that follow.

The Organization of This Book

This book is divided into three parts. Part I is organized around four central questions, each of which is addressed in a separate chapter: What is the history of merging fiction and research? What are the strengths of fiction-based research practice? How do you use fiction as a research practice, and what does fiction-based research look like? And finally, how do you judge, evaluate, or assess fiction-based research?

Part II presents exemplars of fiction-based research. The examples include work done in different genres of fiction: short stories, novellas, and novels. The short stories are presented in their entirety, whereas in the case of the novella and novels, selected chapters have been chosen. Each piece includes an introduction and an afterward crafted for inclusion in this book. I asked each author to write an introduction addressing some combination of the following: how their teaching and/or research informed the piece, why they turned to fiction, and what they attempted to accomplish. Each story is followed by a brief commentary I have written detailing why the piece is an exemplar and how it meets the criteria detailed in chapter 4.

Part III considers fiction as a pedagogical tool. This discussion is situated in the scholarship on teaching and learning as well as in literary neuroscience. This section includes original examples, written exclusively for this book, of how professors use fiction as a pedagogical tool. The appendices include exercises for novices interested in learning how to write fiction-based research, tips for getting your work published, and suggested resources.

Additional Note

As I began to write this book, I had some difficulty labeling the research activity I am describing. For example, I considered using the term "research-informed fiction"; however, I decided that ultimately all fiction is, to some extent, informed by research. That term did not distinguish fiction per se from fiction as a research practice. Without detailing all of the terminology I considered, I want to point out and explain my use of the term "fiction-based research." I am a proponent of arts-based research (ABR) and have written extensively in that area. I decided to take that well-established term and adapt it to denote the practice reviewed in this book. I am sure that other people have used or will use a different terminology, and I don't think it's worth getting too hung up on these terms (for example, a review of the literature on ABR reveals that dozens of different terms have been used, which may not be particularly helpful as we try to grow a field). I think the term fiction-based research makes sense because in some cases the act of writing the fiction is the act of inquiry, whereas in others data are collected in traditional ways and then written up using the techniques of fiction. In both cases, the result is fiction-based.

It is also important to note that fiction-based research is an emerging field, and it is impossible to present a full historical and theoretical review of it. There are other theorists, schools of thought, and genres of writing that could have been covered in this book. I had to make choices. Further, the discussion of research design and evaluation is not intended to be exhaustive or prescriptive. Nevertheless, I hope this book will serve as a useful introduction to the practice of fiction-based research.

Acknowledgments

In the work toward this book I greatly appreciated the support of a number of people. First and foremost, thank you Mitch Allen, publisher extraordinaire. Mitch, I am so grateful you had the idea for this book and the faith that I was the person to write it. Your willingness to innovate has changed the field and your support of my work has been tremendous. Thank you! Thank you Jan Morse for including my project in your series and for your enthusiasm and guidance. I am grateful to the entire Left Coast team—such a pleasure to work with you all. In particular, thank you Stefania De Petris and Ryan Harris. Thank you to the contributors who shared their fictional writing and those who offered their teaching strategies. My hat is off to all of you—I am so impressed with how you are innovating. Thank you for sharing your work with others. A huge shout-out to the world's best research assistant, Shalen Lowell! I couldn't have done this without your help. Thank you to Jennifer Spanier for preparing the index. I am so grateful to my Kennebunk writing group—David, Mort, Ning, Celine, and Alan—and a very special thank you to my weekly writing buddy, the extraordinarily talented Celine Boyle. Tori Amos, my musical guide: the work you have done merging classical and pop has been a driving force in how I understand the fiction and nonfiction continuum. You're right—there isn't a great divide between The Beatles and Bach when they are used to heal, illuminate, and connect. This is the time for me to publicly thank my high-school English teacher, Mr. Shuman, without whom I may not be a writer. I am truly grateful for all that you taught me, your kindness, and your support. Thank you to the best in-laws I could ever hope for, Carolyn and Charles Robins. Finally, thank you to Madeline and Mark. You have both changed your lives so that I can live mine as a writer and I am so grateful. It's a lot easier to try and be brave when you have someplace soft to fall. Mark, this is dedicated to you with love.

Part I

Fiction as Research Practice

Chapter 1
Blurred Genres: The Intertwining of Fiction and Nonfiction

Humanity has but one product, and that is fiction.
—Annie Dillard, *Living by Fiction*

Paige went to the lobby to check the mail for the third time that morning. She had already checked both before and after her daily run, although she knew it was too early. Always rational, she justified this irrational behavior by lamenting that Saturday deliveries were unpredictable, and since the wait from Saturday to Monday was the worst she might as well check, and possibly calm herself. As she turned the tiny key and lifted the icy metal latch she wondered how much longer she could endure this. Still nothing. She waved at Frank, the doorman, and scurried back into her elevator eager to return to the warmth of her home. Although already into April, the last blizzard had blanketed New York with a coldness that had yet to pass. Her slim frame couldn't let go of the chill. She rubbed her hands together wondering if her trembling was from the cold, anxiety, or guilt. "What kind of mother am I?" played over and over in her mind.

Fiction as Research Practice: Short Stories, Novellas, and Novels, by Patricia Leavy, 17–36. Extract from *American Circumstance*, forthcoming 2013, published with permission from Sense Publishers, Rotterdam, The Netherlands.

CHAPTER 1

Not wanting to keep her friend Gwen waiting, she ran upstairs, slipped on her boots, and darted into her bathroom removing a hair tie from a drawer. She took her brush and pulled her long dark auburn hair tightly into a high ponytail, making certain to smooth any flyaway strands. She uncharacteristically indulged for a moment, searching the reflection for someone familiar. As she looked in the large bathroom mirror perfecting her hair, she wondered where she had disappeared to. Then, remembering she was meeting Gwen, she shook her head and lunged back into her routine. She grabbed her workout bag and scoured her walk-in closet for her handbag, until she remembered leaving it by the front door to save time. She hurried downstairs, threw the handbag into her workout bag, and put on her Burberry coat. She cinched the belt tightly as if to confirm that she was in fact there. In an effort to hide in public she grabbed a pair of oversized black Chanel sunglasses from her mail table, slipped them on, and left.

Upon arrival at the health club, she made a beeline to the locker room whizzing past Mollie Johnston, whom she hadn't seen in years. As she brushed past on route to her locker, Mollie yelled after her, "Paige? Paige Michaels, is that you?"

Paige turned around too flustered to recognize the woman at first. She was beaming with an out-of-place friendliness. Her round face and dark blonde curls seemed familiar, but the fullness of her face suggested she was overweight and not pumped up with Botox, so Paige couldn't quite place her.

"It's me, Mollie Johnston! Well, Mollie Cooper back then, but now..."

As recognition set in, Paige interrupted with "Oh, oh hi Mollie," catching her breath and slowly backtracking towards the jolly woman.

"Well, you're practically incognito, aren't you?" Mollie remarked with a bright smile.

Paige took off her sunglasses and leaned in to peck Mollie on the cheek. "I'm so sorry. I'm running late for my squash game... Wow, it has been ages," Paige continued, finally in control of her breathing.

"Since college. Well, you look just wonderful, put together as ever. Still just perfect. Perfect Paige just as always. I'm jealous!"

she said as she gave Paige the once over. "I've been on the wait-list for this place for ages. I'm so glad to see a friendly face," Mollie continued.

"It's nice to see you too," Paige replied in a concerted effort to appear friendly. She could see that Mollie meant well, but she wasn't in the mood to smile through awkwardly worded compliments. "So you live in the city now?" she continued out of courtesy.

"Yes, yes, just about fifteen blocks from here. My husband, you remember Paul?" Paige smiled ever so slightly in confirmation and Mollie continued, "Paul's at a big firm in Midtown and the boys started college last year, one is at Bates and the other at Colby, so I have a lot more time to myself—we have twin boys; gosh, did I even tell you that?" Without waiting for a reply Mollie continued, "Anyway, you can see why I was so desperate for a space to open here! So, what about you? Don't tell me, you're blissfully happy with Spencer of course—what about kids, do you have any kids?"

"Mollie, I don't mean to be rude but I'm terribly late for my match. It's wonderful seeing you. Let's catch up another time," Paige said, already backing away.

"Oh gosh, I didn't mean to hold you up," Mollie replied in a jovial tone. Paige was already walking away but put her hand up in a backward wave as Mollie hollered, "Would love to get together."

With her back to Mollie and several yards away, Paige nodded, one perfect loose curl of her high ponytail bouncing up and down as she continued to walk away.

After changing into her all-whites and restocking her locker with a stack of freshly pressed clothes, she met Gwen who was already warming up on the court. As Paige opened the glass door, the always glamorous Gwen turned around and said, "I can't believe I finally beat you here. It only took three years. Do you want to warm up?"

"I was cornered in the locker room. Let's go, your serve."

The preceding excerpt is the opening of my second novel, *American Circumstance* (forthcoming). This novel explores two primary themes: appearance versus reality (how people's lives look to others versus how they are experienced) and the complex ways that social class shapes people's identities. These are topics that can be difficult to approach—social class and economics, and the personal ways they impact people's lives, are challenging to address in nonfiction writing or lecture formats because they are so intimate, are linked to issues of status and pride, and are highly politicized. The fictional format offers a chance to observe these complex issues in all their nuances and to invite diverse readers into the text in a pleasurable way.

Fiction can draw us in, giving us access to new yet familiar worlds in which we might meet strangers or through which we might reflect on our own lives. Through the pleasure, and at times the pain, of confronting emotionally charged truths, the process of reading fiction can be transformative, as is the process of writing it. *Fiction is engaged.*

Fiction is both a form of writing and a way of reading (Cohn 2000). Fiction grants us an imaginary entry into what is otherwise inaccessible. The practice of writing and reading fiction allows us to access imaginary or possible worlds, to reexamine the worlds we live in, and to enter into the psychological processes that motivate people and the social worlds that shape them. In short, engaging with fiction in our research practice creates innumerable possibilities.

There is a robust and complex history of merging fiction and research (or fiction and nonfiction). This history could be approached and summarized in a number of ways. I come into this field from the qualitative and arts-based research paradigms, so I use those practices as my point of departure.

Qualitative Social Research

Using fiction as a social research practice is a natural extension of what many researchers and writers have long been doing. The work of the researcher and of the novelist aren't as disparate as some may claim. On the contrary, there has always been a winding road between research practice and the writing of fiction (Franklin 2011). Stephen Banks (2008, 155–56) writes that "the zone between the practices of fiction writers and non-fiction writers is blurry," because fiction "is only more or less 'fictional.'" There is a historical interplay, or intentional border crossing, between "fiction" and "nonfiction," as I discuss below with regard to blurred genres such as historical fiction and creative nonfiction.

Fiction writers conduct extensive research to achieve verisimilitude, similarly to social scientists (Banks 2008; Berger 1977). Verisimilitude refers to the creation of a realistic, authentic, and life-like portrayal, and it is the goal of both fiction and established social science practices like ethnography. Fiction writers and qualitative researchers both seek to build believable representations of existing or possible worlds (Visweswaran 1994, 1) and to truthfully or authentically portray human experience. It is not as if fiction writers *created* fantasies and researchers *recorded* facts. The material writers use in fiction comes from real life and genuine human experience. Similarly, qualitative researchers very much shape every aspect of their investigation, imbuing it with meaning and marking it with their fingerprint.

Now, innovative researchers propelled by changes in the qualitative paradigm and arts-based researchers are harnessing the unique capabilities of fiction as a means of engaging in effective and publicly accessible research practice. In order to understand fiction-based research, it is important to ground the conversation in a discussion of the nature of social research and knowledge-building practices, including qualitative and arts-based research. Fiction, more than any other research practice, directly challenges the fact/fiction dichotomy and forces us to renegotiate the boundaries between the two. Understandably, this makes some uncomfortable; however, I choose to focus this book on how fiction has and can be used in research, not on the critiques.[1]

Social research is a process aimed at knowledge-building and meaning-making; at accessing, expressing, and negotiating truths and then effectively communicating those "truths" to relevant audiences. This basic premise is important to bear in mind, since I suggest that when we consider fiction-based research practice the general goals of accessing and effectively communicating those truths is the backdrop of any project.

Characterized as a craft, qualitative research aims at generating deep understanding, unpacking meanings, revealing social processes, and, above all, illuminating human experience. Qualitative research values sensory knowledge and experience, multiple meanings, and subjectivity in the research process. In recent years many qualitative practitioners have reconceptualized the researcher's role in ethnographic studies and the way to best represent that research. The sharp rise in autoethnography and narrative inquiry (Leavy 2009a), as well as the impact of critical area studies such as women's studies (Leavy 2011a), have normalized the active presence of the researcher in his or her writing. Reflexive writing is increasingly common, which Elizabeth de Freitas (2007, 1) defines as writing that "traces the presence of the author in/through the text."

Pushes toward public scholarship have also changed how many view their practice. The academy has long been plagued by criticisms that researchers are in their "ivory towers," shut off from reality and disconnected from the communities in which they are enmeshed. Influenced by a confluence of factors—an engaged public (fueled by social media), the effects of the social justice movements on the academy, developments in community-based research and service-leaning, and changes in technology and publishing that allow for the widespread sharing of knowledge—there is a strong movement toward increasing public scholarship (Leavy 2011a). Researchers across the academy, but particularly in the qualitative community, are seeking new ways of making their work more accessible. Arts-based research is accordingly gaining in popularity.

Arts-Based Research (ABR)

Arts-based research (ABR) emerged between the 1970s and the 1990s,[2] and now constitutes a significant methodological genre (Sinner et al. 2006).[3] This practice developed out of a convergence of factors,[4] and has been further propelled by technological advances in digital imaging, the Internet, Photoshop, sound files, and so forth. As I noted in my earlier work (2009a, 2011a), arts-based research has developed within a transdisciplinary methodological context involving the crossing of disciplinary borders as well as cross-disciplinary collaborations. Arts-based research practices are a set of methodological tools that adapt the tenets of the creative arts and can be used during all phases of social research (Leavy 2009a). Genres of ABR include but are not limited to: poetry, music, theatrical scripts, theatrical or dance performances, visual art, and film, as well as the genres of fiction on which this book will focus—novels, novellas, and short stories.

Pioneers in the field of art education Tom Barone and Elliot Eisner (1997, 214) note seven features of ABR:

1. The creation of virtual reality
2. The presence of ambiguity
3. The use of expressive language
4. The use of capitalized and vernacular language
5. The promotion of empathy
6. The personal signature of the researcher/writer
7. The presence of aesthetic form

For social researchers the appeal of the arts is in their ability to transform consciousness, refine the senses, promote autonomy, raise awareness, express the complex feeling-based aspects of social life (Eisner 2002, 10–19), jar us into seeing and thinking differently, illuminate the complexity and sometimes paradox of lived experience, and to build empathy and resonance. Arts-based research draws on the oppositional, subversive, transformational, and otherwise resistive capabilities of the arts (Leavy 2009a). Suzanne Thomas (2001, 274) writes: "Art as inquiry has the power to evoke, to inspire, to spark the emotions, to awaken visions and imaginings, and to transport others to new worlds." When trying to understand the power of the arts in social research, it is important to remember our general objective. As Ardra Cole and J. Gary Knowles (2001, 211) note, "researchers aim to portray lives." They suggest much of our work can be conceptualized as *life history research*—research that links individuals' personal lives and relationships to the larger contexts in which they unfold—and this practice involves drawing on artistic practice, because imagination and metaphor are needed in order to portray lives sensitively. Cole and Knowles (ibid., 215–17) further delineate seven elements of arts-informed life history research, which ultimately come to bear on fiction-based research:

1. Intentionality (intellectual and moral purpose)
2. Researcher's presence (signature or fingerprint)
3. Methodological commitment
4. Holistic quality (authenticity, sincerity, truthfulness)
5. Aesthetic form (aesthetic appeal and adherence to genre conventions)

6. Knowledge claims
7. Contributions (theoretical, practical, transformative)

If we are attempting to understand and illuminate people's lives, then we need to make our research accessible to the many, not the few. Dorinne Kondo and Kirin Narayan make this point well drawing on the power of metaphor: "Ethnographers should not be like those first class lounges behind hidden doors in the airport, which only certain people, having paid their dues, get to walk through. For ethnography to matter in a multicultural world it needs to reach a wider range of audiences both in and beyond the academy" (quoted in Behar 1995, 21). Free from academic jargon and other prohibitive barriers, the arts have the potential to reach a broad range of people and to be emotionally and/or politically evocative for diverse audiences.

Historically, academic researchers have been plagued with the mandate to publish or perish; as noted earlier, however, the new mantra is *go public or perish*, and ABR has been a vital tool as researchers confront this new challenge (Cole et al. 2004). Moreover, the arts, at their best, can move people to see things in new ways. This is because the arts connect with people in sensory ways—reaching them on a level of humanness that extends far beyond the reach of any one discipline. Moreover, the arts can promote dialogue, cultivate understanding or critical consciousness, problematize dominant ideologies, and unsettle stereotypes (Leavy 2009a, 2011a).

If qualitative research has systematically challenged the foundations upon which positivist quantitative research is built (the subject/object and rational/emotional dichotomies), the explosion of arts-based research over the past two decades has pushed this negotiation even further. As Thomas (2001, 274) notes, "art as inquiry" merges intellect and emotions, cognitive and non-cognitive ways of knowing, and inherently challenges dualistic thinking. This becomes particularly salient when considering issues of evaluation (discussed in chapter 4).

Perhaps more than anything else, fiction-based research practice challenges the fact/fiction dichotomy that has historically dominated our understanding of what is and is not considered research. Barone and Eisner, who have been at the forefront of advocating arts-based approaches to research, posit that the question of whether or not fiction can be a research practice is the "trickiest" issue in arts-based research (2012, 1). They suggest that in the academy we typically have two ways of understanding fiction: 1. All representations of the facts are fiction, because they are created by humans; and 2. The fact/fiction dichotomy, which posits fiction is radically separate from the facts (this is the most popular view in the Western world). Barone and Eisner suggest an alternative or third way to think about fiction as research that accounts for the purpose for which the text is composed, the context for publication, and the way it is used by readers (2012, 103). I agree that in order to understand fiction-based research practice we need a new way of understanding what fictional writing can be, including how it is conceptualized, written, presented, and read. This is elaborated in the following chapters.

Blurred Genres

> If there is a line between fact and fiction, it may by necessity be a winding border that tends to bind these two categories, as much as it separates them, allowing each side to dissolve occasionally into the other.
> —James Edward Young, *Writing and Rewriting the Holocaust*

Although the explicit turn to fiction as a qualitative research practice is an emergent phenomenon, the lines between fiction and nonfiction, and writers and researchers, have long been blurred. The interplay between the two, both outside and inside the academy, has an extensive history of which I offer here only a highly selective review.

When considering the relationship between fiction and nonfiction, it is important to bear in mind that "real life" is the stuff of fiction, which is why these categories necessarily overlap. In this regard, Primo Levi asserted that fictional characters are never "wholly true or wholly invented" (in Franklin 2011, 16). The slippage between fiction and nonfiction can be seen by looking at the beginnings of the 300-year-long history of novels. Ben Yagoda (2010) notes that novels began as fake memoirs. For example, Daniel Defoe's 1719 novel *Robinson Crusoe* contained a title page that marketed the book as an "authentic" account (Franklin 2011). Defoe's novel actually demonstrates a critical issue for researchers using fiction: how the work is presented to readers (this is elaborated in the following chapters). According to Yagoda most narratives, including those which we call novels, occupy "an indeterminate middle ground" between fact and fiction (in Franklin 2011, 10). Thus even the idea of "pure" fiction is problematic.

I now briefly review some familiar genres in which "blurring" has long occurred: historical fiction, ethnography, and creative nonfiction.[5]

Historical Fiction and the Historical Novel

I have friends and family members who enjoy reading historical novels (as well as novels written in other cultures) as a means of gaining access to a different time and/or place. They routinely tell me how much they learn from the novels they have read, and how enjoyable the learning experience is. Statements often begin with, "I had no idea that..." and usually end with, "Did you know about that?" Often this reading experience not only teaches "information" but also builds empathetic understanding by offering a picture of "what it was like" through characters the readers can identify with and/or sympathize for. People report feeling a connection to and resonance with people very different from themselves or who find themselves in foreign places and situations.

Historical fiction can serve as a way to get at issues of inequality—for example, what it means to be a woman, a person of color, a sexual minority, or an economically disadvantaged person in a specific time and place. In this way historical fiction can educate people, document the experience of disenfranchised groups, and build bridges across differences. The content of historical fiction often centers on a particularly challenging time or event and on how people experienced it. In this regard, Holocaust fiction has becomes its own genre. I have elected to explore some of the history and debate surrounding Holocaust fiction because it powerfully reveals the key contested issues that emerge in historical fiction more broadly.

Ruth Franklin chronicles the emergence and impact of Holocaust fiction in her book *A Thousand Darknesses: Lies and Truth in Holocaust Fiction* (2011). Testimonial memoirs are the primary form Holocaust writing takes. Many scholars have urged that firsthand accounts are the only responsible way to represent the event. This argument is guided by two beliefs: 1) The Holocaust is such a unique event that it is not knowable or accessible and can only be preserved via firsthand accounts (Franklin 2011); and 2) Not only is the Holocaust unspeakable but it is also immoral to use such a horrific event as the material for fiction. In this regard Lawrence Langer (1977) argues that it is unethical to turn the suffering of genocide victims into art for "the world that murdered them" (in Franklin 2011, 5). This brings to mind the famous quote by Theodor Adorno, "To write a poem after Auschwitz is barbaric." Whereas this statement has been interpreted in different ways, most suggest it is "a condemnation of the moral callousness of aestheticizing horror" (ibid., 2).

For those who welcome the use of fiction for representing the Holocaust, the response to the preceding arguments is twofold. First, many scholars take issue with the assumption that diaries and testimonials are "pure" nonfiction. In what form would they have to be archived or published in order to qualify as pure? A frequently noted example is Anne Frank's diary, one of the most well-known pieces of Holocaust writing, which was edited or "cleaned up" by her father prior to publication. Different versions of the diary, including some aimed at children, have been subsequently published. But even when the texts we read are the original ones, their authors have been engaging in a narrative process that involves the selection of themes and details. Young (1994) notes that all diaries and testimonials contain narratives and thus merge nonfiction and fiction. In this regard Franklin (2011, 12) writes: "Every act of memory is also an act of narrative."

A second argument made by those who support the use of fiction to represent the Holocaust is that through art we are better able to enter into and understand this "unimaginable" event—fiction allows us to imagine. It is this response that best aligns with the principles behind this book. It is also here that we see the greatest fear that Holocaust fiction evokes: "a more general anxiety about the ways in which we respond to and value art and the uses to which we are prepared to put it" (ibid., 5). Traces of this fear underscore many debates in the research community when fiction and nonfiction are overtly blurred.

It is important to consider carefully the benefits some attribute to fictionalized representations of the Holocaust, since through these we can see the potential for fiction-based research in the social and behavioral sciences. There are three primary experiences fictional accounts of the Holocaust can evoke: understanding, imagination, and empathy. These are interconnected, and they are all vital if we are to learn compassionately from this past horror.

How do you help people to make sense of historical events, particularly those that seem beyond understanding? Jorge Semprun (1998) suggests that understanding is a function of effective storytelling, and that this can't be done well without some artifice—"enough to make it art" (in Franklin 2011, 13). Meaningful understanding also requires imagination. For example, often when people watch a narrative film about a historical event, whether it is the Holocaust, Pearl Harbor, or the sinking of the Titanic, they imagine what the experience was like, who they would have been in that time and place, and how they would have acted and reacted to the larger sociohistorical forces at work. All of this "imagining" is an integral part of the process of learning. Franklin writes: "We need literature about the Holocaust not only because testimony is inevitably incomplete, but because of what literature uniquely offers: an imaginative access to past events, together with new and different ways of understanding them that are unavailable to strictly factual forms of writing" (ibid.). This idea is central to the thesis of this book. It is through the process of imaginatively putting ourselves in the shoes of others that we are able to develop compassion and empathy. In the next chapter I will review the unique ability of fiction to build empathetic understandings across differences.

Despite some resistance, the common wisdom seems to be that fiction can help us understand history. Therefore, a plethora of novels, plays, and films about the Holocaust have been produced. What many have learned about the Holocaust and "felt" in response to this event comes from these artistic renderings. Some argue that the continued production of these representations points to a "cultural hunger for novels, films, plays" (ibid., 5) because they can help us understand and bear witness.

In 1946 what is widely considered the first Holocaust novel was published in Israel. The novel, titled *Sunrise over Hell*, was authored by Ka-Tzetnik 135633, which translates to "Concentration camp inmate 135633." This early novel shows that fictional formats were a part of Holocaust writing from the very beginning. For a recent example of "blurring" within the genre of Holocaust representations, consider the book *Schindler's List* (1982) by Thomas Keneally. Many know the book through Steven Spielberg's award-winning film adaptation. Interestingly, Keneally termed his book "a nonfiction novel,"[6] pointing to the inevitable blurring of fiction and nonfiction in Holocaust literature. Or consider the 2006 novel *The Boy in the Striped Pajamas* by the Irish novelist John Boyne, which was released as a film in 2008. In this same tradition, fictionalized or "blurred" representations of the more recent Rwandan genocide have already emerged.

In recent years there has also been an increase in fiction depicting a range of issues relating to the conflicts in the Middle East, primarily the Israeli-Palestinian conflict. This is arguably one of the most important, complex, and divisive issues of our time. Here fiction may be particularly useful, since it offers the ability to develop empathy and compassion as we "see" into others' experiences and perspectives in a disarming way.

For example, Amy Wilentz's novel *Martyrs' Crossing* (2002) shows how strategically employed fiction can serve as a site to negotiate complex social and political issues and promote understanding across differences. This novel centers on a young American-born woman, Marina, who is the daughter of a prominent Palestinian American academic. As an adult she goes to Palestine, falls in love with a Palestinian radical, marries him, and has a baby boy. All of this is the setup. Her husband is arrested and put in prison. Her child is severely asthmatic and suffers an asthma attack. Because getting through the checkpoint is such a hassle, Marina tries to wait it out. Finally, she rushes to the checkpoint only to find there is a demonstration in progress and the Israeli Defense Forces (IDF) is using a particularly noxious form of tear gas. At this point there is a confrontation between the young IDF soldier who wants to let the mother pass and his commander (reached only by phone) who realizes that she's a family member of a militant and orders that she be held. The child dies, and the rest of the novel follows the cascade of consequences. This is a situation in which everyone feels guilty—Marina for waiting too long, the soldier for holding her up, the child's father for being in jail and therefore making his whole family subject to reprisals, and Marina's father (who arrives for the funeral) who blames himself for having kept Palestine alive in his daughter's imagination. The novel also explores how every political faction tries to use the baby's death—the Hamas people in jail congratulating the father on having a "martyr," the Palestinian Authority (PA) trying to exploit the return of a distinguished professor, and so on. The Israeli-Palestinian conflict engenders strong points of view from most people. The novel format, however, has the potential to invite people with disparate views into the fictional world and imagine what it might be like to be any of the characters in that situation.

Ethnography and Fiction

Ethnography brings researchers into natural settings in order to enter the worlds of the people who inhabit them and to produce "thick descriptions" of social life (Geertz 1973; Hesse-Biber and Leavy 2011). The term "ethnography" translates as "writing culture." This begs the question: How does one write culture?

Historically, ethnographers have been charged with rendering "neutral" descriptions of the field, and that required them to write themselves out of their own projects, or at least put on the pretense of doing so. However, the qualitative research community now widely rejects claims of researcher neutrality as either possible or desirable. The thick descriptions that result from field research come from the researcher's subjective experience, and hopefully from his or her reflexivity about the latter (Hesse-Biber and Leavy 2005, 2011). From research design to data collection, analysis, and representation, researchers bring their assumptions and experiences to bear on their projects. For example, field notes, on-the-fly notes, theoretical memos, and analysis memos all require the researcher to write his or her understandings and impressions of the social reality under investigation (Hesse-Biber and Leavy 2011). John Van Maanen (1988) suggests that we think about ethnography as a deeply personal research experience. Amanda Coffey (1999) notes that ethnographers negotiate and write their identities throughout the research process.

Ethnographers ultimately present partial and situated renderings of particular social realities, and are in many ways interwoven with the tales they tell (Leavy 2009a). The best ethnographic writing can offer bridges between the particular and the universal. In this respect, social scientists often aim to connect people's individual biographies (micro-level experiences and situations) and the larger (macro-level) sociohistorical contexts that shape their experiences and in which their lives play out.[7]

Ethnographic writing, at its best, involves storytelling. Readers are invited into the complex realities of others in ways that promote understanding and connection. In order to tell stories to audiences, many ethnographers compose coherent narratives that require them to engage in a process similar to that of literary narrative (Leavy 2009a). Marcel Mauss (1947, 8) wrote: "The anthropologist has to be also a novelist able to evoke the life of a whole society." Famed researcher Clifford Geertz suggested that writing ethnography "involves telling stories, making pictures, concocting symbolisms, and deploying tropes" (in Visweswaran 1994, 2). Kamala Visweswaran (1994, 16) urges us to consider "fiction as ethnography," and she notes that anthropology has a long history of experimenting with literary genres including autobiography and novel. Social scientists, particularly anthropologists and sociologists, have a history of blurring nonfiction with fiction in order to most effectively "write" culture and get their writing out to public audiences. Two primary examples that illustrate this blurring are feminist ethnography and fiction and the more recent influence of autoethnography and narrative inquiry on ethnographic writing.

Feminist Ethnography and Fiction

There is a long and winding road connecting *feminist ethnography and fiction*, particularly in anthropology. Visweswaran's book *Fictions of Feminist Ethnography* (1994) explores this history and challenges us to investigate the relationship between ethnography and literature. Visweswaran begins: "One of my favorite sets of images is that of Ruth Benedict reading *The Waves* by Virginia Woolf when she was composing *Patterns of Culture* in 1934, and Virginia Woolf reading *Patterns of Culture* when writing her novel *Between The Acts* in 1940" (1994, 1). Ruth Benedict is a renowned feminist anthropologist who used literary models, including those by feminist novelists, when composing her anthropological research (Behar 1995). The writing processes modeled by Benedict and Woolf illustrate how feminist fiction and nonfiction inform and slip into each other. Benedict and Woolf are not alone.

The productive and necessary blurring of ethnography and fiction in feminist writing is most salient when considering work by women of color. While social scientists have been charged with helping the public to understand culture, race, and ethnicity, much of this learning has actually occurred through fictional writings (Behar 1995). As Michele Wallace notes, "black women's most prolific ... intellectual production is found in creative endeavors" (in Harrison 1995, 234). Visweswaran (1994) suggests that the writing tools available in traditional ethnography are inadequate when writing about race. Faye Harrison (1995, 234) sheds light on how fiction has been a refuge for feminist scholars of color and the benefits of considering this work as an alternative form of ethnographic writing:

> Fiction, it appears, has served as a sanctuary offering greater freedom for critical explorations of the cultural, psychological, and historical dilemmas of the black and human experience. Fiction encodes truth claims—and alternative modes of theorizing—in a rhetoric of imagination. In some respects the concealed, coded articulations that fiction allows seem to be opaque interreferences to social sciences' exclusive and monopolistic claims to the verification of social/cultural knowledge and truth ... When radical black women write fiction or ethnography they do so against the grain of a hegemony that peripheralizes them yet appropriates the value of their creative and critical productivity.

Novelists such as Toni Morrison, Amy Tan, Paula Ebron, and Anna Tsing, to name a few, have brought social science concerns into the public domain through their "fiction" (Behar 1995). Perhaps the two most well-known feminist authors to explicitly blur anthropological ethnography and fiction are Zora Neale Hurston and Alice Walker.

Zora Neale Hurston never completed her PhD in anthropology, and endured repeated criticism at Columbia University for failing to conform to standards of "rigor" (Harrison 1995; Visweswaran 1994). Nevertheless, Hurston is widely considered an anthropological novelist. She went beyond the confines of traditional anthropology and decided to use literary tools to write "against the grain" of both the academy and the larger dominant culture (Behar 1995; Harrison 1995). In this way, Hurston's turn to fiction, or ethnographically informed fiction, allowed her to challenge dominant understandings of race, class, and gender as she simultaneously challenged the academic apparatus that excluded the resistive form and content of her work. Harrison (1995, 235, 241) examined Hurston's work, noting: "[Her] fiction was grounded in a contextual, participatory ethnographic subjectivity which during her lifetime had no comfortable home in American anthropology. . . . Hers is a holistic fiction that reflects her vision of a pluralistic yet human-centered set of interlocking experiences. Her creative work boldly envisions and interprets."

Alice Walker's fiction can also be understood as both anthropological and fictive. In composing her work, she drew on historical and anthropological sources as well as literary devices (Harrison 1995). Her fiction seeks to tell complex stories about the social construction of gender, class, and race, the multiplicity of identity, and identity as a source of cultural and political struggles. Harrison has termed her short stories and novels "ethnographic and ethnohistorical," rightly suggesting that her fiction fits within the framework of multiple academic disciplines (ibid., 235). She writes, "Walker's novel is a world cultural history from a pluralistic Third World feminist perspective. As feminist 'her-story,' the novel should be seen as an integral part of the broader literature on the politics of representing gender, race, and culture history" (ibid., 237).

Autoethnography, Narrative Inquiry, and Fiction

Although often credited, and rightly so, with further legitimizing the subjective role of the researcher in the research process, autoethnography and narrative inquiry have also pushed the qualitative research community to think seriously about the form and quality of our writing. The expression of research is what brings it to life and what connects it to "what we have learned, to a tradition, and to audiences" (Banks and Banks 1998, 9). Good stories resonate. Whereas traditional social science writing often lacks the qualities that would characterize good and engaging writing, autoethnographers in particular have pushed us to reevaluate our writing tradition.

Carolyn Ellis and Arthur Bochner have been at the forefront of pushing the research community to think about its writing practices in order to produce meaningful, resonant, evocative, and emotional texts. In their work, Ellis and Bochner have encouraged researchers to explore the intersections of social research and fiction in order to produce well-written, vivid, and engaging texts that have the potential to connect the particular and universal (which, as I noted earlier, is achieved in the best ethnographic research and arguably the best social science research more broadly). Their groundbreaking book series published works in which fiction and social research intertwine—where imagination, authoethnography, narrative, and ethnography merge. Their stated goal was to encourage readers to

> compare their own worlds with those of the people they meet on the pages of these stories . . . [and to] bring the written product of social research closer to the richness and complexity of lived experience . . . [in an] attempt to bridge the gaps between author and reader, between fact and truth, between cool reason and hot passion, between the personal and the collective, and between the drama of social life and the legitimized modes for representing it. (Bochner and Ellis 1998, 7)

Researchers who are turning explicitly to fiction are doing so in an academic and publishing environment that has felt the effects of rises in autoethnography and narrative inquiry.

Creative Nonfiction

Creative nonfiction arose in the 1960s and 1970s to make research reports more engaging while remaining truthful (Caulley 2008; Goodall 2008).[8] In the commercial world (trade publishing and journalism) as well as in academic writing and publishing, writers were looking for ways to use literary tools in order to strengthen their factual writing. Lee Gutkind, founder of the magazine *Creative Nonfiction*, proclaims creative nonfiction to be the fastest growing genre in publishing, and says that at its core the genre promotes "true stories well told" (Gutkind 2012, 6). He further defines the form as follows:

> The word "creative" refers to the use of literary craft, the techniques fiction writers, playwrights, and poets employ to present nonfiction—factually accurate prose about real people and events—in a compelling, vivid, dramatic manner. The goal is to make nonfiction stories read like fiction so that your readers are as enthralled by fact as they are by fantasy. But the stories are true. (Ibid.)

The commercialization of newspaper reporting has normalized the tenets of creative nonfiction within the public sphere. Norms in academic writing have changed as a result. If once purported "objective" journalists could actively engage in crafting good stories through the adaptation of literary techniques, academic researchers were emboldened to do the same. Moreover, as readers have become more accustomed to reading stories rather than reports, expectations have changed, opening up the possibilities for academic writers. The rise of creative nonfiction has put a premium on good storytelling. For many it isn't enough for research to "report" or "chronicle," but it should also do it well. When stories are expressed well, readers are more deeply impacted. Cheney (2001, 1) describes creative nonfiction as follows:

> Creative non-fiction tells a story using facts, but uses many of the techniques of fiction for its compelling qualities and emotional vibrancy. Creative non-fiction doesn't just report facts, it delivers facts in ways that move the reader toward a deeper understanding of a topic. Creative non-fiction requires the skills of the storyteller and the research ability of the conscientious reporter.

In the academic world, researchers are storytellers, learning about others and sharing what they have learned. Whether we go into the field in an ethnographic study or conduct oral history interviews, we are charged with telling the stories of others in creative, expressive, dynamic, and authentic ways. We may also be relying on our own autoethnographic experiences as data explicitly informing the stories we craft. Bud Goodall termed this "the new ethnography" (2000, 2008). When we represent and share our research, our goal is not simply to expose others to it, but to affect those who read our work. The goals of particular projects may vary—educating, raising awareness, exposing falsehoods, building critical consciousness, disrupting dominant ideologies or stereotypes, putting a human face to an issue, and so on—but whatever our objective, we aim to impact our readers. Just like with good teaching, we hope our research is written well enough to make a lasting impact. A well-written "story" has the potential to be long remembered.

Creative nonfiction is such an expansive genre that it is difficult to synthesize it or delineate an exhaustive array of examples. Research articles, essays, op-eds, and books may all be written in this fashion, and commonly are. One example that routinely comes up in the qualitative research community is Truman Capote's *In Cold Blood* (1965), which some suggest can be considered a qualitative research project (Norris 2009). What is clear is that creative nonfiction, within and beyond the academy, has changed how many view academic writing and has brought the tools of literary fiction into the researcher's purview.

Conclusion

I hope this chapter has helped dispel the myth that fiction and nonfiction are binary categories. There is a rich history of blurring these genres, some of which was discussed in this chapter. Fiction and nonfiction draw on many similar practices. Qualitative researchers and arts-based researchers have pushed the boundaries of what is and is not considered research in an effort to better and more fully address research needs and make our research available beyond the academy. Accordingly, fiction-based research is a growing genre. Fiction is uniquely able to draw readers in and express subtlety and connectivity. In these ways and others, fiction carries great potential for social researchers across the disciplines. In the next chapter I review some of the primary advantages of fiction-based research practice, focusing on the distinct strengths of fiction.

Chapter 2

The Possibilities of Fiction-Based Research: Portraying Lives in Context

> The natural history of conventional social science is that of a real world being articulated in imagined details; the natural history of fiction is that of an imaginary world being articulated in real details. The former helps us understand what people are, while the latter helps us understand who people can be.
>
> —Stephen Banks, "Writing as Theory: In Defense of Fiction"

Social research is aimed at generating meanings, creating understanding, and illuminating that which may be concealed in everyday life. Perhaps more than anything else, researchers try to portray lives, complete with nuance and context. As we attempt to interrogate social reality or some aspect of it and share what we have learned with others, we need to use all available tools. Fiction is a wonderful tool for getting at the complexity of lived experience and helping others to learn and feel. It is not surprising that fiction has been used as a pedagogical tool to teach subject matters related to ethics (see for example McCoppin 2008), sociology (see for example Nieckarz 2008; Wolff 2008), psychology (see for example Grosofsky 2008; Simeone 2008), history (see for example Lennon 2008; Schroeder 2008), and

---

Fiction as Research Practice: Short Stories, Novellas, and Novels, by Patricia Leavy, 37–52.

women's studies (see for example Branam 2008), among other topics. What are, then, the unique strengths of fiction-based research practice?

Fiction-based research requires us to conceive of the products of our research practice in new shapes.[1] In this regard, the idea of "findings" in a conventional research report does not apply to this emergent field (Banks 2008). Stephen Banks and Anna Banks (1998) argue that it is the expression of research that brings it to life and connects it to audiences. I concur that the form or "shape" our research takes is what gives it meaning. As we let go of former conceptions of what social research looks like, we open new paths that may bring us closer to our goals.

Traditional research reports are filled with jargon and published in specialized journals likely to be read only by other academic "experts." It is clear that fiction has a much greater chance to reach broad audiences. In addition to reaching a diverse public (which traditional social research publications fail to do), the three primary goals of social research for which fiction is well suited are: 1. portraying the complexity of lived experience or illuminating human experience (linking the particular and the universal, or micro and macro levels); 2. promoting empathy and self-reflection (as a part of a compassionate, engaged, or social justice approach to research); and 3. disrupting dominant ideologies or stereotypes (including building critical consciousness and raising awareness).

Portraying the Complexity of Lived Experience

Fiction allows us to portray people's experiences more holistically than other forms of conducting and writing research thanks to several strategies: 1) verisimilitude; 2) getting at particulars; 3) inner voice and interior dialogue; and 4) narrator's point of view. Although these strategies often overlap in the actual practice of writing fiction, I discuss them separately. (See next chapter for a review of more specific components of a fictional writing, such as plotting, characters, and so forth.)

Verisimilitude

Verisimilitude refers to portraying people and settings realistically, truthfully, and authentically. Achieving verisimilitude is often a goal in qualitative research and the criterion for evaluating the presentation of research findings. Fiction is uniquely suited for capturing verisimilitude.

As anyone who has ever read fiction knows, there is nothing better than entering the pages of a fictional world and feeling a connection to the places and people we are meeting. Whether the fictional worlds and the characters we are introduced to are unfamiliar to us or we share similar characteristics, we are meant to walk into their reality, voyeuristically experience it, and believe it. The world on the page is a virtual world that welcomes us as readers. This is a marker of verisimilitude. The way someone's home is decorated, the smells coming out of their kitchen, the thoughts racing through their mind, and the conversation they just had, are important as writers attempt to portray an existing or possible reality. There is an immediacy to fiction that other forms of representation lack (Banks 2008). Both the details and the larger picture need to ring true. Fiction writers go to great lengths, including conducting extensive research, to achieve this kind of realism and resonance (Banks 2008; Berger 1977).[2]

Verisimilitude is also exceptionally important in qualitative research. In addition to wanting to portray research participants and their worlds realistically for the sake of best communicating their findings, researchers have another motivation for achieving verisimilitude: ethics. Researchers have an ethical obligation to portray people's lives responsibly and sensitively. For example, it is important to achieve multidimensionality and provide context. To do so requires great care during the writing process. People are rarely, if ever, one thing. For example, a teacher may be insecure in her personal life but come to life in the classroom. Someone may be deeply offended by racial discrimination toward some groups and less so toward others. Further, all people have different public and private selves and are known differently by coworkers, family members, and close friends. The examples are innumerable; the point is, people are multidimensional and infinitely complex. Fiction is able to express nuance in ways that appear effortless. Ardra Cole and J. Gary Knowles (2001) suggest that imagination and metaphor are required if we are to portray people's lives sensitively, and explain: "Development of an artful representation . . . relies as much on the imagination of the researcher as it does on the information gathered through inquiry. Artful representations often emerge from intuitive responses to complex interpretations" (ibid., 212).

Combining the tenets of qualitative research and fiction uniquely allows us to create believable virtual worlds into which we may insert a theoretical, philosophical, or socially minded substructure. Wolfgang Iser (1997, 5) writes: "In the novel, then, the real and the possible coexist." As researchers, we meticulously incorporate real-world details into the construction of fictional worlds. This allows us to both create realism and build "possible worlds"[3] that may not exist as such (Banks and Banks 1998). In this way we can present something that is authentic while also inviting readers to imagine the world differently. As Iser (1997, 4) suggests, the act of fictionalizing can make "conceivable what would otherwise remain hidden." Without believability, resonance, and authenticity, we are not able to tap into fiction's great potential to teach.

H. Porter Abbott (2008) suggests that social reality and our perception of it are inextricably intertwined with our engagement with the worlds constructed in fiction. He writes:

> The question of how our understanding of the actual world we live in, including history, plays a part in the made-up worlds of fiction. And the answer to the question is that our understanding of this actual world plays a huge part in almost all fictional worlds. In fact, unless we are told otherwise, we assume that the fictional world is a simulacrum of the world we actually live in. (Ibid., 151)

Marie-Laure Ryan coined the term "principle of minimal departure," which refers to the assumption that the world in fiction resonates with our own reality unless the text itself tells us otherwise (Abbott 2008). In his book, Peter Clough (2002) presents five fictional stories occurring in educational settings. He suggests the stories are legitimate pieces of research because they *could have happened*. Here we can see how the realistic, authentic, or plausible nature of the texts—their ability to correspond with "reality"—is central to the research practice.

Iser has been at the forefront of theorizing about the relationship between the empirical worlds we study and the fictional worlds we create. His concept of "overstepping" indicates that a "literary work oversteps the real world which it incorporates" (1997, 1). Iser details a threefold fictionalizing process: 1. selection; 2. combination; and 3. self-disclosure.

Selection is the process of taking "identifiable items" from social reality, importing them into the fictional world, and transforming them "into a sign for something other than themselves" (ibid., 2). Put differently, selection is the process of choosing bits of data or details from the empirical world or referential world and transforming them. Through the process of selection, we "overstep" the empirical world we aim to reference. Selection happens in conjunction with combination.

Combination is the process of bringing the different empirical elements or details together. The bits of data, empirical elements, or details we select may come from traditional research processes (such as interviews or field research) or they may come to us more abstractly through the accumulation of research, teaching, and personal experiences. Tom Barone and Elliot Eisner (2012) explain that empirical details may arise out of any social research methods, and they further suggest that "empirical elements may also arise out of careful reflections on the previous experiences of the researcher with social phenomena. The research may occur within a preproduction phase, prior to the fashioning of a text; more often it will occur within the process of composition" (ibid., 104). Therefore, descriptions and details written in a work of fiction-based research can be considered "data." The use of details from the real world brings readers into the work of fiction while allowing writers to reimagine what "real worlds" are. Barone and Eisner write: "Familiar elements of experience do help to lure the reader into the text and enable her to vicariously inhabit the world recreated therein.... [T]he imported 'realities' ... must nevertheless remain identifiable and familiar, seen as believable, credible, lest readers no longer be able to relate the recreated world to their life experiences outside of the text." (ibid., 106)

Diane Ketelle (2004) has fictionalized her experiences as a school administrator in order to gain reflexivity and understanding about them. She considers her practice to be a form of autoethnography resulting in stories that represent a "composite truth" because they are grounded in real experience but also fictive (ibid., 450). Ketelle has created the fictional character of Bree Michaels, a public school principal whom she places in a range of scenarios with different characters in order to explore particular aspects of education administration (such as students, parents, teachers, or the broader community). Each character Bree deals with is a composite based on Ketelle's own experiences. In this work, the bits of empirical reality (or "data") are taken from personal experiences and observations. Here is an excerpt in which Bree is meeting with a teacher, Meredith, whom she perceives as difficult. The character is a composite and the story is meant to explore Bree's own limitations in interacting with others.

> This morning Meredith, a teacher, was coming in to tell Bree how to handle a difficult student. Although Bree understood it was her own hard work that had taught Meredith that she should be open and share ideas, she was always amazed that Meredith knew no boundaries. She crossed double yellow lines in conversation constantly, usually defining "what is right" through her own personal worldview. Bree knew this is what life in organizations was like, but this morning she was especially tired. Meredith's diatribe wasn't interesting to her at all and she ended up asking her to leave. As Meredith walked out her heels made a clip, clip, clip sound on the floor and Bree had to laugh. It was too noisy for just one person. (Ketelle 2004, 455)

Ketelle's careful character construction and use of particulars that have resonance to those in the field of education, combined with her imagination, produce works that can be helpful to her and others in her field. According to Iser (1997), the final act of fictionalizing is self-disclosure. *Self-disclosure* refers to the ways that a text reveals or conceals its fictional nature (Barone and Eisner 2012). When a text reveals its fictional nature, as literary texts do through various conventions (which may be as simple as labeling the work a novel), readers engage with it accordingly.[4] Iser suggests that when readers consume fictional works they engage in a process of "bracketing" whereby the real world or empirical reality is "bracketed" off from the fictional world. In other words, readers create a boundary between what they perceive to be the real world they are enmeshed in and the fictional world they are being invited into. Through this process readers are able to take the fictional world as an "as if" world (ibid., 3).

Iser summarizes the fictionalizing process as follows:

> The acts of fictionalizing can be clearly distinguished by the different gestalt each of them brings about: selection results in revealing the intentionality of the author; combination results in bringing about unfamiliar relationships of the items selected within the text; and self-disclosure results in bracketing the world represented, thereby converting it into a sign for something else, and simultaneously suspending the reader's natural attitude. (Barone and Eisner 2012, 4)

While trying to capture verisimilitude, it is also necessary to keep the bigger picture in mind. Whereas the details included in the story are important, the larger narrative is what readers are left with, and must ring true and connect with them. The details are there to assist with the larger narrative. In fiction, truth in meaning beyond any individual fact is what matters (Abbott 2008). Aristotle suggested that the kind of truth that can live in fiction is a philosophical, universal truth that is far more powerful than any other form of truth (ibid., 153–54). So, though details help us achieve verisimilitude, the thrust or overall meaning constructed in fictional stories is greater than the sum of its parts.

Particulars[5]

There is a well-known saying in sociology that goes, I don't know who discovered water but I doubt it was a fish. The implication is that it is very difficult to perceive the environment one is enmeshed in. Similarly, people often fail to see that which is right before them. Fiction is also good for documenting and exploring particulars in order to *reexamine experience* (Ketelle 2004). Ludwig Wittgenstein (1953, 415) has written that a social poetics is needed in order to turn our attention to our "observations ... which have escaped remark only because they are always before our eyes." Fiction-based research is a strategy for illuminating the particulars of daily life, and thus applying focused reflection and analysis on what otherwise escapes our attention. Here we can return to the wonderful example of Ketelle's exploration of school administration via the fictional character of Bree Michaels. Ketelle (2004, 453) writes: "Fictionalizing real world experience affords an opportunity to attend to everyday experience in a new way, to revisit particulars that may have escaped notice the first time around."

Narrative Point of View: First- and Third-Person Narration and Interiority

For social researchers, portraying people's lives sensitively is a responsibility. We try to shed light on what people do and why, on how they feel and act. Their motivations, assumptions, and biases, and how previous experiences or present situations influence their attitudes and behaviors, are all part of building understanding. All of this requires getting inside of people's heads. Psychiatrist Robert Coles explains that regardless of whether we present our subjects through nonfiction or fiction, we should strive to "capture and well express the interiority of those persons" (in Banks 2008, 160). Fiction offers us unique access into interiority. Through the use of first- or third-person narration, fiction allows us to access the interior lives of characters while also providing a context or commentary for understanding their psychological processes. I suggest that the use of first- and third-person narration and the interlinked exploration of people's interiority are what makes fiction distinctive and what gives fiction-based research its greatest capabilities. In this regard, back in 1961, famed literature professor and literary critic Wayne Booth noted that access to the inner life of others was the most distinctive feature of fiction. Similarly, historian Inga Clendinnen has said, "Through giving me access to the inner thoughts and secret actions of closed others, fiction has taught me most of what I know" (in Franklin 2011, 15).

First- and third-person narration techniques offer different points of view within a narrative. In first-person narration, the narrator is a character within the story (for example, the central character). Readers are then invited into the mind, or inner life, of that character and travel the world of the novel through his or her perspective. In third-person narration, the narrator is not a character in the story but rather possesses a general narrator's voice that has access to the inner lives of the characters. Darrel Caulley (2008) suggests that we think of third-person narration as a wide-angle distance shot and of first-person narration as a close-up shot. Choosing the narrator's point of view is a major decision. The style of narration selected can be a great asset as we attempt to impart meaning, weave complexity and nuance into our writing, and provide social, political, or other commentary as a context for understanding individual characters and character types.

Most fiction writers, including those who write fiction-based research, employ third-person narration. Whereas first-person narration at its best can be highly effective, it can also be particularly difficult to navigate, and therefore many opt to avoid its pitfalls (particularly since third-person narration still allows readers access into the minds of the characters through the use of an ambiguous narrator).[6] In this way, I suggest that third-person narration also allows us to present a "close-up shot."

Third-person narration has many advantages. For example, it is a technique for introducing characters and situating them in some social, cultural, and/or historical context. In this way, the narrator's voice can be used to insert some commentary on the unfolding action or, even better, to insert spaces in which readers are likely to critically engage with the ideas embedded in the narrative. Narrators are able to present the "big picture" and show how the different characters fit into it. The third person can thus be used as a means to allow the author to make connections and show interconnections, and as a way for the researchers to explore macro–micro links in their fictional renderings, which is particularly important for researchers in the social and health sciences. Likewise, researchers working from critical perspectives such as feminism, queer theory, or critical race theory may also benefit directly from sketching out complex macro–micro relationships.

For example, in my feminist novel, *Low-Fat Love* (2011b), I employed third-person narration for a variety of reasons. One of the goals I had writing that novel was to show the pop culture context in which women develop their sense of self and how this frames their relationship expectations. Through third-person narration I was able to reveal the cultural context in which the characters came to think of themselves. For example, the main character, Prilly, who suffered from crippling self-esteem issues and found herself in a dissatisfying romantic relationship, was often shown consuming women's media. In this way I was able to explore the kind of commercial media that is aimed at young women and the psychological effect it had on Prilly. Made-for-television movies, tabloid television, music videos, home shopping, and other commercial media aimed at the female demographic were all signposted throughout the book, allowing me to offer a feminist reading of women's media as a part of the subtext of the narrative. This is one example of how third-person narration can be used to achieve specific content goals and forge micro–macro connections.

Another example comes from the work of Elizabeth de Freitas. De Freitas turns to a fictional character as a vehicle to explore issues about how to conduct educational research, and her use of a third-person narrator facilitates her goals. She employs a third-person narrator in her writing about Martha West, a fictional educational researcher. As de Freitas has noted, Martha West engages in an "unrelenting interior monologue" (2008, 3). She writes: "The reader learns about Martha through the descriptive and specular vantage of third person, but the reader also learns that the same detached voyeurism is at the heart of the character's dilemma" (2003, 2).

It is important to note that there are epistemological issues those writing fiction-based research must consider as they select a narrator's point of view. First-person narration can give the appearance of presenting an "authentic I" and thus may render invisible the role of the writer in the construction of the work (de Freitas 2008). In other words, first-person narration gives readers access into a character's mind in a way that might seem natural. When a work is labeled pure fiction, this is not an issue; in fiction-based research, however, writers need to consider how they are representing real people (even if composites). In other words, when presenting fiction-based research it is necessary to consider how the work will be received by readers. Are readers likely to be able to discern the role of the writer in the process (or see the writer-researcher's fingerprint)? Are readers likely to think that something was specifically said by a participant in a study because it is presented in the first person?

Third-person narration poses epistemological challenges as well. Writers have great freedom with third-person narration, since they are able to access and present the inner life of many characters. They can imbue the work with all kinds of assumptions about people and social life. Therefore, writers can construct the entire reality of the novel (the social world presented in the novel and how it impacts the characters) without ever indicating their presence as interpreters. In this regard, de Freitas (2004, 271) observes that the third-person narrator "haunts the novel like the ghost of positivist research." It is important to provide readers with ways of understanding the role of the writer in constructing the psychic lives of characters, the social world in which they are enmeshed, and the connections between their micro-level experiences and the macro level. For example, when presenting as a subtext the idea that media are impacting how a character feels about herself, are readers given any signals as to what experiences, empirical data, or theoretical and philosophical perspectives are guiding the writing? This may be as simple as noting the body of scholarship that informs the work (in an abstract or preface), so that at a minimum the readers understand the vantage point or theoretical agenda of the writer.[7] For example, I have labeled *Low-Fat Love* a feminist novel so that readers understand the framework within which I created it.

Notwithstanding these challenges, fiction carries great potential for researchers. Caulley (2008) rightfully notes that what distinguishes fiction and nonfiction writers is that fiction writers can say what is happening in the minds of characters, whereas nonfiction writers can only infer it (at times) but ultimately have far less latitude. In this regard, Iser (1997, 6) notes that fiction "subsidizes the unknowable." Moreover, by allowing us into the mindset of others, writers are able to create empathetic connections that may be vital in the presentation of social research.

Promoting Empathy and Reflection

Perhaps more than anything else a compassionate research practice, the cornerstone of social justice research, requires the cultivation of empathy—learning about and feeling for others, however similar or dissimilar they may be from us. When we develop empathy, we also grow as individuals. In order to learn about people and about how society (the social structure and the cultural elements) shapes and provides a context for people's experiences, research also needs to promote social reflection. Connection to individual characters with a clear sense of how they are enmeshed in situations and structures larger than themselves provides a way for readers to look both outward and inward. In order to be able to look critically at different social realities, we also need to look critically at ourselves—at our assumptions, values, beliefs, and experiences, and at the way they have been shaped by our social environments. Therefore, the cultivation of self-awareness through critical reflection is also an integral part of research practice.

Self-Awareness for Writers

It is important to note that the self-awareness fiction can bring about may be as true for the author as it is for the readers. In fact, some researchers write fiction as a means of increasing their own self-awareness (in addition to teaching others). Kamala Visweswaran's "Sari Stories" is a short piece of autoethnographic fiction that she incorporates into her larger collection on feminist ethnography (Visweswaran 1994). In "Sari Stories" the author uses the way she dresses and her collection of traditional Indian "saris" as symbols of the struggles she feels both at home and not in her native India. The short fiction touches on issues pertaining to history, culture, gender, and age—all through the symbolism of dress. The story opens:

> Somehow, during the course of that first year in India, I accumulated a lot of saris. I'm not really sure how. Various concerned mamis, surprised and delighted with how "Indian" I looked, determinedly gave me saris at all possible moments: old ones, new ones, cotton ones, and silk; torn, but still lovely ones; others in colors so gaudy I dared not wear them. The logic was, if I looked Indian, surely in a sari, I must be Indian. (Ibid., 166)

Visweswaran has described the piece as "a strategically posed fiction of selfhood and identity" (ibid., 15). At the same time as she seeks self-awareness through writing, she also invites us into her experience. The piece allows us to imagine what it must be like to negotiate two cultures and how something as seemingly simple as clothing can act as a space of tension and a source of identity negotiation. Our perspective is broadened through the imaginative and empathetic act of reading her story, whether or not we can personally relate to the specific details.

Carl Leggo's *Sailing in a Concrete Boat: A Teacher's Journey* (2012) is another excellent example of how the process of creating a piece of fiction-based research can create self-awareness in the writer (as well as the readers). Leggo has created a novel-length narrative composed of a sequence of short stories and poems linked by recurring characters. The book centers on schoolteacher Caleb Robinson, a fictional character that contains many traces of his author. The work explores Caleb's experiences and feelings as he struggles to understand what it means to be a teacher as well as the other aspects of his life—being a husband, a father, a Christian, and a human being. Leggo makes clear that through Caleb he learns about himself as much as anyone else does.

Empathetic engagement, self-reflection, and social reflection are mutually reinforcing processes that can occur as we read (and write) fiction. As we come to understand the experiences of others and correspondingly develop empathy, we naturally look at ourselves as well. Building empathy for others is also a way to change ourselves. This is why Dunlop (2001, 12) states that "we write ourselves as we read."

Empathy, Self-Awareness, and Social Reflection in Readers

Many researchers aim at promoting empathy as a means of creating understanding. Fiction is well suited to elicit empathy and promote "empathetic engagement" (de Freitas 2003). Readers often relate the most to "flawed" characters, allowing writers to develop truly multidimensional portrayals. As readers engage with fiction and develop highly personal relationships with the characters, they are in fact constructing intimate relationships with "the imagined other" (ibid., 5).

Fiction differs from other forms in two ways that are central to the cultivation of empathy. First, as previously discussed we can enter into the intimate thoughts of characters—their internal dialogue. This access to what people are thinking and feeling builds a deep connection between readers and characters. Fiction-based researchers can deliberately link particular concepts or ideas with forms of emotional engagement through the characters readers care about. Abbott (2008, 154) writes, "There is no disputing the power and flexibility of fiction for conveying ideas and wedding them with deep feeling." Second, fictional narratives are incomplete and leave space for the readers' interpretations and imagination. In other words, there are interpretive gaps in fiction, often intentionally included by the authors (de Freitas 2003). Readers fill in these gaps, and in doing so they may actively develop empathetic connections to the characters (and the kinds of people they represent). Further, as we read fiction we engage our imaginations. As Franklin (2011, 15) notes in her review of Holocaust fiction, "[An] act of imagination is an act of empathy."

There are numerous ways that social researchers can exploit the nature of reading fiction to serve purposes such as promoting empathy with others, forging understanding across differences, and developing a sense of how individuals adapt to different situational factors. Consider as an example Cheryl Dellasega's work. Dellasega's nonfiction book *The Starving Family* (2001b) explores how eating disorders impact families (relationships, family members' identities, and practical issues of caregiving and coping). The book features original interviews with family members who are caregivers to a child (sometimes an adult child) suffering from an eating disorder. Because eating disorders are often viewed from the perspective of the individual sufferer, few understand how eating disorders impact families units, and this may impair our efforts to help those who are dealing with this situation. Aiming to address this gap in the literature, Dellasega wrote the novel *Waiting Room* (forthcoming), which details the unraveling of the "perfect" family due to an eating disorder. *Waiting Room* has the potential to offer readers great insight into how eating disorders are experienced by families, including how different people adapt to this set of circumstances.

The ability of fiction to create empathetic engagement, self-awareness, and social awareness, is intimately linked to other strengths: the capacity to disrupt dominant ideologies or stereotypes, build critical consciousness, and raise social or political awareness.

Disrupting Stereotypes or Dominant Ideologies

How do we illuminate that which is taken for granted as "the way things are"? How can we break stereotypes? How do we get others to learn and care about different people they may hold negative assumptions about? How might we disrupt dominant cultural narratives and myths, making room for new ways of thinking and seeing?

Through fiction, readers develop relationships with characters that can serve as guides into different social worlds. As readers begin to care for the characters and develop empathy, previously held assumptions, values, stereotypes, and even worldviews can be challenged. The groundbreaking novel *Jackytar* by Douglas Gosse (2005) illustrates this potential of fiction-based research.

Jackytar tells the story of Alex Murphy, a gay man of mixed racial identity in Newfoundland. Alex was labeled a "Jackytar," which is a derogatory word for a mixed-race person of Mi'Kmaq and French origins. The story follows Alex as an adult as he travels home and confronts the community in which he was marginalized and his own struggles over his identity. Gosse explains his intention as follows: "[to] investigate the intertwining of identity markers of race, class, gender, sexual orientation, ablebodiness, geographical location, and language and culture in the lives of the fictional characters" (2008, 183). By using a fictional format, he hoped readers would identify and empathize with characters, which would lead to both personal and social reflection.

Through flashbacks and memories, Gosse disrupts narrative time and gives readers great insight into Alex and the experiences that have shaped his identity. In one instance, Alex recalls selecting an undergraduate college program that emphasized language acquisition and cultural learning. When he selected this university program, he felt "blessed" to be a "Jackytar" for the first time in his life. Readers then learn how Alex came to take the "Jackytar" label on himself (in the following scene, Genevieve Benoit is a doctoral student and instructor at Alex's undergrad university):

> One day, the beginning of first semester, she took me by the hand and directed me towards the mirror in the common room.
>
> Elle demande: Que vois-tu? Qui vois-tu?
>
> I stared at my dark skin, hair and eyes, the strong nose, somewhat bulbous at the end, the thick neck. . . .
>
> She took the back of my head and forced me to peer closer. . . .
>
> From that moment onward, I saw myself differently. I was a Jackytar, and so was Genevieve Benoit. (2005, 105–6)

By this point in the novel, readers have developed empathy for Alex and learned about how prejudice has shaped his life. In Alex's story, identity forms at the intersection of race and sexuality (and other status characteristics). Through a carefully constructed narrative, the book also draws extensively on queer theory (and teaches its principles to readers).

Jakytar accomplishes several things, all of which are linked to the novel format. It disrupts stereotypes based on race and sexual orientation and challenges dominant prejudices and ideologies. At the same time, *Jackytar* promotes self- and social reflection and critical consciousness, challenging readers to reflect on their own values as well as the larger social system in which biases are created and normalized. An essay, article or monograph about these issues simply could not achieve the same ends. The novel format is disarming, pleasurable, and inviting.

Conclusion

Literature reveals that we are the possibilities of ourselves.
—Wolfgang Iser, *The Significance of Fictionalizing*

After this summary of the unique capabilities of fiction to access and express the complexity of human experience and social life in ways that may not be possible otherwise, it is time to look at what this practice (or methodology) looks like.

Summary of the Possibilities for Fiction as Research

Distinct Capabilities of Fiction	**Strategies for Reaching Capabilities**
Portraying the complexity of lived experience and illuminating human experience	Verisimilitude Particulars Narrative point of view (first- and third-person narration; interiority)
Promoting empathy and reflection	Self-awareness in writers Empathy, self-awareness, and social reflection in readers Disrupting stereotypes or dominant ideologies

In the next chapter I review various approaches to writing fiction-based research. As we think about building a project, it is important to look at the architecture of fiction as well as the literary features that can make fiction compelling. Therefore, I detail some of the building blocks of fiction and how researchers may adapt them. I then review staple features of fiction (plots, characters, description, and so forth) as well as common practices in literary writing.

Chapter 3

Designing a Project: Fiction-Based Research Practice

Every story, every incident, every bit of conversation is raw material for me.

—Sylvia Plath, *The Unabridged Journals of Sylvia Plath*

Writing fiction-based research differs from a traditional research methodology. Fiction-based research practice requires several things from the researcher: creativity, attention to craft and aesthetics, reflexivity, and openness (or adaptability).

This practice also requires researchers to engage in a systematic process of critiquing, copyediting, and revising their own work. Sometimes you have to write a lot in order to get a little bit that really works. When I am working on a piece of fiction, I think of it as if I was sculpting clay. Each bit—scene, segment, sentence, or paragraph—needs to be shaped and reshaped paying attention to language. The more complex the project with respect to purpose, goals, thematic coverage, and emotional timbre, the more involved the process of layering and weaving meanings together.

For those of you who may have considerable experience writing nonfiction, bear in mind that although you can draw on those experiences, which all contribute to writing ability, writing fiction is unique. Writing fiction requires attention to the aesthetic quality of

---

the work. Fictional writing, including fiction-based research, relies on using language well and creating an engaging experience for readers; it requires us to capture the sights, smells, sounds, and atmosphere of the places we describe. In the sections that follow I review the nuts and bolts of writing fiction-based research—data, structure, characterization, and other literary devices. However, it is important not to lose sight of the bigger picture, which is creating an engaging story, developing resonance, illuminating an aspect of the social world, capturing verisimilitude, and inviting readers into worlds that are both familiar and unfamiliar in order to increase their consciousness. At the end of the day, the aim of fiction-based research is to write a good story (aesthetically good and good *for* something).

The Data

The data for a fiction-based project can be garnered in different ways. Sometimes researchers use traditional data collection methods such as interviews, field research, or document analysis and then interpret and represent the data using fictional writing strategies. In other instances, the writing itself is the method of inquiry and representation. Whereas these two primary methods of data collection (traditional and writing) may seem antithetical, I suggest we think about the data used in fiction-based research as existing on a continuum. At one end of the continuum, we have data collected via traditional methods and analyzed and interpreted in a manner that bears close similarities to traditional qualitative practice. For example, interview transcripts may be coded in order to develop specific themes, and the interviewees may be grouped together based on a finite number of experiences and/or traits. Composite characters are then constructed out of each of those "types." While the result would be a fictional narrative, this process is very close to a traditional qualitative interview study. On the other end of the continuum, the act of writing itself becomes the research act, and may be influenced to varying degrees by any number of research, teaching, and/or personal experiences. Elizabeth de Freitas (2003, 1) explains this process as follows:

> The stories are not based on traditional data in the qualitative sense. As a fiction writer, I am always already writing; there is no collecting data before my act of interpretation. There is no

> temporal lag between event and story. My life experiences as a teacher and a researcher inform my writing, but they are not the "indubitable facts" to which my narrative must correspond.... My imagination is immediately engaged in the co-construction of our shared reality.... Honour the ways in which my imagination might furnish a form of rigorous research.

In a later writing, de Freitas further explains that reflexive writing is her research methodology (2004, 262). Similarly, Rishma Dunlop (2001) uses fiction as an act of research. For Dunlop this research practice involves creating an assemblage of "facts" and imagination with literary artifice.

There are many points in between these two ends of the fiction-based research continuum, with researchers drawing on traditional data collection and/or interpretation processes and literary practices in numerous ways.

Data may also come directly from a literature review. Again, in fiction-based research we may not be talking about "data" in the traditional sense. If writing is your research act, you may conduct a literature review on your topic from which you draw ideas, concepts, and even language. If your data are collected via traditional research methods (interviews, field research, content analysis), you may have conducted a literature review prior to data collection and/or you may use literature as a part of your interpretive process. There are many different ways that literature may influence your project. Likewise, you may draw on theory as a part of your data or as a means of interpreting data you have collected. If writing is your research act, you may be influenced, generally speaking, by a theoretical school of thought or more specifically by particular theories. For example, in my own fiction I draw on theories from sociology, psychology, and gender studies (such as feminist standpoint theory, social constructionism, intersectionality theory, and so forth).

Research Purpose and Goals

Before you make design choices, you need to answer the following question: What is the story you want to tell? In other words, what are the issues, experiences, themes, and/or micro–macro connections you want to explore?

In addition to figuring out the thematic content you aim to explore, it is also helpful to identify your research purpose or goal. In other words, what are your objectives? Your purpose or goal is linked to the thematic content you aim to explore but also extends beyond it. In this regard, issues to ponder include:

- What is the content you wish to explore? If you are exploring multiple themes, what are the connections between those themes?
- What, if any, interconnections between people's experiences and/or other topics do you wish to illuminate?
- What, if any, micro–macro connections do you wish to make?
- What do you hope to evoke in readers?
    - resonance
    - empathetic engagement and/or sympathy
    - raising critical or political consciousness
    - learning about particular subject matter/topics/socio-historical issues
    - building bridges across differences
    - unsettling stereotypes and/or disrupting dominant ideologies
- Who is (or are) the intended audience(s)?
    - Who are the key stakeholders you wish to reach with this work? If there are different groups you wish to reach, what are the similarities and differences among those groups?

It is important to spend ample time thinking about and clarifying your goals, both in terms of content and audience, so that the broader purpose can inform design choices. Of course in research/writing practice, which is an evolving process, sometimes our goals change, as do our visions for our audience. It is important to remain open throughout this process.

Design Elements: Structure

The structure of a fictional work gives you its foundation and form. Like with all other design aspects, the structure you build should be linked to achieving your goals. When I use the word "structure" I am really referring to *architectural design*. If we are to envision a physical structure like a house, the structure refers to the foundation, walls, delineation of rooms and closets, windows, doors, and points of access—in other words to the overall framework for the building. When you are building a physical structure, the choices you make are linked to your goals. For example, the size of the structure, the purpose of the structure (residential or commercial), and so on, all impact your design choices. One goes about building a townhouse, single-family house, child's tree house, office building, museum, theatre, or cathedral differently.

When you are writing fiction, the general structure may be a short story, a novella, or a full-length novel. It may be helpful to think of these as three distinct structures. As always in research, you should select the structure that best helps you achieve your intended purpose. You need to think about two major issues: the content you are trying to communicate and the most effective way for readers to process that content.

- Content: How much information are you trying to communicate? Are you trying to tell one story or multiple stories? Can your themes be communicated in a straightforward manner or do they take time to build and perhaps interweave?
- Audience: Can readers access what you want them to take away in a shorter format, like a short story? Conversely, do you want readers to engage at greater length with the narrative or narratives you are building? Do the themes you are tapping require a longer reflexive reading process?

Short stories can be quite powerful and can be an excellent way of making an impact in a relatively short read. Novellas allow you to go further with thematic content, characterization, and so forth. Novels are particularly effective for telling a complex story or multiple intersecting or overlapping stories. Novels are also effective when deep characterization or plot development is needed to communicate the thematic content, or when the story unfolds over a period of time. In short, any one of these formats (or others) may be appropriate for a particular project. What is important to remember is that when you are writing a short story, novella, or novel you are building a specific kind of structure that impacts how you approach other design issues.

It is also important to consider the *interior design* of what you are building. Several years ago, when I completed a draft of *Low-Fat Love*, I asked an editor I am friends with to look it over. When she returned her comments, she said that she did not focus on the overall structure but rather on "the wallpaper." That comment really stuck with me. If you are building a house, the interior design includes aesthetic choices like color, paint, wallpaper, flooring, lighting, flow, etc. The importance of these elements cannot be underestimated, as we all know that when we walk into different spaces we experience varying feelings based on their look and layout. Color choice alone can impact how we perceive the size of the space and how the space makes us feel. In fiction, the "interior design" elements include the genre, style, and tone of the writing. (Interior design also includes elements like furniture, paintings and other adornments, etc.—what is in the space. I address these issues later when talking about characters, description, and details.) In the following sections I review the architectural structure and the interior design choices.

The Architectural Structure[1]

Narrative gives fictional writing its form (Abbott 2008).[2] There are many features of a narrative structure to consider as you build your fictional representation.

Master Plot

Sometimes when we are writing fiction we tap into a very general narrative that has been told in many ways and at different times. Master plots (sometimes referred to as "master narratives") are stories that are told over and over again in different ways. These stories draw on deeply held values, hopes, and fears (Abbott 2008). Master plots frequently reappear in the literature within a given culture and at times across cultures. Some master plots are essentially universal—the quest story, the story of revenge, etc.; however, as Abbott notes, different cultures produce variations on these universal narratives. Abbott suggests, and I concur, that "the more culturally specific the masterplot, the greater its practical force" (ibid., 47). The classic Cinderella story is an example of a master plot that reappears throughout the culture and is continually rewritten with contemporary audiences in mind.

Master plots are powerful literary tools because they resonate deeply with people and therefore carry "enormous emotional capital" (Abbott 2008, 46). Using a master plot allows writers to draw on that emotional capital, which can be particularly helpful for fiction-based researchers. Abbott explains:

> We seem to connect our thinking about life, and particularly about our own lives, to a number of masterplots that we may or may not be fully aware of. To the extent that our values and identity are linked to a masterplot, that masterplot can have strong rhetorical impact. We tend to give credibility to narratives that are structured by it. (Ibid.)

Sometimes writers unconsciously use a master plot, even if it is quite general. As researchers using fiction, it is worthwhile to consider the possible advantages of tapping into a narrative readers are likely to find familiar, and if not explicitly familiar, resonant on a deep level. In this vein it is important to remember that one of the reasons we may turn to fiction-based research is to reach audiences in new ways—through resonance, pleasure, and the disarming nature of fiction in comparison to nonfiction.

Plot and Storyline[3]

Whether or not you are tapping into a master plot, most fictional narratives have a plot (with some rare exceptions, such as stream of consciousness writing and the like, which itself may be considered a plot). A plot refers to the overall structure of the narrative. Typically, the process of plotting involves ordering the major events or scenes of the story and sketching a general outline of the beginning, middle, and end of the narrative. Major "plot points" are typically delineated during this process.

The storyline refers to the progression or sequence of events within the plot (Leavy 2009a; Saldana 2003). Writing the storyline for a fictional work can be a fairly involved process. Whereas you may have a clear sense of the overall plot—what generally transpires in the beginning, middle, and end of the narrative, including the narrative arc—how you get from A to B to C is much more complicated. It is often recommended that fiction writers draft a detailed storyline before writing. This is a strategy that works for many; however, there are writers who prefer to work with a general plot structure and fill in the storyline as they go. Similarly, some writers have a general plot structure and parts of the storyline sketched, and fill in the rest throughout the writing process. Everyone's approach to writing is different and you should develop a process that works for you.

In writing my two novels, I have found it helpful to allow the story to unfold before my eyes, as if watching a movie in my mind's eye. For my first novel I did not use a plot or storyline. However, the further I got in the writing, the clearer the major plot points became, and at some point I did take notes regarding the sequence of events. For my second novel I began with a general plot and a storyline for the first third of the book. As I got further along I wrote a detailed storyline for the rest of the book. However, I continually went back and made changes based on new understandings. In both instances I tried to remain open to where the story wanted to go, making changes based on the new insights garnered through the writing process and critically looking at what was working and what wasn't. So I recommend that irrespective of the extent to which you plan plot and storyline in advance, you remain flexible and open to the new insights and ideas you will accumulate throughout the writing process. You will undoubtedly learn more about the story or stories you are telling as you write them. Strict adherence to a storyline created prior to the writing process, even in the face of new learning, is similar to continuing to use an interview guide with questions that don't work simply because you are afraid to change course during the project. When writing fiction-based research, ultimately the fictional rendering will be judged far more than the methodological process, so it is particularly important to remain open to change.

Scenes and Narrative

There are two basic methods for writing fiction: scenes and narrative. Fictional writing typically draws on both methods.

Scenes are a dramatic way of writing—by showing what is happening as if the action were unfolding before the reader's eyes. In this regard, well-written scenes offer a high sense of realism and appear like slices of reality or episodes (Caulley 2008, drawing on Gutkind 1997). When you are writing in a scenic or dramatic fashion you "write about one continuous action in essentially one place by essentially the same people" (Cheney 2001, 27). Cheney writes: "As fiction writers know, scenes give vitality, movement, action—life—to the story. Scenes show people doing things, saying things, moving right along in life's ongoing stream. Even when writing about the past, writers may play scenes in the present tense, giving the reader the feeling of being eyewitness to the action" (ibid., 11). On a practical note, scenic writing may involve the use of active verbs (Caulley 2008).

Narrative writing, on the other hand, is a means of summarizing or offering readers information beyond what is transpiring in specific scenes. Narrative is less about showing and more about telling (ibid.). Narrative can be very helpful in communicating information that happened outside of the scenes and/or providing commentary on characters and/or situations. This kind of writing typically involves the use of passive verbs. When employing third-person narration, as discussed in the last chapter, the narrator's voice often emerges through narrative writing. For example, narrators may explain background information about characters in order to contextualize or comment on situations that have occurred in the past or present.

Comparison of Scenic and Narrative Writing

Writing Methods	**Description**	**Excerpts from *Low-Fat Love***
Scenes	Dramatic way of writing with a continuous action unfolding before the reader's eyes	"My friend and I were going to go get a coffee, to talk about the reading. Would you like to join us?" Stunned by the invitation from a tall, dark-haired man whose name she didn't yet know, Prilly stammered. Pete quickly responded, "It's ok, no worries, but if you're not busy come along." With that, Pete walked in front of Prilly, opened the door, and let her pass through.
Narrative	Summarizing and offering readers information beyond what is evident in scenes	The next few weeks were the most intense of Prilly's life. Every day she hurried to her apartment after work to freshen up and grab an overnight bag.

It is also worth noting that stories have gaps that the readers inevitably fill in (Abbott 2008; Barone and Eisner 2012; Iser 1980). In other words, fictional narratives are always incomplete. Typically fictional narratives combine scenes and narrative that may occur over some expanse of time, and therefore there are temporal gaps as well as gaps between scenes. Even in cases in which the entire fictional narrative occurs in one dramatic scene (a continuous action unfolding), what happened before and after the scene is still left up to the reader's imagination. Gaps in the narrative allow for a multiplicity of meanings to emerge and may be intentionally carved into the narrative in order to create ambiguity of meaning (Barone and Eisner 2012, drawing on Iser 1980). This is a strength of fiction-based research, but it is also a point to take seriously. Researchers have vested interests in how their work is interpreted, understood, and used that go beyond those of traditional fiction writers. Therefore, it is important to be aware of where the gaps in the narrative are and to make sure those are spaces in which one explicitly wants readers to engage in this imaginative meaning-making process.

Endings, Closure, Expectations

There are several general issues to consider as you structure the ending of the narrative. Obviously the final impression that readers are left with is the ending, so you need to think about what you want to achieve with it. Two specific and interrelated issues to consider are expectations and closure.

Readers develop expectations as they read stories. These expectations are based on: 1) signs and signals the writer has created; and 2) their previous experiences consuming stories (novels, films, etc.). Beginning with the former, there are many different ways that writers create expectations in readers. For example, when the author is working with a familiar genre, readers expect the writing will follow the conventions of that genre. I'm not implying that this needs to be the case, only that those expectations will have been created. For example, in a romance story readers expect the primary characters to fall in love and that love will conquer all. Chekhov famously told an aspiring writer "if in the first chapter you say that a gun hung on the wall, in the second, or third chapter it must without fail be discharged" (in Abbott 2008, 60). The assumption is that by noting there is a gun on the wall the author has set up expectations in the reader, and that the writer has an obligation to fulfill those expectations. While the former may well be true, as readers are accustomed to looking for signs, signals, and foreshadowing, the latter is open to debate.

Expectations do not necessarily need to be fulfilled. In fact, sometimes it is beneficial to violate readers' expectations (Abbott 2008). A surprise ending may illuminate something we wish to highlight, may point to the constructed nature of the genre or master plot we are drawing on, and/or may require readers to reflexively revisit previously held assumptions, which may in fact be our goal. This brings us to the issue of closure.

Closure refers to "resolution of the story's central conflict" (ibid., 57). As readers develop expectations, they anticipate the ending of the story and will often judge a "good" ending based on how well it satisfies their expectations. In other words, readers don't want to be disappointed. Master plots, for example, typically end in anticipated ways, providing closure for readers. However, whether or not we are drawing on a master plot or common genre, we do not need to fulfill readers' expectations. This is particularly salient in fiction-based research in which our goals may be to disrupt readers' commonly held assumptions. Of course as we write fiction we need to be mindful of how the text will be read and the extent to which we are producing a good story (judged not necessarily by whether or not it fulfills expectations, but rather according to literary traditions). This can be a balancing act between understanding the expectations readers are likely to develop and deciding when it is appropriate to fulfill them and when it is appropriate to violate them.

The Interior Design

Whereas the architectural structure or design gives the writing its form, the "interior design" elements give the writing its feeling or gestalt. There are a few key design choices to consider in this regard.

Genre

A genre is a "recurrent literary form" (Abbott 2008, 49). There are very broad genres for writing fiction, such as the novel, novella, or short story, all of which tell stories through a narrative structure.

Within each of those literary forms are thematically driven genres. Some popular examples include romance stories, "chick lit," mysteries, and so forth.

Your selection of the genre within which to write your story is dependent on a few factors. First, the thematic content you wish to cover—your purpose—guides you toward appropriate genres. Second, each genre tends to appeal to a different primary audience. When writing fiction-based research, it is important to consider the audience you wish to reach and select a genre accordingly. Finally, master plots are often linked to particular genres (Abbott 2008). Therefore, your decision to draw on the emotional capital of a particular master plot may go hand in hand with your decision to write within a particular genre.

Once you are writing within a genre, it is important to bear in mind that each genre comes with its own set of conventions. These conventions build expectations in readers. As discussed earlier, it will be up to you to what extent you want to meet and/or violate those expectations. Here's an example of this kind of decision-making: When I was writing *Low-Fat Love*, I decided to adapt the "chick lit" genre in order to appeal to my primary audience, college-age women. However, though I wanted to draw on the pleasure that my target audience derives from that genre, I also wanted to subvert and disrupt the conventions of the genre in order to interweave a feminist subtext into the narrative. So I picked a resonant genre and then began violating the readers' expectations, increasingly so as the narrative progressed.

Themes and Motifs

A theme is a recurrent idea and a motif is a recurrent subject, idea, or theme. Qualitative researchers are accustomed to thinking and writing thematically. Often data are coded so that themes may emerge, which then become the focal point of interpretation and writing. Fictional writing almost always presents themes and/or motifs. Themes and motifs become particularly relevant when writing fiction-based research. Often the writer's goal is to convey thematic content and the fictional medium allows for motifs to be carefully woven into the narrative.

Fiction also allows themes and motifs to appear throughout a text in different forms so that they become part of the subtext underscoring the narrative as well as substantive content within it. For example, one of the themes in my new novel *American Circumstance* (forthcoming) is how social class shapes identity and experience. This theme is interwoven into the novel in different ways, including dialogues between characters, interior dialogues, and descriptions of characters' homes, physical appearance, and life experiences (such as school, work, and travel). The theme is also directly woven into the storyline in several different ways. This is just one example of how fiction allows researchers the opportunity for a careful and nuanced development of thematic content.

Style and Tone

Style is difficult to define, and there are several aspects to this term to consider. Every author leaves his or her fingerprint on his or her writing. This is most salient when writing fiction, which is dependent on the writer's imagination and creative use of literary tools. Style can include things such as: attention to the dramatic effects of language (such as the use of short statements and emotionally weighted language); emphasis on the lyrical nature of language; use of humor, sarcasm, and the like; and the search for a balance between scenic and narrative writing, or between the omniscient voice of a narrator, the interior monologue of characters, and the dialogue or interaction between characters. These stylistic decisions are in part simply a product of a particular author's strengths and personal preferences. However, stylistic choices can also be made with the research purpose and audience in mind. It is also important to consider the tone of the story. Is the story meant to be uplifting, hopeful, tragic, humorous, sarcastic, or something else?

Design Elements: Characterization

One of the primary decisions to make is: Who peoples your story? Constructing characters that will engage readers and help you achieve your goals—such as empathetic engagement, resonance, or unsettling of stereotypes—requires great attention. All fiction writers have the burden of creating authentic character portrayals. However, writers who use fiction-based research have the additional task of making sure they are sensitively, compassionately, and responsibly portraying people (whether they are portraying research participants or constructing imaginary characters who are meant to reveal something about real experiences).

How one develops characters depends first on how data have been collected for the project. When data have been collected via traditional research methods, such as interviews or field research, characters may be based on real research participants. There are two major issues to consider in these instances. First, as in any research practice there is an ethical obligation to protect the participants' identities. Second, decisions need to be made regarding whether characters will be composites based on aggregates of data or if some participants' stories and experiences will be highlighted over others. In other words, how many of the participants will in some way or another make their way into character representation, and to what extent will characters be composites? When writing is the research act, and authors are drawing on cumulative research, teaching, and personal experiences, decisions need to be made about what kind of characters will be portrayed and the function of each of them.

As discussed in chapter 2, decisions also need to be made about the narrator. Is the narrator a general, omniscient chronicler that has access into the perspectives of all of the characters (typical in third-person narration)? Or is the narrator a main character in the story (typical in first-person narration)?

As with all other aspects of writing fiction-based research, there are many different ways to approach characterization. Although it is impossible to provide a model of character design that will fit every project and writing style, there are different aspects of characterization that can be considered.

Types and Character Profiles

There are recurring kinds of characters referred to as "types." Character types are often linked to master plots, so if you are working within a master plot to structure your narrative, you may work with a character type as well. For example, a battered wife is a character type and her story (which centers on a cycle of abuse) is a master plot (Abbott 2008, 49).[4] Just as master plots, character types can carry emotional and symbolic weight for readers, and this makes them potentially useful tools. However, reliance on a character type can be likened to walking a tight rope—you really need to tread lightly. When a character type is used well, it can help readers relate more easily to the character and his or her circumstances. However, when a character is not written sensitively and authentically—with dimensionality, nuance, specificity—the type doesn't come to life and appears instead as a stereotype (Abbot 2008). Reverting to stereotypes is problematic from both a research and a general writing point of view. Researchers have an ethical obligation to sensitively portray people and "types" of people; further, fiction that relies on stereotypes is generally poorly written.

The issue of readers' expectations emerges again here. If you are drawing on a common type, you need to make decisions about when and how to challenge the readers' assumptions about the character. These decisions should be made in service of the research goals and the benefit to the story. So, for instance, a story may begin with a stereotypical character portrayal in order to ultimately disrupt, unsettle, or challenge that stereotype.

Whether or not you are developing your characters out of recurrent types, it is important to develop robust character profiles. Some issues to consider in the development of each character are:

- Physical description. What is included in this description and how detailed it is should be based on the research purpose and on what is needed to help readers get to know the character. The physical description may include everything from status characteristics (gender, race, ethnicity, etc.) to age, clothing, facial features, and perceived attractiveness. A related decision is the point of view from which we learn about the character's physicality. For example, are readers introduced to what the character thinks of his or her own appearance, do we see what a character looks like through the eyes of other characters, or do we learn what a character looks like only through descriptions by the narrator?
- Activities. How does the character spend his or her time? What is he or she shown doing? How does he or she feel about these activities?
- Personality. What is this character like? Is he or she funny, shy, loud, boisterous, sarcastic, etc.? What are the character's core

values, morals, and ethical guidelines? What motivates this character? What makes him or her tick? How does the character make other characters feel?
- Name. Names can carry all kinds of symbolic meanings. For example, character names tend to denote age, nationality, religious background, and so forth. Names can also be used to make characters more distinct or to give them a common "every person" quality. You may also consider whether or not the character will be referred to by one or more nicknames and what those nicknames are signifying either about the character or his or her relationship to other characters.

Beyond these dimensions of a character, I think it is important to keep an eye on the big picture and on capturing who this person is—his or her essence or core being. It may be helpful to think about what characters might have in common with others (how they illustrate or tap into culturally specific or universal themes) as well as what makes them unique (the specific details about who they are and what differentiates them from others). In my own writing I have also found it helpful to think about characters strengths as well as their flaws. Very few people are universally good or bad. Most people have strengths and weaknesses, which is what makes them valuable, interesting, and relatable.

Dialogue

Nothing brings a character to life more than dialogue (with others as well as internal). Through hearing their voices, seeing how they interact with others, and listening to their streams of consciousness and/or private reactions to people or situations, readers learn who characters truly are. It is not surprising that many writers find writing dialogue the most joyous and/or the most challenging part of their work. There are two main techniques for incorporating dialogue into a fictional work: dialogue with others (via interaction) and internal dialogue.

Dialogue and Interaction

Fictional narratives often feature "captured conversations," which enhance characterization and are meant to be snippets of the way people communicate daily (Caulley 2008, 435). Writing dialogue between characters illuminates who individual characters are and how they relate to one another. Realistic dialogue—that which rings true—is an important feature in most fiction, particularly with respect to character development. Things to consider when writing dialogue include:

- The way that a character uses language. This includes the use of formal, informal, and slang language, culturally specific expressions, and so forth. A character's particular style of talking can also illuminate things about the character or the way he or she reacts to particular people or situations.
- The relationships between characters. Through dialogue authors denote familiarity between characters, the comfort level of the characters with one another, and many other aspects of their relationships.
- The tenor of conversations. The tone, feeling, or mood of conversations/interactions is also communicated through dialogue.
- Additional features of dialogue. It is important to consider the pace of a conversation, pauses, audible signals other than language (such as sighs or exaggerated words), gestures, expressions, and the context in which the dialogue is unfolding (for example, if there is a conversation between characters sitting in a restaurant consider how the waiter coming over to the table might impact the conversation).

When writing dialogue, the most important thing to consider is that you are giving voice to your characters. It is important that the dialogue rings true. Well-written dialogue can engage readers, whereas poorly written dialogue (that which appears inauthentic) can disrupt the flow of the narrative.

Internal Dialogue and Interiority

As discussed in the last chapter, the ability to reveal internal dialogue and represent a character's interiority is perhaps the greatest distinction between fiction and other writing forms, as well as fiction's greatest asset. Representing interiority allows writers to make conceivable what is otherwise hidden (Caulley 2008). Internal dialogue should be used carefully in fiction-based research to the extent it facilitates research goals. With respect to the interests of researchers, internal dialogue can be effectively used for:

- Exploring sociopsychological processes (readers are given access to what a person thinks and feels in regards to him or herself, in response to interactions with others, and in response to particular events, situations, or circumstances).
- Creating empathetic engagement (getting to know, care for, and sympathize for or empathize with characters).
- Establishing micro–macro connections (illustrating how larger social, political, economic, cultural, or other forces are interpreted by individuals and/or how they impact individuals).

As noted in the last chapter, when revealing interior dialogue researchers need to be mindful that they are in essence speaking on behalf of others in a way that gives the appearance that the characters are speaking for themselves. While this may not be a significant issue in traditional fiction writing, there are potential ethical concerns that researchers using fiction have to consider (as discussed in the last chapter).

Internal dialogue can be written into the narrative in different ways. For example, during a dialogue with others we may also have access to what a character is privately thinking. In these instances we are learning not only about the individual character but also about the relationships between characters. Internal dialogue can also be used when characters are by themselves. In these instances characters may be engaged in an activity (such as exercising), they may be consuming art or media (such as reading a book or watching television), or they may be engaged in a passive activity (such as sitting on a train or lying in bed). Access to the characters' internal dialogue during these moments may appear as a stream of consciousness.

Design Elements: Literary Tools

There are a variety of literary tools writers use in order to make their fiction good. Based on the needs of particular projects and the style of each writer, these tools can be used in different ways.

Description and Detail

Similarly to ethnographic writing, fiction often requires descriptive writing. Rich descriptions of places, people, and situations help to draw readers into the narrative. As readers enter into the social world represented in the story, they want to see, hear, and smell what the characters in that space are experiencing. In this regard, the robust descriptions that often characterize fictional writing bear striking similarity to the "thick descriptions" found in the best ethnographic writing (Geertz 1973). The way a room looks, its size, color, lightness and darkness, its mood, smell, the objects it contains, how a character feels in that room—all of these elements may be important. Note that even in the preceding example, the description aims to capture both the physical aspects of the space or situation and the emotional or lived experience of that space or situation.

During the process of building descriptions it is important to incorporate concrete details. Realistic details "conjure emotions and images in the reader" (Caulley 2008, 47). The use of details accomplishes several things in fiction-based research. First, these details create mood or atmosphere and can help develop the tone of the narrative. Second, incorporating realistic details can help achieve verisimilitude. Achieving authenticity paves the way for building resonance and creating a connection between the reader and the narrative. Finally, as researchers we are incorporating empirical data/details into our stories, whether these empirical details come from traditional data collection or our cumulative experiences that shape the writing process. Selecting and combining this empirical data, as Iser (1997) suggested, is an integral part of the fictionalizing process. As researchers writing fiction, the selection and combination of realistic details or data is one of the main strategies available for expressing our key messages, themes, or motifs. Weaving together these details is an act of interpretation and meaning-making and, in part, it ultimately guides the readers' interpretive process.

Language

At the end of the day, the only tool that writers really have available is language. Whether writing dialogue, describing places, or reaching a narrative arc, language is the medium with which we communicate.

Good writing requires attention to craft and language. There is great artistry that goes into writing fiction well. This is a practice that demands time and patience. There are no shortcuts. Elizabeth de Freitas (2004, 269–70) explains her attention to language as follows: "In my own fiction writing, I plunder my experiences, my language, and my very being, to achieve an exactness in my sentences and paragraphs, grooming them over and over until they match my intentions and my sense of potential impact. Nothing is sloppy in fiction. . . . Composing fiction is a rigorous act."

Similarly, in my own writing practice once I have completed a draft or part of a scene, I go back and rework the language, sometimes over and over again. As noted earlier in this chapter, I liken the experience to working with a piece of clay. I begin with a big lump and use my fingers to work and rework and rework each small area until it has been sculpted properly.

Although writing fiction and using language well mean different things for different writers, there are some commonly used literary tools.

Specificity

Writing fiction well requires specificity. It is important to use language clearly, crisply, and effectively in order to achieve your intention. You will have choices about how you use language to achieve specificity. For example, there are words that imply emotion (Caulley 2008, 432). So if you are interested in reporting the temperature of a bathtub that a character is dipping her toe into, you could say that the water was "X degrees" or you could use a word that implies emotion and say something like the water was "frighteningly hot."

Metaphors and Similes

Creative writing often draws on the power of metaphor and simile: "The use of metaphors and similes make for richness of writing. They are figures of speech that compare an abstract concept with something concrete—an object we can see, hear, feel, taste, or smell" (Caulley 2008, 440). Qualitative researchers are adept at thinking metaphorically and symbolically (Saldana 2011). This dimension of interpretation and construction of meaning allows us to see connections between data. As Cole and Knowles (2001) note, as researchers aim to sensitively portray lives they engage in a process that requires thinking metaphorically. Metaphors and similes can be used to enhance the aesthetic quality of any work of fiction, but there are added benefits for fiction-based research. Metaphors and similes can be used to:

- Create micro–macro connections
- Challenge, disrupt, or subvert taken-for-granted assumptions
- Create subtext

Metaphors and/or similes should serve the quality of the writing as well as the research purpose, and should not simply be thrown in or overused "for good measure."

Summary of Design Elements

Design Elements	**Building Blocks**
Architectural Structure	Masterplot Plot and Storyline Scenes and Narrative Endings, Closure, Expectations
Interior Design	Genre Themes/Motifs Style and Tone
Characterization	Types Character Profiles Dialogue Internal Dialogue (Interiority)
Literary Tools	Description and Detail Language Specificity Metaphors and Similes

Presentation of the Fiction

An important consideration for those writing fiction-based research is how to present the fictional work to an audience. Generally speaking, a text discloses or conceals its fictional nature (Barone and Eisner 2012). There are various conventions by which the text reveals its fictional or nonfictional status. The simple act of labeling a work as fiction or nonfiction is one way of signaling the status of the text.

Depending on the structure of the text (short story, novella, novel), the venue in which it is published and how it is disseminated, you are more or less likely to use particular conventions. When a work is published on its own, as is most often the case with a novella or novel, you can signal the fictional nature of the text simply by labeling the front and/or back cover. You may also choose to include information about the fictional/nonfictional status of the text in a foreword, preface, introduction, or afterword. When the work is published as a part of a collection, for instance in the case of publishing a short story in an academic journal or literary magazine, you may choose to signal the status of the text in an abstract, preface, introduction, or afterword. You need to be mindful of the norms of the venue in which you are publishing, which may restrict your options.

Writing fiction-based research is an act of border crossing, and so the issue of disclosure is particularly complicated. It can be difficult if not impossible or just plain undesirable to tease out the "imaginative" aspects of the work from the real-world experiences that have informed the writing, and I am certainly not suggesting that you do this. There are no universal guidelines about how much information to disclose about your research practice—this needs to be determined on a case-by-case basis in accordance with the format in which you are writing and publishing as well as your purpose. I personally prefer that the fictional writing stand more or less on its own as an artistic work. In this vein, I advocate a short preface or afterword briefly describing the project. More in-depth treatment of methodological issues can be left for discussion in separate articles, essays, book chapters, or blog posts.

Douglas Gosse took a different approach and created two versions of his novel *Jackytar* (2005). In an attempt to bridge public writing and academic writing, Gosse included extensive footnotes as a "hypertext" in one version of his novel (Gosse 2008). In this way he was able to directly reference his literature review, including queer theories he was extensively citing. Gosse also published a version without footnotes, so that the novel could stand on its own. While this idea may be very appealing to those who wish to work within both academic and literary circles, of course it poses the additional challenge of being able to publish the work in more than one format. As an alternative, one might consider offering a short supplemental text where academic citations are made—this could be offered as an electronic supplement available for download on the publisher's website when the book is adopted for courses.

Additional Suggestions

In the spirit of strengthening your writing I have a few additional suggestions. First, *proofread, proofread, proofread*. Second, *revise, revise, revise*. Good writing doesn't just happen, it takes practice, care, and critique. Each time you go back to reread something you have written consider looking at it from a different point of view. For example, in one instance you might consider content-based issues such as the chronology of the plot, how the storyline unfolds, and unintended gaps in the narrative. During another read you might consider structural issues such as sentence structure and flow. You may review the text again and pay particular attention to literary details such as use of language, repetitions, and wordiness.

Inviting others to read part or all of your manuscript can also be very useful. A common way of doing this is joining writing groups. Often you can find an established local writing group by checking out your local library's website or a local community center or adult education facility. If you are unable to find an established writing group, consider starting your own. A good place to begin is by contacting your professional and/or personal network through social media or email to see if there is any interest. In my experience it doesn't matter what the other people in your writing group are writing about. In fact, it can be very useful to be in a group of people working in different genres. This can add a level of neutrality to how they approach your work. One of the great benefits of writing groups is that they often put their members in the position of reading their work out loud. This can be enormously helpful and can even be done on one's own, outside of the context of the group.

As opposed to joining a writing group, you may opt to find a writing buddy. I consider a writing buddy one other writer with whom you regularly exchange work. Although you may exchange your work via email to give yourself more time to read, think about, and offer suggestions on each other's work, optimally this does not replace face-to-face meetings. The process of talking through your work with someone can be very helpful as you clarify your intention and sharpen your writing. Sometimes you can find a writing buddy from a writing group, and if you have time for both, all the better. When you work regularly with a writing group and/or writing buddy the process you engage in bears similarities to the analysis cycles that qualitative researchers often engage in. Of course you can also share your work with colleagues and/or students as well as trusted friends to gain their perspectives.

Despite how important it is to revise and revise, in the end you also have to be willing to let the piece go. I don't think there is any piece of published writing that an author would not at least minimally adjust if he or she had another crack at it. This is the nature of writing. At some point you need to decide the piece is as strong as you are able to make it at that time, and you need to let it go and trust yourself. This takes some courage and self-confidence—but the fact that you are writing fiction in the first place means that *you are already brave*. While you may feel like the piece isn't "perfect" or that it will never be perfect, your writing doesn't do any good for anyone by sitting in your desk drawer. When you're writing fiction-based research, you have a larger objective—to teach, illuminate, or shed light on something. In order to achieve your goal, you need to get to a point where you trust yourself and your work, and simply let it go. When you do, I suggest you make peace with it. Feel good about what you wrote and allow others to engage with it as they see fit.

Conclusion

The practice of writing fiction-based research is not a linear methodology (like one might expect in quantitative research). There is no one way to do it, no set of procedures that can simply be followed. The data (or empirical bits) exist on a continuum, and data may be collected and analyzed using a traditional method and then fictionalized or the writing process itself may be viewed as the generative act. While there is no model for how to write fiction-based research, there are narrative features and writing strategies one can consider. I hope this chapter will be helpful as you consider the elements of a fictional work and how you might go about developing your own writing process. The next chapter considers how we might evaluate fiction-based research.

Chapter 4

Evaluating Fiction-Based Research

> I love reading social science done as fiction because as Richard Sennett once pointed out, we can learn more from a reasonably good novel about social life than we can from reams of fairly mundane scholarship.
>
> —Bud Goodall, Facebook Post, July 6, 2012

How do you judge, evaluate, or assess fiction-based research? Before getting into specific evaluative criteria, it is important to briefly review four issues that are central to evaluation. First, the issue of research "findings" is not relevant in fiction-based research and must be reconceptualized. Second, different methodological genres or genres of research practices require different sets of evaluative tools. Third, within the confines of a particular project, evaluative standards should be linked to specific research goals. Finally, the evaluative criteria detailed for any arts-based approach to research are not intended to be prescriptive, but rather should be applied as appropriate to a particular project.

Typically we think of research findings as the result of research practice, whether qualitative, quantitative, or involving the mixing of methods. This remains true of many arts-based research practices as well. While arts-based researchers have challenged the notion of research findings more than other social researchers, the term still persists. For example, in poetic inquiry we often talk of research findings being represented as poems. Certainly there is nothing wrong

Fiction as Research Practice: Short Stories, Novellas, and Novels, by Patricia Leavy, 77–91.

with using the term "research findings" when it is appropriate; however, in the case of fiction as research the term "findings" is simply irrelevant (Banks 2008; Cahnmann-Taylor and Siegesmund 2008). The practice of writing fiction-based research results in a fictional work. Therefore, we are not left with "findings" but with a fictional rendering, which may or may not include a nonfiction component (for instance a preface or afterword).

Fiction-based research has to be evaluated on its own terms. Qualitative research is assessed differently than quantitative research, arts-based research is assessed differently than qualitative research, and so too fiction-based research should be evaluated based on a specific set of relevant criteria. In chapter 1 I noted some of the major features of ABR, which can be used as assessment criteria. However, here I prefer to get more precise and present criteria specifically aligned with fiction-based research.

There should be a tight fit between the research purpose/goals and the standards by which we evaluate the research outcome. For example, some projects seek to make macro–micro links, foster self-awareness or social reflection, disrupt stereotypes, challenge dominant thinking, and/or contribute to our understanding in a substantive area. The extent to which the resulting piece of fiction meets any of these research objectives, or at least can be said to have made reasonable efforts to do so, is intimately linked to the particular goals. The same is true for the structural features of the narrative. For instance, research design choices such as the use of a master plot or a particular genre are judged, at least in part, with reference to the research objective. When considering the fit between the research purpose and the standards by which to judge the fictional work, issues of audience also come to bear. The design choices should make sense with respect to the intended audience.

Like other forms of arts-based research, although there are many different criteria that can be used to assess a specific piece of work, there is no one-size-fits-all model of evaluation or checklist of criteria that one can simply tick off of a list. There are, however, a range of criteria that can be considered as appropriate to a particular individual project based on its content goals and intended audience.

Before detailing specific criteria, I briefly review some standard qualitative evaluative criteria and how those might be trans-

Traditional Qualitative Evaluative Criteria Transformed for Fiction as Research

Traditional Evaluative Criteria in Qualitative Research	Traditional Criteria Transformed for Fiction as Research
Validity	It could have happened; Resonance
Rigor	Aesthetics; Use of literary tools
Congruence	Architectural design; Structure; Narrative congruence
Transferability or Generalizability	Empathetic engagement; Resonant or universal themes/motifs
Thoroughness	Ambiguity
Trustworthiness	Resonance
Authenticity	Verisimilitude; Creation of virtual reality
Reflexivity	Writer's personal signature

as we consider the merits of a fictional rendering (see table on the next page).

My goal in presenting the chart is merely to suggest that whereas fiction as a research practice is not a traditional qualitative method, there are ways of reimagining traditional assessment tools (for those who feel more comfortable working that way). However, instead of transforming criteria used to evaluate a different genre of research, I think ultimately it is much more effective to develop alternative criteria designed specifically for the practice of writing fiction-based research (see Richardson 2001). This is partly because as we move from traditional qualitative research to fiction-based research, we are moving from methodological practices to writing practices. As we move away from a methodological practice that produces "findings" to a writing practice that produces a fictional rendering that reflects research, teaching, and/or personal experiences, it is important to evaluate that work on its own terms.

Criteria for Evaluating Fiction-Based Research

In this section I present eight criteria that can be used to evaluate fiction-based research. While I have tried to create a comprehensive list, it is by no means exhaustive nor is it prescriptive. As the field of fiction-based research continues to develop and grow, the research community will continue to negotiate how to make sense of this work. Further, these criteria do not apply to every project and should be used on a case-by-case basis, not as mandates. I also offer checklists of questions that can be asked to evaluate a work of fiction-based research.

The Creation of a Virtual Reality

When readers enter into a short story, novella, or novel, they are entering into the world represented in that story. The story world may be quite familiar to readers or someplace new, but in either case it comes to represent a virtual reality. The creation of a virtual reality is a primary standard by which we can evaluate fiction-based research (Barone and Eisner 1997, 2012). It is important that readers can clearly see and imaginatively experience the virtual world represented on the pages. Fiction writers have many tools at their disposal as they build virtual realities. For example, detailed descriptions can be used to create sensory scenes that provide readers with a sense of how a place looks, feels, and smells. Well-written scenes also paint an emotional landscape for the reader, conveying ambience, mood, and feeling. When building descriptions of people, places, and activities, it is important to incorporate empirical details that ring true for readers.

As I have already noted, achieving verisimilitude is a hallmark of quality fiction-based research. The importance of portraying people and settings realistically, truthfully, and authentically cannot be underestimated. Whereas in traditional qualitative research authenticity is considered a primary evaluative standard, in fiction-based research capturing verisimilitude is what imbues the work with authenticity (de Freitas 2004). Here are some questions to consider as you evaluate fiction-based research:

- Are there rich descriptions? Can you envision the people and places portrayed?
- Is the mood of this reality expressed clearly?
- Have details been incorporated into the descriptions? If so, do the details resonate as truthful?
- Do the descriptions of people and places ring true? Do they feel authentic?

Sensitive Portrayals of People and Promotion of Empathy and Empathetic Engagement

A primary goal of social research is to sensitively portray human experience (Cole and Knowles 2001). It can be difficult to portray the complexity and nuance of human experience and in doing so afford people their multidimensionality. Characters in fiction should appear as people, not caricatures. The thoughtful portrayal of characters in fiction promotes empathy and empathetic engagement in readers (Barone and Eisner 1997, 2012; de Freitas 2003). Therefore, the promotion of empathy is both a goal of fiction-based research and a standard by which to evaluate it. There are three primary literary tools writers use to foster empathetic engagement that can be considered during evaluation: narrator's point of view, interior dialogue/interiority, and characterization.

The selection of first- or third-person narration impacts the perspective from which the story is told. Writers can use narrative point of view to their advantage with respect to promoting empathy. Similarly, the ability to represent interiority through interior dialogue is a powerful tool at writers' disposal as they develop rich characters and build connections between characters and readers. The stronger the connections that are built, the more readers will develop empathy for the characters. It is important that interior dialogue resonates with readers. This can be challenging when characters are dissimilar from readers; however, herein lies an opportunity to build bridges across differences. By representing interiority we are able to develop much richer characters. Fiction-based research can be evaluated, in part, by the extent to which it offers rich characterization, illustrates multidimensionality, and provides a context for understanding individuals—all of which culminate in the sensitive portrayal of people and their experiences.

In addition to literary tools, writers can also make substantive choices to promote empathy. For example, fiction writers concerned with social justice issues can disrupt stereotypes and/or challenge dominant ideology. When this is done well, the author's fingerprint is subtle and the characters, situations, or issues speak for themselves. In other words, the fictional rendering provides moments in which readers are likely to engage in the kind of self-reflection or social reflection that has the potential to build understanding across differences. This is also a form of empathetic engagement. Questions to consider include:

- Are there rich character portrayals? Are the characters multidimensional?
- Do the character portrayals ring true? Do the characters seem authentic?
- Whose point of view is guiding you through the story? How does the narrator shape your point of view?
- Do you have access to the interiority of characters? If so, does this help you to understand the characters? Do you understand the motivations, values, hopes, and/or fears guiding them?
- Do you feel an emotional connection to the characters?
- Do you feel sympathetic or empathetic towards the characters?
- Do you feel invested in the characters?
- Have the characters challenged any stereotypes?
- Have the characters helped you to learn something new about yourself or the social world? Have they exposed you to new ideas, experiences, or perspectives? Have they triggered a reflexive process?

Form, Structure, and Narrative Coherence

It is important in social research that the form and content are closely aligned. So, prior to considering specific elements of the fictional rendering it is important to consider the use of fiction more generally. By using fiction the writer should have achieved something that would not be possible in a different format (which may be as simple as rendering the work in a pleasurable medium or as complex as representing interiority in order to reveal social psychological processes). Questions to consider include:

- What does the fictional format offer that a nonfictional format does not?
- What has the writer been able to tap into or create through the use of fiction?
- Does the medium help communicate the content? Is the delivery of the content enhanced by the medium?

Creating a fictional rendering requires attention to architectural design elements (see previous chapter). One approach to evaluating fiction-based research is to consider the logic of design choices as well as the quality of their execution. Compositional design elements should be chosen in accord with the research goals (Barone and Eisner 2012). Of course, as with any art form, the execution—how well design choices are realized—should also be taken into account. The major architectural design features to consider include: structure, master plot, plot, storyline, scenes and narrative, and ending. Here are some questions to consider:

- Structure: Does the selection of the structure (short story, novella, novel) make sense? Was this form utilized for its advantages?
- Master plot: If a master plot has been employed, does tapping into it facilitate the research purpose? Has the master plot been used well? Is the emotional capital that is part and parcel of a master plot exploited in order to create resonance, empathetic engagement, or something else? Has the master plot been used in order to aid the delivery of the content as opposed to being used as a crutch (common in low-quality writing)? Has the master plot in some way been subverted? In other words, does the writer draw on the emotional capital of the master plot while also challenging and/or rewriting it in ways that are relevant to the delivery of content?
- Plot: Does the plot make sense? Can you follow the plot? Does the plot aid delivery of content pursuant to the research goals?
- Storyline: Does the storyline make sense? Can you follow the storyline? Does the storyline aid delivery of content pursuant to the research goals? Does the storyline move the plot along? Does the storyline engage you?
- Scenes and narrative: Are the scenes vivid? Did you feel like you were there, watching the action unfold? Is narrative writing used well to summarize and provide additional pertinent information? Does the balance of scenic and narrative writing (or exclusive use of one) make sense?
- Ending: Does the ending provide closure and/or ambiguity—as linked to the research purpose? Are expectations met or challenged in ways that make sense? Does the ending leave you wanting more? Does the ending promote reflection over the entire story? If

you are reading with others, does the ending promote discussion among readers?

It is also important to consider the narrative as a whole. Another evaluative criterion is narrative coherence:

- Do all of the pieces of the narrative fit together? When considering all of the previously discussed design elements (structure, master plot, etc.), do they all work well together? Are you left with a story that hangs together? Does it make sense as a contained fictional work? If not, has the writer provided additional clarifying information (for example, in an afterword)?

The Presence of Ambiguity

The presence of ambiguity is both a feature of fiction-based research and a standard by which we can evaluate it (Barone and Eisner 1997, 2012). For many social justice–oriented scholars, particularly those coming from critical theoretical traditions, research produces a multiplicity of meanings. In other words, instead of closing off meanings by providing an authoritative text, research renderings allow a multiplicity of meanings to emerge. Fiction-based research has an advantage over other forms of expression when it comes to presenting multiple meanings. Fictional stories can be read and interpreted in many different ways by diverse audiences. Readers bring their own unique perspectives to fiction. Furthermore, even when the author has a specific target audience in mind, it is more likely that diverse audiences will have an opportunity to engage with the fictional work. Differing from traditional research reports, fiction-based research involves a process of weaving meanings, creating subtexts, and offering one or more points of view. A great deal of fictional work, particularly when written in scenes, involves showing as opposed to telling. This allows readers to engage with and interpret fiction differently from nonfiction. While the fictional format itself nearly ensures that writers will build ambiguity into their work, there are some specific strategies that can be used.

All narratives contain gaps (Abbott 2008). These gaps can be strategically placed within the narrative (in the storyline) in order to open up spaces of imagination and interpretation for readers. For example, how closely scenes appear with respect to chronological time can create gaps in the narrative. How much information is provided about the characters before and after the action presently unfolding in the storyline is also a decision that impacts ambiguity. The extent to which readers' expectations are violated, how much closure is provided, and how the story ends also contribute to crafting ambiguity. Some questions to consider include:

- Are there multiple ways to interpret parts of the story as well as the story as a whole? If you are reading with others, does conversation among readers produce multiple interpretations, perspectives, and understandings?
- Where are the gaps in the narrative? Do the gaps in the narrative help you to contemplate themes or motifs in the story?
- Is the ending open or closed? Does the ending push you to further reflect on the story as a whole, including your own expectations?

Substantive Contribution

As any other research project, fiction-based research contains substantive content. One evaluation criterion, therefore, is the substantive contribution of the work (Cole and Knowles 2001; Richardson 2001). This is an important criterion that distinguishes fiction-based research from "pure" or literary fiction. Fiction-based research is always about something, and the researcher-writer's goal is to share knowledge about that topic. While all fiction is judged by how well it is written (the writer's skilled use of literary tools), research rendered as fiction also needs to be evaluated by its substantive contribution to a knowledge area or disciplinary field.

Fiction can contribute to our understanding about a historical event or time, a culture or subculture, a certain kind of experience, and so forth. Fiction can make various kinds of contributions to the particular subject or subjects explored. These contributions may be in the form of educating or sharing knowledge, building micro-macro links, raising awareness, or cultivating understanding.

When evaluating the outcome of any arts-based research project, including fiction, it is also important to consider the potential use of the work. Fiction-based research should be *useful*.[1] Maura McIntyre suggests that we ask: "Can its artfulness increase its usefulness?"

(2001, 220, drawing on Finley and Knowles 1995). Some other questions to consider include:

- What have you learned from this text? Have you learned something new? Has something you thought been challenged or reinforced? Are you seeing something familiar in a new light?
- Are micro–macro links forged? Can you see the connections between the characters' lives and the larger context in which they live?
- Has reading this text increased your awareness about a particular issue or issues, or about how different issues are connected to each other?
- Do you understand something about the topic covered differently or more fully?
- Does the thematic content contribute to your understanding?
- What can be taught/learned from reading this text? What kind of reflection or discussion may be promoted, and how, if at all, might that stimulate further learning?
- For what is this story useful?

Aesthetics

All researchers using an arts-based practice need to pay attention to aesthetics. When adapting an art form, it is vital to pay attention to the craft you are borrowing from (Faulkner 2010; Leavy 2009a). In projects where the act of writing is the act of inquiry (i.e., data are not collected via a traditional method), attention to the craft of writing and aesthetics is how one achieves rigor. As Elizabeth de Freitas (2004, 269) notes, when the fictional rendering has "deep aesthetic impact," then rigor has been achieved.

The aesthetic merit of the fictional rendering is an important evaluative marker (Barone and Eisner 1997, 2012; Bochner 2000; Cole and Knowles 2001; Richardson 2001). One of the reasons researchers are turning to fiction in the first place is because so many traditional research write-ups lack the qualities of good, engaging writing (Banks and Banks 1998). Aesthetic pleasure engages readers and fiction has the potential to offer readers enjoyment. As a consequence, fiction-based research is uniquely capable of truly reaching audiences (Banks 2008; Bochner 2000). Again, *the writing has to be good.*

There are many literary tools that can be used to strengthen writing: description, detail, language, specificity, metaphor, and simile. Here are some questions to consider:

- Is the story well written? Is it engaging? Does it flow well? Do you feel present in the story as if the action was unfolding before your eyes?
- Are there rich, lustrous, detailed descriptions?
- Is language used well? Are words carefully chosen? Does the language convey details and nuance? Is there richness in the language used?
- Is there specificity?
- Are metaphors and similes used, and if so, are they well executed? Have clichés been avoided?
- Did you enjoy reading the story?

Personal Signature

The personal signature or fingerprint of the writer may also be used to assess fiction-based research (Banks 2008; Barone and Eisner 1997, 2012). Just as with any other art form, every writer has his or her own personal style. Cultivating a personal writing style takes time and skill. The writer's personal signature is important for several reasons. First, it shows a rigorous commitment to the act of writing (paying attention to the craft and the aesthetic merit of the text). Second, good writers keep their audiences wanting more because of their own unique style of writing (which is an integral part of engaging readers). Finally, writers are present in their fictional rendering. Writers cannot disavow their role in the creation of the fiction—in fiction the writer is inextricably bound to the text. By imprinting the fictional rendering with one's personal signature, the writer is accounting for his or her active presence in the resulting text.

There are two main literary tools that writers have at their disposal to imprint the work with their trademark: style and tone. Style varies but may include the particular ways that a writer pays attention to the dramatic effects of language; the lyrical nature of language; the use of humor, sarcasm, irony, juxtaposition, metaphors, and similes; the balance between scenic and narrative writing; the balance between the omniscient voice of a narrator, the interior monologue of the characters, and the dialogue or interaction between characters.

Stylistic choices also influence the tone of the work—the emotional tenor or timbre of the story.

There are also content-based choices that reflect the personal signature of the writer. For example, some writers revisit similar topics, subjects, or themes throughout their work. Sometimes writers produce stories focused on different subject matter but draw recurring themes or motifs from earlier works based on their theoretical or political commitments. The repetition of characters across different fictional works is another strategy that some employ to mark their work. Questions to consider include:

- Is the writing style unique? Do you enjoy reading this style of writing?
- How does the writer use language to convey mood and emotions?
- What is the tone of the story? What has the writer done to convey the tone?
- If you have read other work by this author, what similarities in writing style are present? Is the writer committed to particular topics or subjects? Have themes, motifs, or characters from earlier works reappeared? If so, has this added to the aesthetic pleasure in reading the text?

Audience

When writing fiction-based research, it is important to bear in mind issues of audience. There are three primary considerations with respect to audience, each of which may come to bear on evaluation: the fit between design choices and the intended audience, how the text is presented (disclosing the fictional status of the text), and the audience's response.[2]

When writing fiction-based research, it is important to consider design issues in relation to the target audience. For example, writers can consider which genre is likely to be most effective in reaching their target audience. Ultimately, the hope is that the writing will resonate with readers. A range of stylistic choices—genre, writing style, tone—can help achieve resonance. Moreover, by making design choices in relation to the intended audience, a fiction-based researcher can capitalize on the pleasure of reading fiction. Remember that fiction is as much a reading practice as it is a writing practice (Cohn 2000). By making choices that tap into the pleasure different audiences find in reading particular genres and styles of fiction, researchers have a greater ability to reach and engage their public.

The presentation of fiction-based research also affects the way it is received and can be used as an assessment tool. A fictional text reveals it fictional status (Iser 1997). This can occur in several ways. A text may simply be labeled a novel, novella, or short story, thereby signaling its fictional status. A fictional work may also be presented with a nonfiction component, such as a preface, introduction, or afterword. In some cases a piece of fiction-based research, particularly something like a short story, may be presented with more extensive nonfiction writing. For example, a traditional research article may contain a short story or short stories as well as the nonfiction features of a conventional research report. It is important to disclose the nature of the text in fiction-based research, which is a "genre straddling" category of writing (Barone and Eisner 2012, 113).

Finally, one can consider how the audience has received the fictional rendering. Researchers can seek feedback from readers in order to gauge how successful they have been with respect to their goals. For example, researchers can assess whether or not readers enjoyed the text, what they learned from it, if it promoted reflexivity, if it fostered discussion among readers, and so forth. Researchers can seek feedback from readers and their target demographic even prior to publication. Once the piece is published, this kind of feedback can most easily be garnered when the text is used in classrooms; however, there may be opportunities for researchers to receive additional feedback at conferences, book talks, or through Internet surveys. Some questions to consider as you think through issues of audience include:

- Have design elements been chosen in ways that make sense with respect to the target audience? Have design elements been used in ways that are likely to engage the target audience?
- Is the fictional status of the text disclosed? How? Does this make sense given the nature of the text (i.e., if it is published as a self-contained text or alongside other content) as well as the venue in which it is presented to readers?

- How have readers responded to the text? Did they find the story engaging? Did the story resonate with them? What, if anything, did readers gain from the story (self-awareness, social reflection, education about a particular topic, pleasure)?

Criteria for Evaluating Fiction-Based Research

Criteria	Summary
Creation of virtual reality	Capturing verisimilitude
Sensitive portrayals of people, promotion of empathy and empathetic engagement	Using narrator's point of view, developing interiority, and creating multidimensional character profiles
Form, structure, and narrative coherence	Linking design elements and content
Presence of ambiguity	Opening the text to multiple meanings, structuring gaps in the narrative, and considering reader expectations
Substantive contribution	Contributing to a knowledge area or disciplinary field and usefulness
Aesthetics	Paying attention to the craft of writing and readers' aesthetic pleasure
Personal signature	Imbuing the text with the writer's personal fingerprint (style, tone, and content choices)
Audience	Linking design choices to the target audience, including presentation/disclosure, and gauging audience response

Conclusion

In conclusion, let me emphasize again that the list above is suggestive, malleable, and should be used as appropriate for a particular project. As I have previously noted, I believe that *usefulness* is perhaps the most important criterion for judging arts-based research (Leavy 2010). This distinguishes "pure" or literary fiction from fiction-based research. Remember, although writers creating fiction-based research use many of the same tools as literary writers, they have, at least in part, different goals. With this said, there is always a balance to be struck between artfulness and usefulness (between aesthetics/craft and substantive contribution). It is also worth considering how literary craft or artfulness and usefulness are related to each other, inform each other, and enable each other.

At the end of the day, perhaps the most important questions are:

- Did you enjoy reading the work?
- Did it engage you?
- Did you learn something?
- Is it well crafted?
- Is it well written?
- Did it stick with you?

I also want to leave those who are exploring the possibilities of fiction-based research with another thought. Once your work is published, make peace with it and let it go. No matter how your work is evaluated by others, you need to make peace with it so that you can continue to write. Those who are unafraid to explore new approaches to research and writing, to innovate with form and content, and to push themselves creatively are putting themselves and their work out there with no guarantee of what will come back to them. This takes courage and self-confidence. As anyone in the arts knows, readers can interpret your work and form relationships with it in unexpected ways. It is important to develop your own relationship with your fiction-based research that is not dependent on the judgment of others. When you're able to do that, you are far more likely to move forward on your creative journey.

Part II
Exemplars with Commentary

In this section I present exemplars of fiction-based research. I consider these pieces exemplars based on the evaluation criteria detailed in the previous chapter. I have selected pieces written in different genres, including short stories, novellas, and novels. The two short stories are presented in their entirety, whereas three chapters of the novella and two chapters of each novel are excerpted. I tried to select pieces that cover a range of substantive content and are stylistically distinct from each other. While the exemplars presented in this section by no means cover the full range of possibilities for fiction-based research, I hope they serve as useful illustrations of this approach to research.

I have asked each author to write a brief introduction to their fictional rendering. I offer my own brief commentary after presenting each fictional work. My commentary centers on why I think the work is an exemplary piece of fiction-based research. Instead of considering all eight evaluative criteria for each exemplar, I have decided to select two criteria to discuss in relation to each piece. Beyond showing why I consider the selections exemplars, it is my hope that this process will highlight how the evaluative criteria outlined in the previous chapter can be applied to a reading of fiction-based research and how different criteria are more or less relevant in different cases. This is not to imply that any of the works does not achieve the other criteria—each piece excels in far more than two areas. I have selected criteria to apply to each work based on its unique strengths in relation to the particular strengths of the other pieces (making certain to apply each of the eight evaluative criteria to at least one exemplar).

Short Stories

Chapter 5

The Scrub Club

by Elizabeth Bloom

Introduction

When I began my career as a middle-school social studies teacher in rural Upstate New York, I noticed that students from economically impoverished backgrounds were sure to lag behind others in the classroom and did not participate in school activities such as sports, music, or clubs. I noticed them slipping to the margins, banding together at the back of the class, getting into trouble, smoking in the parking lot before school. They were often the subject of eye-rolling gossip; of stories of teen pregnancies, adult boyfriends, and fights.

Early on, my principal asked if I would take a small homeroom that was made up of students who had been retained from the previous year. This I gladly did, and again I noticed that most of these students were poor, had difficult personal lives, and were considered very at risk by the school community. Amazingly, they were almost always children whose parents or aunts, uncles, cousins, or grandparents I already knew, or knew about, from growing up in this community. These students came with bad reputations already established, their

---

Fiction as Research Practice: Short Stories, Novellas, and Novels, by Patricia Leavy, 95–145.

family names well known in the police blotter of the local daily paper. Many of the teachers were also from the local area and were aware of the backgrounds of the students. "The apple doesn't fall far from the tree" was a refrain frequently heard in the teachers' lounge.

My homeroom kids thought of themselves as losers and they hated school, sometimes with a passion. My job was to provide nurturance and a safe haven. Sadly, I learned that what I had to offer wasn't going to be enough and that these students would more than likely drop out and go to work before their senior year had come around.

One of my reasons for leaving middle-school teaching was frustration with what Erickson described as the school's attempt to "cool [poor kids] out of the system" (deMarrais and LeCompte 1995, 189). With few exceptions, my homeroom students appeared to be repeating the experience of institutional and social exclusion and eventual disappearance that characterized their parents' school careers. As a result of this observation, I came to have great empathy for the plight of these students and frustration with what I perceived to be their systematic marginalization in school.

I knew these things only intuitively when I was a teacher. No one in my teacher preparation program, workshops, conference days, or the teacher's lounge ever mentioned anything about the reproduction of structures of domination. It wasn't until I read *Schooling in Capitalist America* (Bowles and Gintis 1976) that the full weight of the lie struck me. Like others I've known, I felt angry. I was angry that I'd been complicit in a system that I felt was morally wrong and felt that I'd been duped into serving as a paid functionary of the state.

At the same time, it began to dawn on me that this was a subject worthy of scholarly pursuit; not just for itself, but for ethical reasons as well. As Janet Fitchen notes in her classic ethnography of nonfarm rural poverty, one of the potential areas for breaking the cycle of educational, economic, and social inequity is to study schools. She says, "The study of school should provide very useful insights into what really happens, what doesn't happen, and why both parents and school, as well as children, are often disappointed with the results of schooling" (Fitchen 1981, 215).

When I began a doctoral program in education theory and practice at Binghamton University, I also began working on a long piece of writing that chronicled the experiences of my last year of teaching.

As a member of a writers group, I had already written several short stories about school over the previous year. As a habit, when I was a teacher, I collected and saved material from school that I had experienced or observed; notes left on the floor, poems students had written, vignettes that I witnessed, anecdotes, dialogue, observations, and desk graffiti all found their way into my notebook. This collection served as the basis of my writing. Perhaps my earlier training as an ethnographer at SUNY Albany in the 1980s led me to create this record. Perhaps it was an intuitive desire to preserve something that I believed was deeply important.

The most important motifs in my ethnofiction, *The Scrub Club*, involve answering three questions: First, what do working-class and poor adolescents have to do to survive socially and emotionally in an institutional climate that (a) overtly privileges their middle-class counterparts and (b) places submission to a middle-class authority structure above all other virtues? Second, given the systematic reliance on discipline and punishment to enforce compliance by students and faculty, how are the relationships among young people and between young people and adults affected? Third, what happens to students from economically disadvantaged backgrounds whose best shot at middle-class success happens in an academic environment that fails to inspire curiosity, critical thinking, or personally meaningful learning?

Though I initially undertook this project privately, in an effort to come to terms with my teaching experience and what I perceived as a personal failure, it later became an attempt to bear witness on behalf of my former students. This realization unfolded as I continued to write and to read the politically inspired work of many authors such as James Gee, Michelle Fine, Patrick Finn, Paulo Freire, and finally Laurel Richardson and Carolyn Ellis, who opened up the possibility of taking my creative writing and transforming it into what Laurel Richardson (2004) terms "creative analytic practice ethnography."

I write almost entirely in the voice of my narrator, a fourteen-year-old Puerto Rican girl named Mercedes Vasquez who was a newcomer in town, placed in my "at risk" homeroom. The choice to write in Mercedes's voice is a risky one. There is the danger of being accused of a discourse of colonization as I *use* Mercedes for my own suspect academic purposes. Who am I to speak for Mercedes? Why not let her speak for herself? I choose to take this risk for several reasons.

First, Mercedes was a forceful presence, someone you had to notice, listen to, and think about. In addition, Mercedes reached out to me when she was my student and in the process disclosed a great deal of her personal history. I admired her very much for her courage and resilience in the face of extremely difficult personal circumstances. She did what she believed she had to do to survive every day. On the outside she may have appeared very tough and even cruel sometimes; but I also saw that she was a sensitive and intelligent person with a keen awareness of others and deeply held values. Second, Mercedes and I are, to a great degree, fused in her fictional character. In the story, Mercedes is recounting events that I observed or that she told me about. Third, choosing Mercedes as the narrator plays on the notion of the traditional ethnographer as the outsider who arrives from afar to study the natives as a classic participant observer. She was raised in a cultural and geographic milieu that was in almost every way alien to the one in which she was thrown in rural Upstate New York. Creating her character as the outsider/ethnographer provides a mechanism for reporting her observations of the daily life, rituals, beliefs, and economies of the subject population.

Some might argue that the choice of Mercedes as a narrator could confirm a suspicion that I, as a middle-class person, cannot identify with the white working-class and poor neighborhoods of my childhood, and that it is Mercedes's "otherness" that makes her a strong ally and lets her stand in for me. This is mostly true. As a kid growing up, I had a strong sense of my liminal status among my peers. As the last in a large single-wage-earner family, I grew up lower-middle class in terms of income but upper class in terms of social/cultural capital, since my father was an English professor. I was attracted to anthropology as an undergraduate precisely because I identified with the outsider positioning of the ethnographer.

Last, as the narrative bears out, I had an opportunity to exercise powerful and compassionate agency at a critical moment but failed to. The piece is a fictionalized biography of the kind of children whom Freire (1998, 22) refers to as "the rag pickers of the world, the 'wretched of the earth,' the excluded." Recording their stories, heavy with violence and abandonment, meant that I had not completely forsaken them.

The Scrub Club

Prologue

I don't mind sayin that when I come before the judge I was scared shitless. The attorney they give me say me and Crystal and Tiffany and Sierra all equal in this crime. He say it don't matter who hold Bethany head under the water, we was all there with the same plan to hurt her so we all gonna go down for it together too.

When they brought me in I was thinkin that Bethany was dead so I guess it all came out the best way it could in the end. At least they let me stay at my house with my cousin Alma and her baby Little Dennis. Cause of the trouble I been in already at Binghamton the judge give me probation. He also put a order of protection on me so I don't go near Bethany or her sister, Fawn, and say I'm not allowed no contact with nobody else involved. That's o.k. cause Crystal and Tiffany over in JD in Syracuse and it happen on the last day of school so I didn't have to go back there again with nobody to hang out with. When all this mess over me and Alma goin back to NYC anyhow.

They also say I got to get a counselor for my anger issues, but since we got no insurance I got to go to the County Mental Health Clinic and the lady there can't squeeze me in till July. The counselor send me a letter though and tell me to get a notebook and write about my story to get prepared for seeing her. That's cool too since the judge make me have a electric ankle bracelet and I can't go nowhere but the county office and home without my probation officer givin permission. I got nothing to do in but sit around and smoke cigarettes and think.

Cause I'm fourteen the judge say he want me to be rehabilitated and not punish so he give me the chance. If I fuck up again he gonna charge Alma with neglect and put me in foster care.

My homeroom this year was 414 and we call it the Scrub Club on account of how everybody in there failed eight grade last year. Tell you about how we got that name later on. There only seven of us down there and the teacher. There Tiffany, Tom, Shawn, Sierra, Dale, Taylor and me, Mercedes.

First there's this girl name Tiffany down there and she real messed up. She be big and fat and she stink like piss so bad, my eyes be waterin some time when I have to stand next to her. She be kickin! Me and my girls let her hang out with us sometime anyway. The teacher tell her she got pretty blue eyes though and it true, she do.

The teacher, she so funny, she always be bustin on everybody. She even dis the principal. We never say the pledge in 414 cause the teacher say we can choose for ourselves and she say she don't like the "under God" part anyway cause she think they only talkin about a Christian god in the pledge and we got all types of religions in this country like Hindu, Muslim and so on. So we don't say it in there. The principal, she so fake, she come by there everyday and pop her big head in the door and say something like, "How're my favorite kids in the whole world doing this morning?" All cheery and happy like.

The teacher she say, "Great!" All cheerful back but then she roll her eye when the principal walk off. This one time the principal pop her head in right before the pledge and when it come on she stand at attention but we all keep on doin what we doin.

The teacher she look up at her and say, "We've made a pledge not to make pledges."

Straight up, just like that. The principal give the fakest smile yet and walk out. We all fell out laughin, even the teacher, and she say, "Jesus, you kids make me look bad!"

But she don't care. The principal don't pop her head in at pledge time no more.

Now Tom in the room, he a freak. He got black nail polish and he bleach his hair. He real skinny too. He in a band with Matt P. and them other boys call it Ritalin and they play metal or some shit like that. He has this bright yellow tee-shirt that say, "The Jesus is Fun Club" he got at Salvation Army. The teacher, she love that shirt. She always laugh when he wear it, she say, "WWJD if I stole it?" You know, like those What Would Jesus Do bracelets them kids who call themselves Christian wear? She like that; she say anything.

We felt bad that time Tom dad got arrested on a felony cause of some law about race discrimination. Tom father menace this black dude who give his brother Paul a ride home from Wal-Mart. He swing a bat and call him a nigger. What they didn't say was that the dude was Paul's boyfriend and the problem Tom dad got with it. They make it a race thing in the paper but it was a gay thing in real life. Tom just come in the class that day and put his head down on the desk and we all leave him alone but Shawn sit over by him and say, "It sucks when your old man's in jail don't it?"

Then he stop a second and say, "Or, your mom, in my case."

Then he do a Ba-dum-bump with his fingers. At least he make Tom smile a little.

Now Shawn, he a problem, and the teacher too soft on him. She always give him second and third and sometimes fourth chances. He always showin off and he say some outrageous stuff to teachers and I hate to admit it but he definitely hot for a red neck. Just the other day he jump right out the window in the homeroom and he get his foot caught in the string for the blinds so he land on the ground in a pile and the blinds come rollin down, brrrr rump . . . She don't even get mad when we all look out the window and he pretendin to be hurt on the grass. She just laugh and tell him to get back in before somebody catch us actin stupid. He always late cause he got to smoke a cigarette in the parking lot after he get off the bus.

Sometime the teacher get mad though. In fourth period one time he be leanin over Pam desk with his back to her and she keep sayin, "Shawn, sit down. . . Shawn sit down!" But he keep ignorin her cause he hittin on Pam. You know Shawn, he a skater boy so he wear his jeans down low. She raise her voice and say, "Shawn sit down or I'm going to pants you!"

He don't miss a beat and he say, "Yeah and it'd be the best piece a ass you seen in a long time."

Snap! Just like that. Everybody got all quiet then and the teacher say real serious,

"Now you've crossed the line Shawn. You are not welcome in this room right now. You need to go to the principal's office."

And Shawn, he know he gone too far that time, but he stroll out the room slow anyway, but you could tell he feel bad cause he shut up.

I told him later he shouldn't dis her cause she mostly nice to us kids. Like this one time. I got these big black eyebrows so I decide to pluck them and I'm pluckin along but, my bad, they don't come out even so I say fuck it and I shave them all the way off. So I just use some of my cousin Alma eyebrow pencil and come to school. The teacher look at me the next morning and she say, "Sweetie what happened?"

And then she make me laugh cause she tell me about how her nephew is brain damage and he shave his eyebrows off one time when he suppose to be shavin his chin. The trick was I didn't know that swimmin was startin in gym class that day so the pencil all come off in the pool. Right? So I go back to 414 and ask the teacher if she got a eyebrow pencil and she say no but she let me stay in the room while she go ask teachers until she find one for me and she write me a late pass sayin that she helpin me with homework.

Sometimes she be mean though. Don't let her catch you writin on the desk. She hate it when kids write on the desk. She saw me write, "I love Eric Edwards, #72 Binghamton Style" so she make me come in at lunch to wash all the desk off. You should see the dumbass shit kids write in there. Check it out: Mitchum sux cock, Ashley G. Sucks, Hope for the best but don't expect it, Jill stuffs her bra, Nick Howard is so hot, Hell yes, He's gay, school blows, penis, I love my mom.

Next in 414 is Dale and Taylor. I put them together cause they like bookends. They always be fightin with the yard sticks before the first bell doin their LARP . . . Live Action Role Play. You probably seen them in the park playin that shit with swords and shields. They freaks. Dale really little and dark and he wear a dog collar with these red rubber spikes and these oversize tee-shirts that say stuff like, "Look on the bright side, no one despises you as much as I do." His mom work at Frito Lay so he always bring us food in the morning. He pop the can or the bag right under the teacher nose and she say, "Don't give me any no matter how much I beg," but she end up eatin it anyway and then she say, "Dale if I turn into a fat slob it will be your fault!"

Then she ask for just one more handful.

Taylor, he taller and he could be hot if he dress better and cut that hippy hair off. He like a genius though, he got, like, a photographic memory, but he still fail eighth grade. He never do no homework, no projects, nothing! But he always got his hand up with the right answer in class.

The last on the list is Sierra and she the reason we call the Scrub Club. She fat like Tiffany, but she clean. She either in a good mood or she in a bad mood, nothing in the middle. Her mom a waitress at the Artemis Diner over on South Side. This one time she was in science class and the preps talkin and laughin all through class and the teacher get mad and he say he gonna give the whole class a zero for the day. So Sierra say right up in they face, "Jesum, we're supposably learning here, so shut up!" Well these preps don't like gettin dissed so one of them say to Sierra, "At least I'm not a dirty scrub."

Now Sierra is my girl and I would back her up if she want to fight that prep bitch but Sierra say no, she got a idea. So that night Sabrina and us girls made these tee-shirts say, "Prowd Member of the Scrub Club since 1980" and put pictures of flies on garbage cans and stuff, and we all just about died laughin the next day cause you should have seen them prep's faces. They all embarrassed and shit cause we made them look stupid. The principal called us down though and made us turn them inside out cause she said we were making trouble and it wasn't "appropriate."

I got my own story too. I pretty much got kicked out of my last school for fightin and what not. When I come over here to live last November I tried to keep this info on the down low. But the teacher she ask me right away why. Day one. "So how come you're coming in the middle of the year? Did your family just move in?"

I say, "Nah, I'm livin with my cousin and she already been here."

She ask another question. "So you came over from Binghamton public school?"

"Nah, I got kicked out over there."

"For what?"

"For fightin."

"Were you in a gang?"

"Somethin like that. But I ain't wearin no colors here. Your not gonna see me wearin nothin but blue jeans and grey or black. Nuh ungh, that's how it's gonna be this time around."

The teacher say, "That's great Mercedes. If anybody tries to drag you in let me know, o.k.?"

"Shore Ms. B. You da bomb." That was my first day.

The teacher she try to give me some lessons on fightin. Like once in January I went back to this teen club in Binghamton and I was lookin forward to it all week and tellin her about it cause they don't have none of that down here and she say on Friday, "Have fun but be careful Mercedes. Don't get too wild on me."

And then on Monday I have to tell her how I got kicked out, boom! Fifteen minutes into the party. Some girl got all up in my face sayin I be lookin at her boyfriend and I gotta say, "Step off bitch! Cause if you wanna go I'm gonna kick your skinny ass."

So the girl jump the bait and I gotta go cause she wanna get nasty with me. But before I even throw a punch or pullout a chunk of her hair the bouncer he kick me and my friend out. I didn't even get to dance.

Sometime though fightin bring good things, like the way I met my best girl, Crystal. This one time I come into 414 and I was too jacked up cause these girls come up to me in the hall and tell me this other girl wanna fight me. I don't even know who this bitch is so I ain't even got beef with her.

The teacher say, "You don't want to fight someone you don't even know, do you?"

And I say, "Yeah that's right."

But I keep thinkin that she got no right to say she wanna fight me so I'm gonna fight her so I can show her that she got no right to say she wanna fight me. The teacher she go find this girl name Crystal Fleming. She bring us both to the office cause she say she wanna give us a safe place to work it out so we don't have to fight. So I'm waitin in the office and the teacher bring Crystal in and she sit between us on them chairs that face the secretaries where you wait when you in trouble. She talk us through it. And guess what? It turn out this girl don't want to fight me. She heard I wanna fight her from the same girls who come up to me. Ah snap! Them girls were just tryin to stir it up, that's all.

Crystal, she got a bad streak in her. The teacher let her come into my study hall sometime and this one time Crystal come in and we got a project we need to do for Spanish and so the teacher gotta write us a pass. She tell us to go in quietly and get to work so we don't get in no trouble. That library teacher kick us out though before we even sit down. She say, "You girls don't belong in here, I'm sorry but you have a bad reputation and I'm not going to have you in my library making trouble."

Can you believe it? So we storm back into 414 and the teacher say, "You back already?"

And we tell her how the library lady kick us out and say we got a bad reputation. And she say, "No offense girls, but I really don't think she was talking about Mercedes because Mercedes is always so polite to the adults around here."

The teacher she always mention how I'm so polite and nice. I told her that my Grandma back in the Bronx would smack me hard in my face if I showed disrespect to any old people, Womp, and she did it too. More than once.

"I really think she was probably talking to you Crystal."

Crystal just look at her and smile and say, "I do got a bad rep around here and guess what? I'm proud of it."

One other time I got called to the principal office this year. This time she got the vice-principal with her and she definitely not lookin all sweet and cheerful and she say, "Mercedes, I have reliable information that you're carrying drugs in your purse. I'd like you to take each item out and put it on the table.

Now this bitch can be cold and she got no right to ask me this and I got to know who rattin me out so I ask, "Who told you?"

"That's not important," she say and the two of them stare me down like they was the FBI so I say fine and I take it all out one by one real slow to keep them hoppin. First I unsnap the latch, but I pretend it's hard to do. My bag look like a old style back pack but real small. It all patchwork suede of different kinds of blue and it got a tassel with a silver bead on the latch. First I pull out a pack of Big Red cinnamon gum with four sticks left but I kind of wrap my fingers around it so they can't see what it is till the last second. Then a bottle of Cover Girl Clean Make-up, color Tawny, then a pink and green tube of Maybelline Great Lash mascara, and I keep takin my time cause they lookin at my hand and my bag like two hungry dogs watchin a bone. Then a tampon with the end of the wrapper ripped. Then a can of Dax Wave and Groom Hair Dress in the red and black can. Next come my blue brush and a silver mirror in a compact.

"Open it up please," the principal say.

I look at her like it make me extra nervous and then I unsnap it and I make my hand tremble just a little. I'm holdin off on the last things cause I know they be gettin excited now. I pull out my lighter but they don't know it a lighter cause it look like a little silver and black cell phone with a key chain on it with my house key on it. They fooled by this one. Then come the only thing they gonna find on me, a pack of Newport Light 100's with three and a half cigarettes left in it. They eyes light up when they see my smokes. They make me take them out one by one. And I do it, real slow, glancin up at them through my black eyelashes.

"Now rip open the package," she say. And I do that too.

"That's it," I say.

And she say, "Shake the bag upside down."

And I say, "Suit yourself," and I shake it out for them on her desk and little bits from my cigarettes and a bobby pin and some crumpled up toilet paper all fall out on her desk. She got nothin to say but, "Cigarettes will not be tolerated in this building and I'm going to have to report home that you have cigarettes in your purse at school."

And I say, "Yes ma'am, I understand," but inside I be laughin my ass off cause my cousin Alma bought them cigarettes for me and she gonna be pissed off cause that shit be costin mad money these days.

CHAPTER 5

I.

One day back in winter we have extra time in homeroom on account of a big snow storm the night before. I was sure they was gonna call school all the way off but they didn't and we had to wait in homeroom till all the late busses come in. We get mad snow around here sometime in the winter and this day it was serious. We sittin there in 414 lookin out the window moanin and groanin about how come we gotta go to school and we listin off all the schools in them little towns around that were close for the day cause we heard it on the radio. On those snowy mornings you know there a whole town full of kids with their ears pinned to the radio waitin to see if school close. You know there some happy kids out there when they do call it off.

So we just sittin around bullshittin when somebody, probably Tom, say, out the blue, "What's the earliest thing you can remember?"

Shawn pipe right up with, "Dude, I can't remember what I had for lunch yesterday, my head's so fried!"

And Sierra say, "I remember being at the fair with my dad and we ate all these French fries and candy apples and stuff and he took me on the ferris wheel and I threw up all over myself and we had to just keep going around and around with that smell coming up in my nose."

Tom say, "That is so sick dude."

And then I check in, "I remember my grandma brushin my hair. I used to have real long hair and she would brush it back real hard and real tight and put it in one of those bands with the colored balls on the ends and then she would braid it and put another one of those bands in at the bottom. The end of my braid bounce off my butt. That's how long it was."

What I don't tell them is that I'm tryin to be real quiet cause it hurt real bad and I know she gonna slap me if I cry out. And I don't mention that I'm wearin a school uniform. It's plaid; blue, black and white, and the skirt have those folds in it called pleats and it got bands that come up over my shoulders. I'm wearin a white button down blouse with short sleeves underneath, white knee socks with a pattern in them and black shoes. It's hot in there even though she got a old air conditioner that make a rough buzzing noise. She pullin at my hair like she wanna rip it out and she talkin fast and mad. My real mom is lyin on the couch like she sick. I feel sorry for her but I ain't seen her for a while and I don't know what to say. When I woke up on this morning she was lyin there. She look real skinny and I seen that her fingernails were black underneath. She wearin a red sweatshirt with a hood. Her face look yellowy. When I look back on it I knew she was in trouble, not really sick, but what was I? Maybe five or six year old. What I got to say to her? All the while she lookin out at me while my Grandma be pullin at my hair and yellin at her sayin this and that. My mom finally just roll away and turn her face to the back of the couch. That's the thing I remember as the first thing.

And moms aren't the only problem. Down in 414 we got seven kids, right? Out the seven, three got fathers live with them. Sierra dad live with her but he disable. The way Sierra tell it, he spend his time bitchin and drinkin and watchin TV and tellin her how fat she look. Tom dad live with them too, when he not in jail. Shawn live with his grandma and his dad work for the railroad in another town, so he only come home every couple weeks. We know when Shawn dad home cause Shawn always got stories to tell when his dad there like how he and his dad ride they snow mobiles five mile in the dark through the woods to get to a redneck bar over there in Mt. Vision. Or he show us scabs he got on his knees cause him and his dad be wrestlin mad hard on the livin room rug. Taylor dad and mom still together and that a surprise cause he told us they was only fifteen when they had him. Tiffany mom got a order of protection against her dad and he can't come closer than 100 yards from them or they house, cause he beat them and worse, I think. Dale dad live in another town too but his mom got a boyfriend who live with them. He told us after Christmas that he thought Christmas was gonna suck and there he was lyin on the couch watchin a Christmas movie on TV on Christmas day. All a sudden he hear a voice that he know behind him. The voice say, "This is my favorite part."

Dale turn his head quick and see his real dad standin there. Dale didn't tell us this part but I know he jump off that couch and hug his dad up real close cause he love him and miss him so much and they so far apart. Dale say it make the worst Christmas ever the best.

Now me, I never seen no dad at all. I don't even know what he look like cause everybody say I favor my mom.

In a way, fathers the reason I come to live over here in this little town. When I was thirteen I was livin over there in Binghamton with Alma and her husband Big Dennis cause after my grandma died, Big Dennis and Alma decide they gonna get out the city and move Upstate. Big Dennis got hisself a job in a mechanic shop over there and everything goin good cause he got good pay and benefits. Alma workin for a old lady, sittin with her givin her food and shit like that. But when we was over there, Big Dennis started doin drugs. Alma don't drink much and she don't do drugs so she pick up on it when he start to go bad. Little by little nasty stuff start poppin up. He out late, he don't call, he don't got money to pay the bills.

That when Alma got pregnant with my baby cousin, Little Dennis. Once she pregnant, Alma lose patience with that man. She screamin at him day and night cause she think he need to act like a man now he got a baby on the way. But Big Dennis just slide from bad to worse. First he stay out a whole night, then two, then three. Alma always on the phone tryin to track him down. Then Big Dennis lose his job. He straighten out for a while then and he get another job and he make promises to Alma and everything was cool for a while. But then little by little Big Dennis start to slip away from us again.

Alma so broke up over Big Dennis then she hardly notice me at all. Since nobody watchin I start skippin school. We just go hang around the basketball court and watch the guys play, or we catch a bus to the mall and lift shit we want like CDs or clothes. Sometime we smoke a little weed. I got me into some mad fights round those days, mostly with girls but sometimes with some guys too. School start callin Alma bout me bein in trouble. She get call in for a meetin. The guidance counselor tell Alma that they wanna PINS me. That stand for Person in Need of Supervision and if I fail that they wanna put me in foster care or send me to juvi. Alma promise my Grandma that she gonna care for me so this got her scared. What with me playin crazy, Dennis all fucked up and her pregnant, Alma decide she got to pick up and go. She start workin the phone lookin for a way out. She got a friend who used to go to the Job Corps over here and she tell Alma we can stay with her till we get on our feet cause she got two kids and Alma could baby-sit for the rent. That day Alma was happy cause she thinkin she gonna get her and me and the baby set up at least. That was the same day that Big Dennis almost die cause he got shot in his head. They told us later that it was a dealer who Big Dennis owed money. Now me and Alma was sick as hell of Dennis shit but when it come down to this, we cry for him in the hospital that night. Dennis didn't die but he wasn't never quite right no more. He couldn't work and he got messed up seizures but at least he got the SSI money comin in and Little Dennis get a check every month cause of that too.

That night at the hospital Alma lean over Big Dennis and she tell him that she want better for her son and him gettin hisself shot wasn't gonna change her mind. We only saw Big Dennis one more time after that. It was just a couple months ago. We seen him at the Salvation Army over there in Binghamton and he got to play with Little Dennis. I never seen a more sad and sorry man when we was walkin out of there. I looked over my shoulder at him and he looked at us with these eyes that showed just how alone he was. A few weeks after that he seized up so bad he just died. All alone over there in that hotel. Around it goes, Little Dennis ain't never gonna know his father neither.

I love school and I hate it too. What I love is the commotion in the halls. They packed wall to wall with kids and you josslin and bumpin up against people and you use your elbows to get past when you late and you lay your shoulders back and walk smooth when you not, you know, just to delay traffic a little. When you see a friend you touch hands or you give them a hug, just a quick one, and then you walk on without sayin goodbye even, back in the flow. Sometime somebody get knocked over or lose they grip and drop they books. Then they gotta scramble on the floor to gather up the papers and pencils. Most kids got they binders filled to the max so when they hit the floor they truly explode all over the place. Now traffic can't stop, cause you can't be tardy to class, so some of the papers, maybe that day's homeworks, get kicked up the hall. Meanwhile there a jumble up of people buildin up behind the one on the floor.

Hall also the time and place to pass notes cause you always know what class your friends been at so you meet and hand them over. Usually it have to do with what's goin on with us and our friends. Here's the one in my pocket now, "Hey sexy sup? Notta lotta here. Ur friend Shawns a fuckin dick wad and I ain't apologizin to him cuz I didn't do shit. Yeah I hit him but that was after I told everyone NOT to touch me or my hair or I'm gonna smack em. Shawn did. I bit him. Then Shawn was stupid enough to, so I hit him."

The only class I like is Spanish cause the teacher nice and he talk with me real fast Puerto Rican style. That is, a mile a minute. The other kids just hang they mouth open like, what? He ask me questions like I'm the expert so I get respect from the other kids in there.

What I hate is every other class. It's like I'm in the water and the tide keep risin and every day I gotta struggle harder to keep my nose out in the air. Now my homeroom teacher got the social studies class and she got kids in there that know it all, I mean, they real brains. There this kid Elijah. He got blond blond hair cut short and neat and gold frame glasses. He always wearin a plaid shirt or a rugby shirt and you know it button up to the chin. He that religion we learned about in class, the one where the leader got killed cause he have more than one wife. (You know I wouldn't be puttin up with that shit!) Well that boy know every answer no matter what she ask. He sit next to David, another brain. He wear a shirt say, "Be nice to nerds. Chances are you'll be working for one some day."

Me and Sierra sit in the back with another girl name Shayna. We just kind of like to stay out the limelight in class, you know, on the down low. I always do my homework and I take the notes real careful. I make my letters round and pretty to show I care. Some kids always come what they call unprepared but that ain't me. I got my dark blue binder. It got three big silver rings on the inside. I have a zipper pencil case attach to those rings and inside it I got pens with blue, black, pink, and pale green ink. I got three pencils, a pencil sharpener and a pink and green eraser that say Power Puff Girls on it. It have white line paper under the pencil case. On the other side I got notes for my classes. Each class section be separated by a plastic sheet with a tab on it to show where the section start and the plastic sheet have a pocket to put papers in. That where I put my homeworks so they don't get lost. Once the teacher say, when she checkin our notebooks, "If you need a good example to follow, take a look at Mercedes."

So I know how to make things look good and I keep quiet in the back but sometimes we play a game when we gettin ready for a test and everybody gotta answer questions in that game. When she ask me a question I just don't know what to answer. I know she tossin me a softball but I don't dare pick it up cause I know that if I'm wrong I'm gonna look stupid as shit. Like when we was reviewing about the Civil War she askin questions about I don't know who and I don't know what. While I'm waitin for my turn I just feel my guts twist up and my breath come short. So now when it my turn she pick a question she think I know and I know she doin it cause some kids roll they eyes when she ask it and some kids whine shit like, "How come she gets the easy one?"

Here it is, "Mercedes, which side had slavery at the start of the Civil War?"

But I really don't know the answer. The teacher holdin her breath for me now. What does she want me to say? The name of the people? The places they come from? I can't even try to think of the answer cause what if I'm wrong? I just shrug and the teacher let her breath out and that brain David say like he almost bored to death, "The South."

Lord I want to smack him upside his head but I don't do nothin' cause I know if I'm good and I keep my binder neat and I treat her with respect she gonna pass me.

This one time we learnin about the pioneers goin out west in the olden times. The teacher set it up so that the brain, Elijah, gonna talk to the class cause it was his religion that went out there. He tell somethin about all these women walkin all the way out there pullin they wagons and they children walkin too. And sometimes these women get sick and even die by the side of the road. And sometimes they have babies out there and sometimes the babies die too but the women keep goin cause they think it gonna be better out there and they gonna live free. Elijah call those women saints. He say it they faith that keep them strong on the trail, and you can see he embarrass to be up there but he real proud too that he got women like that backin him up.

Now I went to Catholic school when I lived over there in the Bronx. My grandma make sure that I'm clean and neat for school and she bring me to mass with her too. They teach us about sin at school and my grandma teach me about saints at home. Elijah's saints all dusty and dirty but my grandma's saints be clean and beautiful. She got what she call a shrine in her bedroom on her dresser and this what it look like. First, the whole thing lay out on a white cloth with lace on the edge that she made herself. She got four or five candles lit there all the time and they in these little blue glass cups with bubbles in the glass, they make the light glow in there. At the back there a mirror and she got rosaries hangin on the corners, one with white beads and a white cross made out of shell and one black one with a gold tassel on it. There a ring of pink and yellow plastic flowers layin there and in the middle of that wreath stand a little statue. The statue is of Our Lady and she so beautiful! She wearin a blue robe that fall from the top of her head to swirls of soft cloth down around her feet. Close around her face is a white band that go across her forehead and under her chin. The only part of her skin that show is her face and her thin white hands with a rosary wrapped around them in prayer. She gazin up to heaven. Her mouth is open a little and she got tiny white teeth. Her eyes are turned up and she look so sad and mournful like she got to ask God to forgive all of us. There a bead of glass on her cheek for a tear.

Now Elijah talkin about his church as it stand today and he say his people believe that the spirit good and the body bad. He say he believe that our spirits be royal in God's eye but that our natural bodies be God's enemy. He say he God's servant.

My grandma wasn't his religion but she definitely God's servant. She use to kneel there in her bedroom sayin her rosaries, prayin for me, prayin for my grandpa who's dead too and prayin for my mom. She was makin a deal with God that she gonna keep on prayin for our souls no matter how long it take so she can get us into heaven. Elijah say he gotta work all his life to get hisself into heaven, but my grandma, she plan on doin it for us.

When I was little I would go sometimes and kneel with her when she prayin and I would look at that little statue and I would think, "Please save us Lady. Save us." Now I'm grown though and I ain't positive anybody up there listenin anymore but I pray like my grandma did for my mom and now I pray for other people too. I pray for my cousin who got shot and I pray for Crystal (cause she need all the help she can get). And when I do it I think about that statue of Our Lady lookin to heaven. And I think on how she the real saint cause she give up her only son for us, for our sons, and I gotta stay true to her even if she ain't listenin no more.

Elijah talk about how he gonna get to heaven by makin what he call covenants with his Lord. Covenants like promises to do this or that and he take them real serious cause he make them in his heart with God and if he break them he got to repent and ask forgiveness. He say he do this with his studies at school. He promise God he gonna do his very best at school.

Me, I got my own set of promises with God, they my own rules that I don't break no matter what. First off is to believe in God and Mary and Jesus. Second, always keep your body and your clothes and your things clean. Third, never show nobody no weakness, and last, always stick by your friends, no matter what kind of stupid shit they do. In the end, it was them rules that get me in trouble over here in this town.

2.

So it was a Thursday night and me and my girls were going to the Cheap Skates over on the highway by the trailer park. We got a ride over there with Crystal big sister and I'm lookin good. I cut my hair that day into a bob style and I greased it down flat and smooth and I made these little curls stuck nice and flat to the side of my face with the hair that grows in front of your ear. I got on a black velour tank that cut real low and it say HOTTIE in little diamonds across the chest. I got on some mad tight jeans and they sit down real low and I got a black thong with sparkles on the triangle in back so it sparkle nice when the light hit it. There's no doubt I got a body on me.

We went out there around 7:00 and all my girls be tricked out too, so we all feelin real good. We smoked a cigarette quick before we go in cause once you in you can't go back out and get back in again. It real hard to sneak out. When you first get in there it always smell nasty, like feet and b.o. at first, but then you used to it. There this dumb ass guy who take your money. It cost $3.00 for the night and that include skates. That's how come they call it Cheap Skates. The guy working the door got them old style glasses, the glass part real big, and he got a fat face and he look greasy. He wearin the uniform they got out there, which is a black and white striped shirt, and he got a coach whistle on a string around his neck. That night I bought one of them lights for a dollar you bite down on and keep in your mouth. When you open up your mouth a real eerie type of blue light come out. You flash people you like with it.

When we first got in there it real dark. We knew where we goin though. We head over to the squares which are right by the doors. The squares are these kind of low tables that covered with carpet. You can sit there to put on your skates or you can lounge about. That's what we do so, you know, so we can see and be seen. I didn't even get my skates yet cause I got another plan. Crystal know the plan too. She say, "C'mon ho', lets show these white motherfuckers how to dance."

And I say back, like I'm mad, "Who you callin a ho', ho?"

But she know I'm jokin cause Crystal a "wanna be" Puerto Rican. She got long soft brown hair, pale white skin and blue eyes. Me and her saunter over there real slow cause we gonna tear the place up, that's why.

The dance floor at the other end past the rink. Some people already skatin, warmin up, and lots of people sittin on the benches by the snack bar puttin they skates on. That night start out real cool. The first person we seen over there by the dance floor was Dom Williams. He was lookin fine, I'll tell you what. He got a wife beater tank on, new Junco jeans with the big label on the back written in grafitti style and basketball sneakers. Dom should be in high school but he quit and he still hang out with middle school girls. He wearin' gold chains, a red du rag with a red baseball cap on top turned off to the side. Dom got café au lait skin, cause his mom white, and the kind of eyes that half close so he look high even when he not. He got a little goat on his chin and a thin line of hair that stretch along his jaw to his ears. He wear two gold hoops in both his ears. That boy look hard.

The music playin loud so it hard to hear but Dom say when he pass by, "Yo baby you look good tonight."

And I know he right so I say back, "So what you gonna do about it nigga?"

And he me. And I do mean warm up cause Dom gonna make it all blow up that night. Here's how it happened.

CHAPTER 5

Me and Crystal stepped on the dance floor and we were rockin it. That dance floor real small at Cheap Skates but hardly anybody there yet so we got it mostly to ourselves. It got a mirror ball that hang over it and mirrors around the back wall and a smoke machine but that ain't turned on this early. Crystal put her hands on my hips and stand behind me and we swing our hips together side to side and then rock our shoulders back and forth. We been practicin these moves at her house like we seen on MTV. We move together perfect and it look real cool. We know cause we seen ourselves in the mirror.

While we dancing, Dom made his way over to the squares. This seventh grade girl Fawn and her eighth grade sister Bethany come in then. That's when Dom first seen her. The girl Fawn is real pretty, even though she dress from the Wal-Mart sale rack, but she like a baby and she only twelve or some age like that.

Dom pinpoint her right away and he make his way over ready to pimp. While Fawn and her sister puttin on they skates he started up his smooth shit with her. He lean right up on Fawn kind of slumped over talkin in her ear. She don't know what to say so she don't say nothin. Her sister say, "Frig off, Dom, if you haven't noticed she's not interested."

This only got Dom more interested cause he think she playin hard to get so he keep up the talk. Finally, Bethany say, "Dom, you friggin retard, just go the frick away and leave her alone."

That girl Fawn just sittin there lookin down. Now Dom take this as disrespect. He stand up so his dick right in front of Fawn and he say loud enough so the kids around can hear, "C'mon girl suck it, I know you wanna suck it," and then he look about at his friends and they laugh along with him.

And that girl, Fawn don't say nothing still but she keep her head down. Dom want his respect from this girl now so he grab her wrist and she look up at him finally and her face look scared now and she start cryin. Her big sister be a big girl, she got to outweigh Dom by twenty pounds, she push Dom aside so he stumble a little bit, and she grab Fawn arm and pull her away. It look funny as hell cause Fawn only got one skate on one foot and a sock on the other. Bethany pull her along to the girls room.

Dom shout out for all to hear, "You better watch yourself bitch cause one of these nights I'm gonna track you down and rape your ass!"

Dom and the others just laughin and shakin they heads as Fawn and her sister limpin off.

That's when me and my girls came back in the story. Tiffany and Sierra run over to me and Crystal on the dance floor and tell us what just happen. They laughin and happy cause it so funny. We just had to see the rest so we headed over to the girls room to check it out. We all rush over in there and there this little bitch is with her back to the wall with one foot up in the skate and the other one gettin wet on that nasty floor, cryin and snottin on herself. Bethany got a cell phone and she talkin to her mom, "I know but could you just come now?"

Then she look over at us, "Could you step off?"

Then back to her mom, "Now . . . O.K. . . . We will . . . Bye."

And there we was. I got my elbow on Crystal shoulder and we standin in front of the girls room door and Tiffany and Sierra with us too. That place got three toilets; the first two in the row work and the middle lock don't stick so you got to have somebody hold it for you. There a red rubber mat on the floor cause of the skates but it always wet. One of the sinks always dribblin water. The walls made of white tiles and for some reason they always kind of wet too.

Crystal, was actin all nice, "What happened?"

"None of your business," say Bethany.

She got a brown paper towel now and she wet it and tell Fawn, "Wipe your face."

Fawn do it and then she spoke up for the first time, "I can't deal with that retard."

I say, "You better learn to deal with him bitch or you ain't never gonna make it out here."

Bethany say, "Are you deaf? I said step off!" And she use her big shoulder to shove us out the way, and she drag Fawn with her to the parkin lot.

3.

One thing you notice in school is how the kids from the trailer parks and the apartments in town have rotten, messed up teeth and how the kids from the big houses have braces. Maybe its me but it seem like all the rich kids got braces even when they don't need to.

Take Crystal teeth. She got a place growin between her front teeth shape like a oval with pointed ends. It brownish grey and it smaller than my pinky nail but I been watchin it grow. Another girl we know name Cara got this yellow crap growin on the top of her teeth like it added on bone. I'm watchin that too and it gettin thicker and thicker and her gums up there always puffed up and red. Me, I got a crisscross in front with the left one layin over the right. I like it though cause it like I always got somethin crossed for good luck.

The preps get different color braces on they teeth. Pink or green little boxes glued on with a silver wire runnin through. Some have silver screws or bolts or joints in they jaws. Some got a red rubber or a sparkle retainer that they click in and out they mouth. All this color supposed to make havin braces fun. They have to run to the nurse from class cause a wire pop loose, or they got to get wax from they locker, or they rubber bands jump out they mouths and hit somebody. When they get they braces put on they lips puff out over the metal and they talk like they got wadded up paper in they mouth till they get use to it. They get cuts and sores inside they cheeks and on they tongues. They ain't supposed to have candy but they do and then they gotta stick they pointer finger way back in they mouth to pick off the Blow Pops and Laffy Taffies.

This one girl name Isabella got them on this year. She the prettiest girl I seen in this school. She got giant brown eyes with eyelashes about a inch long. Her nose tiny and it turn up and she take all kinds of dance lessons so she got a nice body too. Her hair long and it blow dry perfect everyday. You ain't never gonna see a zit on her face. You know nothin ever bad touch this girl cause she cry if she get a bad grade on a test. There was only one thing about this girl ain't perfect and that was her teeth. That girl got a gap in her front teeth wide enough to stick a pencil through. I always smile to myself when I see that big ugly gap when she battin her eyes and suckin up to the teachers. When she got her braces put on she make such a fuss the whole school gotta know about it. She whinin to the teachers before class how her mom tearin her hair out tryin to figure out what to feed her cause all she eat is mashed potatoes and ice cream.

When the preps get they braces off they gotta make their big entrance in to school to show off they straight even teeth. It make them all look the same to me. The only thing I like better than the sores and cuts they get in they mouth is when the braces come off and it leave they teeth stain grey from the glue. Tough shit for me though cause now I heard they got bleach that make they teeth pearly white again.

Talkin about teeth make me think of my boy, Eric Edwards, number 72. Eric Edwards sit in front off me in English class back at my old school. Eric Edwards got his hair cut in a Ricky Martin style. It real short and tight to his head and it cut with a razor around his ears and across the top of his spine. When he first got a new cut you only see the faint holes where the hair grow on the back of his neck. As it start to come back you can see that the hair grow in a upward direction then swirl around like water goin down a drain. His brown hair thick and stiff looking so that it would press back against your hand if you rubbed up to the top of his head. When he turn sideways you can see that it a little longer right in front and he gel it up so it stand away off his beautiful forehead.

Eric Edwards got a dimple in his chin and when he chew gum you can watch two muscles on the corner of his jaw flex and relax. His nose straight and narrow with the nostrils pointed flat down. He got a deep v cut in the middle of his top lip. That lip hide the best thing about Eric Edward's face. Eric Edwards could have braces if he want but he don't. He got four top front teeth slant in a little and they small and white. When he smile big you can see the eye teeth. They slant outward and cross over the others and they have points on them. I guess his teeth crossed for luck too.

Eric Edwards shy and he never say nothing to me that he don't have to. I know he number 72 on the football team cause when they got a game the kids always wear they team jerseys to school to get theyself psyched. The school colors purple and white over there and they sign a tornado. Any team does the same type of shit. The girls on soccer wear they jerseys and put purple and white ribbons over pigtails. The softball girls wear they jerseys and they pajama bottoms and fuzzy slippers. Basketball write they numbers in eye pencil on they cheeks. It all mean the same thing. They showin off that they in a team. They do the same stuff over here in this school.

Eric Edwards got nice manners. He pick up my pencil if it roll off the desk. He wait till I reach out for the papers when he passin them back. He push in his chair when he leave. He don't raise his hand but he try to answer when the teacher call on him. I don't think I ever heard him disrespect nobody though he know how to laugh along when somebody crack a joke.

I write Eric Edwards name on the desks in this school like he my long distance boyfriend. I listen when the boys be talkin about they football games cause I wanna know if we ever gonna play my old school. If we do I'm sure as hell gonna go to the game. Sometimes I run over in my mind ways I could get Eric Edwards alone. There ain't nothin I want more than to feel the back of Eric Edwards neck with my hand while I run my tongue across his crooked teeth.

4.

The day after all that shit happen at Cheap Skates I went up to the smokers spot near the school and I seen my girls all in a cluster. I seen that somethin big be goin on cause you could see the spit was flyin from a mile away, and them wavin they arms and cursin.

"What up?" I say in a rush.

Crystal start talkin first and then they all jump in. One hoppin on the words of the others. "That little bitch from last night got Dom in jail!"

"Nah, nah," I say, "unh unh, you lyin."

"Hell no she ain't!" say Sierra. "He's in jail and that little bitch done it to him."

I come back, "Dom in jail? Cause of her?"

"Little jail bait!" say Tiffany.

"What you talkin about?" I ask.

"Her mommy called the cops!" say Sierra.

Crystal tell me, "Yeah, and the cops went to his house and they brought him in."

"What you mean?" I ask again.

"Un huh, and now he's down at the police," add Tiffany.

"She done it," finish Sierra. Now while we all yellin in a circle who walk up but Dom himself and we open up the crush and let him in. He tell us that it true that the cops pick him up and bring him in.

Crystal say, "I'm gonna get her, Dom, for what she done to you."

That's when the schemin start. We got lot's of time to think today cause today we got final exams and you know that otherwise we be bored shitless sittin in there waitin to get let out. Now we got somethin to really think on.

5.

That day was the first really hot sunny day that spring. All through May and June it was grey and rainin outside and we all be cooped up in school or at home with it rainin and rainin and now that it was nice out it like we all gonna explode. It was hard to stuff that genie back in the bottle but we had to go in there and take a test before we could carry on with our own business.

You know I finish the test quick. It was math. All year I been usin my skills at lookin like I understand what's on the papers and the board. I put my head to the side and squinch up my eyes. I tap my teeth with my pencil and I punch numbers in on my calculator. This all a big show on my part cause this algebra be true bullshit. I'm stuck on, why this one called a *x* and why that one call a *y*? You can tell me about it a hundred times but it like I got a brick wall in back my eyes. I *see* the *x*'s and the *y*'s and those fucked up triangles but they only paper deep. How those brain kids come up with the number the teacher want in the end I just don't know.

So here it was, almost the end of the year and I been sittin here all these months and I just know I'm gonna fail cause the math teacher ain't gonna pass me no matter how good I act. He all about the numbers, that's why.

Now there's twenty-five minutes left till we can get out. I got nothin to do but look around and think about Dom and that girl Fawn and what we gonna do when school get let out. The math teacher set the desks in perfect rows, one by one, each desk exactly the same amount apart. The chair and the table part be stuck together. The chair part is dark blue and cold and it hard like stone so it make your butt hurt after sittin there for a while. The table part be light grey and wide enough that you could open your binder and lay it flat and still have your elbows on it and you could do some nice drawin on it but you know the math teacher won't have none of that. The desks in that room be clean all the way across. The math desk smooth and cool and if you run your flat hand over it feel like polish stone. The wall behind the blackboard and around the windows is cement blocks painted mustard yellow. The back wall and the side wall is a dark orange color and it made of metal. I know it metal cause he got magnets holdin up posters. None of them have a picture but they got sayings. The first one say,

"The dictionary is the only place where success comes before work."

The second one say,

"Success is 1% inspiration and 99% perspiration."

And the third one say,

"What is popular is not always right. What is right is not always popular."

I'm sittin in the back by the windows cause my last name begins with a V and you know he got us seated alphabetical. I can see the white brick wall of the gym and the walkway that lead up to the gym door from the outside playin field. Usually when it warm you can look out at the kids comin and goin from the gym. You see if you can catch someone's eye and then maybe they shout your name, "Hey Mercedes! What's up!"

Then everybody in math class see that you got friends. This is the way you can stick the teacher too cause he hate being interrupted but he can't get mad at you cause it not your fault that somebody shout from outside the window. He hate being interrupted so bad that he don't even pick up the phone when the office call, he just let it keep ringing till they give up on the other end. He just pretend it ain't ringin and he keep on talkin and writin numbers and letters and lines on the board.

When he in a good mood and the class start driftin off he say, "Let me see your baby blues now people."

But when he pissed, look out. He say, "I'm sick and tired of you little punks!"

That what he call us, punks.

This one time the outside janitor, we call him Cupcake on account of his size, was mowin the lawn out the math window on the rider machine. Now you notice Cupcake. First off, his ass so big it hang over the seat of that thing and it loud so you hear it comin way before you see it. He got a midnight blue uniform with a white oval on the chest with his real name sewn on it. When he make his first pass by we got the windows open cause it a June afternoon and it stuffy in there cause you know we got a class full of boys who been stampin and trompin through puddles and creeks all spring and when they feet start to warm up, well, let me tell you, the smell just start to rise. Now the sound of that thing fade away but you know it ain't over cause Cupcake like to mow that grass down to the dirt. So we sittin and waitin for Cupcake to make another pass by. The sound start gettin louder and then here he come, but this time he one step closer by the window. Now Cupcake got a mustache that curve round his fat chin and down to his fat neck. He got wrap around mirror sunglasses too and if you squeeze up your eyes you can see a pair of woman's legs on a tattoo hangin down from under his rolled up shirt sleeve. When he make that second pass by somebody sing real low from behind me, "I am the walrus koo koo ka choo," and people start laughin real low along with it. So RANHHH that mower with Cupcake on top of it pass by and the teacher start lookin tight around the mouth and he start talkin louder and writin harder on the board. When Cupcake mower start to fade away you can hear his chalk rat-a-tat-tatin on the board. We know this game ain't up too cause there a foot worth of grass next to the wall that he ain't mowed yet and I think Cupcake like to show them teachers that they can't tell him when to mow and when not. So around he come again and now everybody lookin out the window and gigglin cause don't nobody got the nerve to interrupt the math teacher three time in a row. Cupcake lookin straight ahead, like he ain't straight up against the window with his big self makin mad crazy noise.

The teacher stomp over to slam the sliding window but he so pissed he do it too hard and it don't catch the latch but it bounce off and slide back open again. Next he snap the roll up shade and it come rollin down but it stuck on one side and so only one end roll down and it at a angle. The math teacher face all red now cause the kids start laughin out loud. He take his chalk and he throw it full force against that orange metal wall at the back like that's the final word. We all got the last laugh though cause that chalk pop off the wall and it land right in Matt Jacobs curly hair!

6.

While I was waiting for the test to get out I let my mind come back to the serious business at hand. I was thinking about Dom, Fawn, and Crystal. First off I know it gonna go down in the park after school. We all gonna face off where there ain't no teachers, no parents and no cops. I know Crystal wanna beat Fawn ass. I'm thinkin I'm probably gonna help. Why? Cause Fawn show she weak, number one by cryin like a baby and actin a fool at the rink. Number two by tellin her mom what happen. This girl got to learn to act strong, even if she ain't feelin it. She got to know that her bein so pretty there gonna be another Dom gonna come along and bump up against her. She got to learn to knock him down, laugh in his face. Spit in it if she got to. Second, I got to back up Crystal cause she my best friend.

Now Dom another story cause he weak too but in a different way. Don't you know he male for starters. No offense, but truth be told I don't think I know a man who ain't stupid, trippin, dead or gone. He just want his fun and his respect where he can get it.

On the other side, Crystal just lookin for people to lay her fists on. That girl just pissed at the world. And I guess she got a right knowin what I know about her. But when I really ask myself why she wanna beat Fawn it come down to this. Besides bein mad, the other thing Crystal be is hungry. She want a man so bad that she do anything, even fight for a sorry ass fool like Dom, who ain't worth two cents when it come down to it. She lookin at Fawn like a ticket to get Dom. Only you know that maybe Dom sleep with her, maybe he hang out at her house and eat her mom's food. But there ain't no way Dom plannin to stay by her, even if he was to get her pregnant. Crystal don't see all that. She got her own calculator in her head and she workin out the problem so Dom come out for the answer.

When the test finally over and the bell ring the first thing we did was bunch up around Crystal locker. Crystal know that Fawn and Bethany gonna walk through the park to get to they house over by the railroad tracks. The park the place where there ain't no grown ups except once in a while you see some fool walkin they dog or joggin. We were makin a crowd. Maybe ten or twelve kids. Word spread fast when somebody gonna get they ass kicked and a crowd always grow cause everybody wanna see it happen.

When you walk out of school you got to walk across the high school kids' parking lot. Then you walk through a gate in a high chain link fence that go around the school ground to get into the park. They got a chain link fence for one reason. It keep the high school kids from smokin on school property. It show where the school stop and the park start. If the kids smoke on the school side of the fence and they get caught then they get detention.

The park have two levels on a big hill. The bottom part, which we call the Lower, have a swimmin pool, tennis courts and places for cookin out. The school on the second level up and we call that the Upper. After the Upper the park just be woods that go off up the hill. Between the Upper and the Lower there a creek. In the summer it dry and the water go down to a trickle. You can walk across on the dry rocks in there without gettin your feet wet. In the spring though the water high and deep in some spots and the water move fast enough to knock you on your ass if you was to stand in it. You can't see no rocks stickin out then and you gotta find a tree to walk across.

There a road that start where that chain link fence at. There a fork in it. One way lead down to the Lower. It loop around the hill and end at a bridge that go over the creek. There a yellow guard rail after the bridge. The other fork lead to a road that run about a half mile between the fence and a big green wood pavilion that got picnic tables and a bathroom and a soda machine in it. On the other side of the pavilion there a basketball court, a playground and a pretty garden with paths that was made for some lady. Where the pavilion at there a yellow guard rail that go across the road so no cars can go toward the school on that road neither. When kids skip school or want to get lost they go in there where cars can't follow.

On the chain link end where kids smoke there always garbage on the road, you know, wrappers and what not. There a big blue plastic garbage can by the school fence but it always nearly empty cause kids rather throw they junk on the ground. As you go down the road there ain't nothing but trees and bushes and the path. All year long I been watchin this tee-shirt somebody probably drop out they gym bag. I been watchin that tee-shirt disappear in the dirt. It was there from the fall and through the winter and now it spring. First it was clean and plump up. Then it start to flatten out. First it got rain on, then pine needles and leaves fell on it, then it got snowed on. Now the wrinkles in that cloth be folds. It just keep gettin dirtier and dirtier and nobody ever pick it up. It make me think on how sometime the teacher hold up a sweatshirt or some gym shorts and say, "Does this belong to anyone? Does anyone know who it belongs to?"

And nobody ever answer. It like we all shamed by these clothes, like a loose thread or a cheap label, gonna point us out for what we are. Most kids would rather take the heat at home for losin they clothes than raise they hand and say it belong to them.

That day my posse head past the chain link fence into the park. There were the other groups there too like the skateboarders, the pot heads and guys and girls lookin for a private place to hang out. We was all feelin high cause the sun was shinin and we was out of school and there was gonna be a fight. Us girls was gettin each other goin. We had to move fast and find Fawn and her sister before they got to the pavilion or the bridge. Everybody was loud when we under the sun in the parking lot but we got quiet once we in the woods. Your feet don't make much noise in there cause that road half blacktop and half dirt and it be covered with pine needles. The sun mostly block by the trees, and the leaves make the shaded air look green and dark. The trees tall but the bushes tangle up underneath so it hard to walk off the path. We was all talkin but now it in whispers. We have our shoulders hunch up and we keepin our eyes movin. We have our arms loose. Ready. We was eggin each other on too. "I heard she told the cops he raped her," Tiffany tell the crowd.

"That little bitch. I bet she did," say somebody else.

"I bet that chicken shit ran home to her mommy already."

"Poor baby."

Then Crystal say, "Maybe we should split up."

Other people got ideas too. "We could circle around and cut them off."

"We could come at them from two sides."
"Then they couldn't run away."
"She'd have to stand and fight."
"Crystal's gonna fight her alone."
"But if her sister jump in..."
"Then we all gonna jump in."

I'm startin to look at my girls. Crystal and Tiffany definitely the most jacked up in the crowd. We walkin fast. Most of us shiny from sweat but Tiffany cheeks all red too. It make her blue eyes show up even more. Her hair pull back in a pony tail but it have all these loose pieces springin out around her face. She got dark round patches under the arms of her light blue tee shirt. Crystal got a bounce in her step and she look ready to pounce on Fawn and bite her to death with her bared teeth. She talkin low to herself about what she gonna do. I ain't no follower in this hunt. I'm walkin out in front too. Still, I'm startin to think.

We come up on this big tree I been watchin all year. It crack off near the base in some storm but it not all the way broke. It look different dependin on which way you comin from. From one side it look like a dragon with it neck stretchin out and wings flappin, it mouth open and it tongue stickin out like when dragons breath fire. From the other side it look like a man runnin up the hill wavin his arms like he tryin to get away.

7.

Tiffany and Crystal decide to back track with a few girls leading them off the right fork headed down over the bridge to the Lower. Me and Sierra lead the girls on the Upper. The two bunches of us separated by the creek and the hill with all them trees goin to the Upper in between. Without them other girls we was quiet enough so that when a warm wind pick up we can hear the hush noise the trees make when the leaves rub together. We hear Crystal yell out, "Yo! Fawn! Hold up."

There wasn't no call back and we couldn't see what was goin on down there cause the trees so thick. We broke out toward the voice and hop over the cliff and slide down the soft dirt grabbin at the baby trees and steppin on the knotted up roots for breaks. My heart poundin so bad not knowin what was gonna happen now. We hit the bottom at a place in the creek where it swollen up and deep and there ain't no where to cross over. The bank overhang with tangled up roots and bushes. Me and two other girls standin all up on each other on this little mud patch on the edge.

I couldn't see Crystal but I hear her voice, it have a high sound in it, "Go ahead and run you little bitch baby!"

Then the bushes on the side of the creek across from us started to shake and the branches was crackin and some leaves was poppin off in the runnin water. A top of a blond frizzy head show up first and then some big shoulders in a navy blue hood sweatshirt crawlin into the open. The head look up and it was Bethany. She just stop dead in her track when she seen it's us standin on the other side. Her big gold hoops were shinin in a patch of sun that made its way through the trees. That moment go so slow when I think back on it and we were all in a freeze frame but then we hear Fawn say, "Bethany, hurry up!" all crazy and scared, and then Brittany move back into action and she step right into the water and stand up straight. Then Fawn, pullin on the back of Bethany's jacket, stumble into the water too.

There wasn't nowhere for them to go. While we was standin there eyeing each other, Crystal's group come up from behind Fawn and Bethany, cursin and pushin there way into the open creek. They were hangin on to branches and standin on hunks of rock and roots just barely able to keep they feet dry.

Crystal say, "What the fuck, Fawn. We only want to ask you some questions."

Bethany speak up. "What's your frickin problem, Crystal? We don't want to fight you. Just leave us alone."

Crystal step into the water then too and walk up close to Fawn so they faces close and Crystal puff up her chest the way guys do. "Just tell me Fawn, did you or didn't you call the cops on Dom last night?"

But Crystal couldn't wait for an answer and all this anger in her burst out in one sharp shove and Fawn fall backwards into the water but scramble up quick and start to back away. Her jeans was wet and clingin to her legs and the water was comin down in streams from her wrists. And Crystal move in on her but then Bethany come up from behind and twist her arm back hard so that Crystal cry out and she trip up on somethin hidden under the water and go down on one knee. This give Tiffany the green light and she stride into the water now and grab Bethany by the elbows from behind and even though Bethany fightin to get loose she can't do it cause Tiffany big and strong. Fawn back away into the bushes with her hands over her mouth. The fight was about Bethany now. With Tiffany holdin Bethany's arms back, Crystal hand free to clock her and she wind up and she punch Brittany in her jaw so hard you could hear the crunch.

Bethany fall back on top of Tiffany and the two splash down into the water. The heavy water pull hard on these two girls sprawl out in the water and Tiffany sputter and holler, "Jesum. You stupid fuckin..."

Tiffany get herself up and jump on Bethany, who on her hands and knees tryin to stand, and she grab the back of Bethany head by the hair and she shove her face down under the cold fast water. Crystal jump in behind Tiffany holdin Bethany down. Bethany was workin her back and shoulders trying to get up on straight arms. The rest of us was standin by just watchin strands of Bethany long frizzy hair break loose from her hair clip, it look like soft sea weeds in the runnin water. That when my voice come to me full force, "Crystal! Crystal! What you wanna do, kill her?"

Crystal look up at me and her eyes look real crazy but she do back off and she yank hard on Tiffany shirt so she look up too, "What the hell. . .?"

But once the pressure off, Bethany body float up to the surface, and with them two not holdin to her she start to float away downstream. Her arms and legs fan out so she look like she jump out a plane and was waitin for her parachute to open. She stopped flyin when she hit on a rock that was stickin up out the water. Fawn woke up then too, "Oh my God, you killed her."

Crystal don't miss a beat. "You say she fell in, you say it was a accident. You say it or we're gonna kill you too."

We was all scared shitless and we take off like we was on fire scramblin back up the bank. My breath wouldn't go no deeper than my throat and my hands and feet get a electric buzz in them. When we get to the Upper we was all pantin and Crystal and Tiffany was all dirty and they clothes and hair was hangin and wet.

I cry out, "What's wrong with you girl? You know what you done? You know what you done?"

Crystal put on her hard face like she was ready to fight me now too. "Don't sweat it, Fawn is so chicken shit she won't tell nobody."

"Wake up, Crystal. You drown that girl down there. This ain't no game no more!"

And she look at me and I look at her and I seen that I got no choice but to cut her loose.

"I gotta bounce girl," I say, and I take off runnin and I don't look back when she holler, "If you tell you ain't my friend no more Mercedes."

But I keep headin back toward school cause it bright and not dark over there, and the bricks and the blackboards and the sidewalks and the teachers gonna make this whole scene disappear.

8.

As soon I was out in the sun of the parkin lot again I start thinkin that I gotta make a decision, quick. I could see the windows of the homeroom teacher's room across the way and that one of them was wide open. I know I couldn't go back in the park just yet cause I didn't want to be near any of them girls but I need to get me some shelter from the hard bright sun. I take off at a run for her windows.

The school building only one floor high so you can stand at the window at waist level and talk to somebody inside. I didn't want to go direct so I set my sight on the brick wall between her room and the next teacher down. I slide along the wall so I can peek in her room to see who in there first. When I first look in there I couldn't see nothin but my own reflection in the glass. I don't look too good. I lick the sweat off my top lip and I could see I been cryin cause my mascara been all smeared down. I didn't want her to see I been cryin so I rubbed my fingers under my eyes and sniff up the snot. I need to get in that room and out of the sun cause I was thinkin maybe God can't see me as good when I'm under a roof.

"Yo, Ms. B." I was tryin to play it off like normal but I know my voice got panic and tears in it. The teacher sittin at a table with a pile of test papers, her water bottle, a coffee cup that say *2 teach + 2 touch live*s = *4 ever* and a calculator. She must have change out her work clothes cause she was wearin chino shorts and a black tank top and her brown hair was put back in a pony tail.

She look up over the top of her glasses like she bein woke up from a dream. "Hey Mercedes," she say in voice that sound kind of tired and bored.

She smiled but she didn't get up and she didn't invite me in cause I guess she got a lot of work to do for our report cards. Still, I gotta get in so I said, "What up?"

"Just correcting finals. I have about a million to go, want to help?"

"Sure, Ms. B," I say, and I hopped up on the windowsill and swing my legs over it and jumped down into the room. The room have two big tables in it, one on each side. She sittin at one, I hopped up on the other swingin my legs back and forth. She bein polite but I could see she wanted me to go and I can't think of nothing to say to stall her out.

After a minute she asked, "How come you came back to school? I thought you were dying to get out."

"I was lookin for some people."

She started lookin harder at me. Her eyebrows draw together. She was puttin two and two together. "Are you ok Mercedes? You look kind of upset."

Then she sat up straight and looked at me like she really see me now and she put down the pencil she got in her hand. She push herself away from the table, not takin her eyes off me and she walk across the room, zig-zaggin through the rows of desks, to my table. As she walk toward me I was feelin a lump begin to grow and ache in my throat.

"Things are so fucked up Ms. B," I choke out.

"Mercedes, what's going on?" She say it in a voice that demand a answer.

That's when I started to bawl so bad that I got hiccups and I couldn't talk and tell her even if I want to, which I didn't.

She say, "Oh sweetie, what's wrong?"

And she give me a quick tight squeeze with her cool bare arms and I can smell her perfume and the coffee she been drinkin and the sourish smell of pencil lead. She break away and say, "Let me get you a drink of water."

I was just sittin there snivelin and she quietly go over to her yellow teacher cupboard and get a plastic cup out a sleeve and take it to the fountain outside in the hall. I was thinkin back to when I first came over here at the beginning of school and how one time there were these seventh graders who were makin noise out in the hall by the fountain. She go out and see how they stuck some gum in the spout and were watchin people take a drink and get squirted all over from it. On accident one kid squirted her and she act all mad and disgusted with them in the hall but she come back in the room with her hand over her mouth and burst out laughin after she shut the door. She shake her head sayin, "My God, the look on their faces! That was priceless."

But now she came back in with the water and she picked up a square flowered box of tissues and she give me a minute to wipe my nose and take a drink of that half warm metal tasting fountain water. I was still havin that feelin in my throat where you can't get a regular breath without it bein all shaky.

"O.K. Mercedes, so what happened?"

"I swear I can't tell you Ms. B," and I can't help it but I start to cry again.

"Is somebody hurt? Are you in a fight?" Her voice be gettin harder now like she was gonna use it to make me tell her. I looked down at my hands and at my gold rings and I shake my head back and forth.

She say, "Hang on a minute," and she walk over to the tan teacher phone hung up on the wall by the hall door. She dial three numbers and she pull the tangle spiral cord out into the hallway. Whether she was callin the principal or the counselor or whoever, I knew that I got to go. The choice made for me by the teacher callin in those others.

Quick and quiet as I could I slid off the table and swung myself back through the window frame out into the bright sunlight and I run like I was on fire back across the parking lot, through the chain link fence and into the dark cool silent park and run, tracing back over the path we gone on before. I don't go back down the hill where it happen. I pick up the pace in that spot and I don't think about Bethany or Fawn or Crystal or Tiffany and what we just done. I don't think about where they was right now and I don't think about whether Bethany really dead and what Fawn done after we all took off. I just run flat out past the dragon tree and around the yellow guardrail and past the green pavilion across the playground and through the iron gates at the end of the fancy garden that some old man had made for his dead wife.

I run up the steep part of Central Street by the pretty wood style houses that got porches with furniture along the outside of the park and turn down North Fifth where the houses ain't so nice. It's in one of these houses where we got our apartment. It's good for Alma cause she can walk to work at the nursing home where she a aid right in back of the hospital across the way.

I was wearin my keys on a chain around my neck and just as my shaky hand finally got the lock turned in the door, an ambulance come out the distance makin it's way into the emergency, blowin that wailin noise let you know that somethin terrible happinin to somebody. I flashed on the thought that this time the somethin terrible was happinin to me. Or because of me. I just start lookin through Alma's jacket pockets and old purses on the coat hooks in the front hall lookin for a stray cigarette cause I gotta calm my nerves.

9.

Back in the fall, after that day we met in the office, me and Crystal started hangin out. Crystal live at Messina Trailer Park over on the highway near the skatin rink. The first time I go over there I feel shock. When you little and you think of the Upstate you think of Old MacDonald or Goldilocks. But Lord, when you see some places up here for yourself, you see some of the sorriest dirtiest white people you ever could dream of. Messina's kind of like a little farm only they got people in there but might as well be cows cause they so dumb and dirty and helpless. Some of them people got no pride in theyself at all.

Now Crystal didn't ask to come from there so you can't blame her for it. Her mom got four other kids, some of them grown and some still be little. Her big sister got her own two kids and they all livin there too.

Crystal got a brother, Andrew, only one year younger. He don't look nothin like Crystal though. Her eyes blue and her brown hair smooth. Andrew hair curly and dirty blond. His eyes so dark brown that you can't find the black circle in the middle. Andrew take medicine cause he hyperactive. He in what they call the BAP, which mean Behavioral Adjustment Program, in school cause he don't know how to act right. He pretty short for his age and he skinny and he always on the move. He got a best friend name John who live over there in Messina's too. Both those boys slow. They don't got sense. Sometimes we let them hang out with us when there ain't nothin else to do. They always got some kinda project, like tryin to make they own fishin poles.

On the opposite side of the highway, behind the rink and the gas stations, there a river. There a dam over there and a big old tree with a rope tied on it for swingin on. Anybody with two eyes can see that Andrew got a crush on me. That kid always sniffin around when I'm over there and he showin off. Like when we go over to the rope swing him and his friend act like they gonna kill theyselfs tryin to catch our attention. Me and Crystal sit on a old log and talk and smoke while these two hollerin and splashin and carryin on.

One thing you notice when you pull into Messina's is all the grass be dead over there. Then you notice the puddles in the dirt path they call the road. The trailers they live in look like those long boxes the tractor trailers carry with windows cut in. Every one of them trailers rusty. The rust drippin and spreadin from the corners of the windows and the doors. Most have home made wood steps in front. The trailers layed out in rows, but they ain't no math teacher rows. They sloppy rows. Each one front door face the ugly rusty back of somebody else's trailer. Some got plastic lawn chairs and a place to barbecue. Most have some old broken-down-nobody-want-it-no-more car or snowmobile or lawn mower dumped outside. Outside Crystal's there a Tickle Me Elmo, a few Hot Wheels and a Easy Bake Oven all scattered around and left outside to rot. There a naked Barbie lyin with her legs scissored open in a split and her thin arms sticken up over her head. Her blond hair is frizzled and it look like somebody step on her face. Somebody at Crystal's make a porch by stretchin a dark blue tarp between the trailer and two silver tent poles.

Crystal trailer be packed to the top with people but we hang out there anyway cause Alma don't want nobody hangin out at our apartment. She strict about that. She wanna keep the place straighten up and clean. She think these kids nasty anyway. So packed as it is, we hang out there cause don't nobody seem to care who comin or goin or when.

Crystal share her room with her little sister and her big sister's kids. They got gold carpet goin through the whole place. Crystal bed still got a Cinderella blanket on it with her dress like a princess. Crystal say she have that blanket her whole life and she ain't gonna never take it off her bed. She got maybe twenty stuff animals on her bed too. She got bears, snakes, a fox, and a tiger. Most she got at the fair last summer. She went out there with her big sister Tami and stay in a tent the whole week that the fair on. Her sister got a job workin one of the rides. Crystal met this guy who work a booth, he like nineteen or twenty. She tell me the game he run got a rabbit that run away from the player and the player got a gun shoot water to kill the rabbit. Don't you know she was layin on her back for him after two days? That why she got so many stuff animals.

It turn out I went to that fair last summer myself. We move over here on the first of August and the fair come that week. Alma friend Pauline who we live with when we first got here say we gonna go so we pack up her kids and Little Dennis who was just a new born baby and off we go. We went on the last day of the fair so everything kinda run down by the time we got there.

We went to the barns where the farmers show they cows and pigs and shit. That where the country people look like the ones you read about or see in pictures. Those kids clean and so they animals too. The girls got braids in they hair and boys wearin cowboy hats and they cheeks all pink and they look healthy. There they are rakin out the stalls, brushin they animals, goin about they business. Ee-I-ee-I-Oh.

We went the carnival part in the afternoon. Crystal talk about that place make you think it gonna be the bomb but what I seen made me want a long hot shower. The sun beatin down on the dirt over there and the air smell sweet and sour like rotten garbage and beer sweat. You see people with every type of sickness and problem you ever wanna know about.

Everybody showin skin too so you see all they got hangin out. One lady had a hole the size of a orange in the top of her leg, like somebody cut a circle of meat out. A old guy in a wheelchair with a big white beard and white hair stickin out every which way have the stump under his knee stickin out his pants and covered with white scaly skin. Another guy missin a leg got a fake one that dark blue and it say Go Cowboys in big letters on it. I saw a kid with that thing where they gotta sew up the top lip only this one look like the doctor done it with a rope. Then there the retarded people, there lots a them wanderin around lookin lost. One girl had the parts of her face slid into the wrong places with a ear on one cheek and a eye on the other. Another one on chemo had brown circles under her eyes and thin pieces of pale hair lookin like spider webs clingin to her skull. You see every kind of fat over there too. The kind where the belly flap hang over they crotch, or when they ass and legs big as a house but they slim on top, and the type where most the fat in they tits and they hardly able to walk with the weight. Then there the people on crutches with dirty towels tape around the armpit pads and there the ladies with they leg veins look like they tied up in knots under the skin. And everybody over there got a tattoo, specially the workers, and you know every one of them mothafuckers seen jail time. And all of the people over there standin in that sun watchin they kids flyin around on the Twister, the Flyin Bobs, the Typhoon or the Crazy Bus but it make my stomach turn to watch so I look down at the cigarette butts and the sno cone papers and the cotton candy tubes and the dusty bits of sausage and pepper and the candy apple sticks and the chicken bones and the flies buzzin in the ketchup on the cardboard french fry trays. And always over the different music comin from the rides you hear kids wailin cause they didn't like the prize from the rip off game or they want another ride or they feel like they gonna puke. You see they tears mixin up with the candy and the dust and the sweat coatin they little red faces. So that what I think on when Crystal start talkin about the fair. No way in hell I lay my ass one night in that place much less seven. If you ask me, that place a freak show.

Crystal got a baby brother too name Jamie. He only three and he got asthma real bad. She also got a lot of pets over there. They got a rabbit, mice, two guinea pigs and a bird. Sometime the cages stink pretty bad. When the sun make it through the little windows in the trailer you can see the dust from them cages floatin in the light. Sometime when I'm over there I clean out the cages cause don't nobody need to live with that filth in they house. That why Crystal mom like me.

One time we got over there and the ambulance in front of they trailer. We scared so we run in the house and her little brother stretch out on the couch and he got a oxygen mask on his face. It cover almost his whole face except for his eyes. Jamie starin around at the EMTs and the white stretcher they got and pantin so hard it look like his little chest gonna pop open. One of the EMTs say, "Please put out your cigarettes or go outside sir."

Crystal sister boyfriend, Dougy, sittin in the plaid easy chair smokin a butt and he say, "No," with a attitude like he got a beef with the EMT.

The EMT say, "Oxygen is highly flammable sir so you better step outside with your cigarette." He say it real calm but I know he thinking, "Put it out unless you wanna burn this shitbox down asshole." The EMTs roll that child out and carry him down the broken up steps and into the back of the ambulance. They don't say nothin more to nobody on the scene cause they ain't worth talkin to. Crystal big sister climb in the back with her child and the EMTs drive off leavin the rest of us standin there, watchin them go.

10.

That day it all went down with Bethany in the park, I ran home and busted in and the first thing I did was find me a wrinkled up Kool at the bottom of Alma brown suede jacket hangin on the white metal coat rack we got by the front door. I smoothed it out and then tapped it butt end down on my palm so the loosed up bits of cigarette packed down enough for a good smoke. There wasn't no matches or lighters on the kitchen counter so I turn on the electric stove burner in the kitchen to high. I stand there and watch the black spiral rings turn grey then orange then glow red. I cover up my eyelashes and eyebrows while I lean in with the smoke between my teeth. The heat from the stove makes my hot cheeks hotter. The end of the cigarette sparked then a wiff of smoke curled up. I sucked in and the burning edge spread across the round end. The smoke gave me a head rush and I held on to the edge of the stove cause I was so dizzy for a second. I started to get a ashtray from habit. I fit my fingers through the pounded copper handle on the cabinet but then I just stood there. I said, "Fuck it," out loud and just flicked my ashes in the sink. How much more trouble could I get in anyway?

Alma is particular about the way she keep the house. This apartment is like the other ones we had, it's sketchy cause its so old and the landlords just keep slappin on more paint and more linoleum like it's gonna cover up what's underneath. The corners of the windowsills and the rooms gunked up with old grime which include soot from the cars, dust, hair and dead and alive spiders. When we first come over here Alma take a paint scraper trying to scrape up all that stuff. She pull up the black mold around the bathtub and smooth on new white caulk. She repaint the walls and the baseboards. Somehow though the black gunk always creep back up on her. The linoleum start peelin up on the bathroom floor and let out the stink of a hundred years of piss soaked in underneath. A tile fall off behind the kitchen sink and leave a pile grey crumbling wall on the counter. Alma always buying new bottles of cleaning stuff hoping that this time she gonna make the mold and mildew disappear forever.

I didn't realize I'm even thinkin when I went to the bigger bedroom I share with Little Dennis to get some things together. He got his crib and a changing table on one side and I got my bed and dresser on the other. It came to me that I been concentrating on the thought of Shawn and how he got a place in back of his house where him and his skater friends party and play they music. It's like a old garage or somethin. He talk about it in homeroom. How he got a sweet set up with a couch and a cooler for beer.

I lifted my red back pack off the hook on the back of my door. I carried it over and set it on top of the dresser we got for me at the Salvation Army. It's wood with two round knobs on each of the three drawers. I opened the top one where I keep my underwear. The undies folded and stacked on the right. My two extra bras go in the middle and my sock pairs are on the left. I took two pairs each of socks and underwear and poked them down smooth on the bottom of the bag. In the middle drawer I got my shirts. I took two shirts off the short sleeve pile on the right and one long sleeve out the middle and put them neat into my pack. In the bottom drawer I got my pants and I take the pair of jeans in the jean stack in the middle. When I go to put in the jeans I seen the order all wrong so I take it all out and put it back in with the jeans on the bottom and the socks on the top.

On top of my dresser I got a jewelry box I got when I was little. When you open it up it have a ballerina in a white suit that pop up and tinkly music which used to come on. It's got a lot of crap in it like cheap earrings and loose beads but I dug around to get out my grandma's white rosary and put it in my pocket. I also looked for something secret I got in there which I need for good luck and which I don't want nobody to find out about. I got it wrapped in a piece of folded up kleenex under the other stuff. That thing I was lookin for is a man's golden wedding ring. I stole it off Big Dennis' finger at his funeral.

When I first walk up to look at him at the funeral home he looked totally fake to me, like he made of wax, especially in the suit they put him in which wasn't even his. He look like a big rubbery doll. The suit is black and his shirt is white. He wearin a light grey tie with dark grey diamonds on it. They put a red flower on his jacket pocket. They have combed the hair over to the side and it look kind of powdery. The real Big Dennis was always movin around and jokin and for real, the man was a slob. So this big doll that was lyin in the coffin so still and hard, with glue on his eyelashes, must have been put there while they did something else with his rotten old real body. I was gonna yell out that somebody stole Big Dennis when I see something shine down by his side. I focus my eyes down there and see that the doll wearin Big Dennis weddin ring.

When the different people were done lookin at him and most of them went home I pretended to go up for one last look myself. I flopped my hands over the edge and lean my forehead on the coffin like I'm prayin to God. I seen people touch the face and body in there all that day so I reached out like I'm gonna hold the hand lyin on the side. I run my own hand over the surface of the left hand in the coffin, feeling for the edge of the ring. The hand was hard and the skin was stiff over the muscle and bone underneath. The only thing different about the feel of the ring from the skin was the smoothness of the ring. I had to wiggle the ring over the knuckle bone and edge it past the fingers on both side. I tried to pull it straight off the way you do with a tight ring where the skin bunches up behind it and turns white and then gives way. But Dennis finger stay rock hard in place. I was gettin sweaty tryin to ease the ring off and hold my back perfectly still. I edge it off the tip of the finger and bunch it inside my fist. Nobody see me slip it in my pocket and nobody notice it missing before they bury him. I didn't take it out to look at until the people with us left and Alma stop cryin and fall asleep. I hold under the light by my bed and look on the inside ring. It said, *Yo soy amor, 1996,* just like it was supposed to.

When I found the ring at the bottom of my jewelry box I took it out of the tissue and put in my pocket with the rosary. Then I go back to the kitchen and take a bottle of Gatorade out the refrigerator and two mini boxes of Rice Crispies cereal and put them on top of my clothes. I zip up the red back pack and slide the straps over my shoulders. I don't look back as I head out but I stop at the cabinet by the front door. I take out the phone book and look up Kyle's phone number. I write it down on a scrap of paper along with the address. Then I open up a little cookie jar shaped like a pink pig to see what's in there. There a five dollar bill and some silver and I scoop it out and put that and the address in my pocket too.

I got a one track mind now like a bee goin back to the hive when I walk out the apartment. I got Shawn's garage as the only thing in my mind pulsin with the blood in my brain. I know he live up on a hill behind the college on one of them back roads. My shoulders all bent over to stay out the lime light but there come the college bus with its rattlin engine and black smoke. It cost fifty five cent to ride and I got that much in my pocket. It so hot in this summer air that the cold air of the bus hit me hard. The driver slump over the wheel don't even take his eye off the road. That's cool with me. There ain't one other person ridin so I pick a seat toward the back and slide down low watchin out the window. The bus go past the school and the driver kind of slow down there thinkin I'm gonna get off but I just slide down deeper in my seat to let him know I ain't gettin off yet.

The bus travel up hill to the college which sit up high lookin over the town. I ain't never been there before cause I never took the bus further than my school. He pull the bus in by a mad big building at a bus stop. There nobody there so I guess this the last stop and he mean for me to get off. He don't say nothin and neither do I as I slip off the bus down the step in front of the building say Library on it. There a big red and white cloth hangin over these big ass front doors with a picture of a open book in the middle with a computer clicker comin out of it and it say Open the World on there. When you go in there they got some kind of metal detectors you gotta walk through and then you facin a big long desk. Two girls with long hair talkin to each other back there and they don't see me comin in.

The place be so big and it nice and cool in there. Off to the left where the shelves of books start there a lady sittin at a desk with a sign on it read Reference Librarian. The lady skinny with a long bony neck. She pale as paper and she got blond hair cut blunt under her ears make her neck look even skinnier. She got a big book open up on the desk and she stickin her pointy little nose out at a computer screen. She don't notice me comin up even when I'm standin right in front of her. Finally I gotta say, "Excuse me."

And she look up and her blue eyes blankish like she don't know how to read a person face no more.

"Where the maps of this town at?"

She put me in focus then and she give me a papery little smile. "Do you mean maps of Oneonta?"

"Yeah, I guess."

"The map room is on the second floor, down the corridor directly across from the elevators. You'll find local maps displayed there."

"So I can just go up there?" I ask her.

"Certainly. Just take the elevator or the stairs in the foyer up to the second floor. If you're looking for more specific information you'll find that the maps are organized by location name in the card catalogue. Here, just a moment."

She get up and kind of lurch forward and walk over to a rack of papers on the wall and she take a blue folded up paper out of there. "Here, this should give you more information. If you need help you'll have to come back down to ask. There won't be any staff upstairs at this time of year."

"O.K. Thanks ma'am," I say, cause I take pride in bein polite.

The blue paper say Maps at Milne Library, with a picture of the building on the front. It got all this shit in it about geologic and topographic. I just drop it in the trash when I get back to the lobby. Up the stairs there a picture of a man in a suit from old fashioned times and he just smilin away lookin down on me as I'm goin up. The steps are made of stone and they real wide. On the second floor there a sign say what's in there and Map Room on the list. When you go through the double doors into there you hear... nothin. It like the most silent place I ever been at. The floor and the walls got carpet so it soak up the sound of your feet and even your breath. The hallway go out to the left so that's the way I walk. There more doors to go through and when you push through them you in a room with rows and rows and rows of grey metal book shelves and they all filled top to bottom with books. Its like a maze of books all different colors, some fat, some skinny. Like sideways bricks in a wall. It would be so cool to play hide and seek in here. It make you want to run and sneak around. It's off my track but I gotta walk down the aisle and run my fingers over them as I go. I'm thinking about if any these books ever get taken out and who write them in the first place. Stoppin to look up close I see the names of some, The Memoirs of Napoleon Bonaparte, The Algerians, The French and Their Culture, and some other crazy shit like that.

I'm standin there thinkin about the books when I look up and see Map Room written up over a door. It darker in there and they got big grey file cabinets with long skinny drawers in there all along the walls. Nobody in there, nobody on this whole floor, but me. I pull open the top drawer on the first cabinet I see. There giant sheets of paper in there and the top one got big light green splotches on it and these little lines in a weird shape like a amoeba only the lines one inside the other kind of like a tree ring only they get skinny and closer together toward the middle. I'm squintin down close but this shit don't make no sense so I slide the drawer shut. That's when I see a big map on top the cabinet say City and Surrounding Town of Oneonta. This map wide as my arms stretched and I know Shawn road got to be here someplace. I bring the map to one the big tables in the middle of the room and pull the paper out my pocket. 680 Ketchum Hill Road.

Right away my eyes blur over lookin at the map. I can't see nothin but tiny lines and boxes. I bend over almost touchin it with my nose but nothin I recognize come up. My eyes are burnin so they start to tear up. I close my eyes to rub them and lay my head down on my arms for just a minute.

I'm lyin in a big big bed and the covers are real soft and fluffy and the pillow is deep. I'm lyin on my side with the bottom arm crook under my head. I'm pressed up against someone too. We touching all along our bodies. Our forehead press together and our toes tangle up. We got our top arms wrap around each other pullin us even closer together. My eyes closed but I can smell his breath. We press our mouths together, not kissin exactly, just breathin into each other. I open my eyes and I see it Shawn eyes I'm lookin into and they look like pieces of soft green blue sea glass up close like this. He is so warm. I close my eyes again and I say with my lips still pressed against his, I love you, and the words are breathed into him. He say nothin back so I open my eyes again and he change into my grandma and I look into her cloudy black eyes and she say, I love you too, mi amor. Go ahead and cry, I know you didn't mean for that girl to be killed. And then I do start to cry real hard and my tears start to make me and my grandma all wet in the bed and the bed in a stream all a sudden and me and my grandma are holding on to the bed and the bed swirlin around and I'm afraid she gonna get blown off and I can see, tangled up in the bushes is a bunch of hair and its long and blond and kinky and then I know who it is and I let out a scream that actually come out into the air so it jar me awake but the sound that poured out got soaked up in the walls of that place before anybody else know about it.

My mouth taste like shit and my head so heavy and my eyes itchin. There the map still in front of me but it still don't make no sense so I think I just gotta ask that white lady downstairs again. In the ladies room I see that I look like shit too so I wash my face and drink some of my Gatorade to rinse out my mouth and open up one of the boxes of Rice Crispies and eat half of it dry.

Downstairs the white lady gone and there a man there now. He do the same routine about not lookin up till I say, "Excuse me. Do you know where Ketchum Hill at?"

He wasn't expectin this question so it take him a minute to focus in. "Um, well, if you drive off campus at the West Street exit and you go past the tennis courts you'll go along West Street for about two or three miles. Ketchum Hill is off to the left."

Outside it was startin to get dark and that was cool by me cause the more I kept on the down low the better. It was when I was walkin off the campus that the cops pulled up. I was gonna run but then I figured it wasn't no use. They ask me my name and tell me to get in. I did what they said cause at least they couldn't get me with resistin.

II.

Sometime when I'm feelin bummed I like to take a certain day out of my mind and relive the whole thing. This day stand out above all the rest and I take it out and I run over all the parts like maybe a selfish king count out his gold pieces one by one. It happen the summer before sixth grade. My grandma was still alive and Alma and Big Dennis was just datin. For my twelfth birthday Alma and Dennis decide to take me down to Manhattan to see the Central Park Zoo.

As usual I got my long braid but my grandma let me wear shorts for once. She old style Puerto Rican so she think kids gotta be dress up to go out. This time Alma got me a new outfit. It had hot pink shorts with white and yellow daisies on the back pockets and a light pink tee shirt with ruffles on the sleeves and more daisies on the chest. So I got to wear shorts and it was just me and them two and the whole day was about me.

We take the number 2 train down from the Bronx. The three of us sittin in a row on them orange plastic seats with me in the middle. Dennis playin stupid games to make me laugh like he lick his finger and stick it in Alma ear when she ain't lookin. Alma pretend she mad but she laughin too.

He make jokes about the signs they got in there for some guy name Dr. Zitzmore and one about Got Hemmoroids? Call 1-800 and so on. Dennis just crackin us up. We all surprise we there already when the conductor say we at Columbus Circle.

We push our way through the steamin subway and come out at Central Park South. We walk along the bottom of the park. There all these horses with fancy carriages over there for takin people on rides. They line up along the avenue. The horses swishin away flies with they tails, pawin at the street. I remember one had a cloth bag hooked up to his nose that he was eatin out of. The drivers just stand around in they tall leather boots and long jackets waitin for a customer. I remember just wonderin how you get a job like that, like you in Cinderella every day.

Dennis know this place real good cause he use to work in the mechanic shop they got in the park. He so excited to show us everything he know. We stop on the corner by Fifth Avenue where Dennis tell us we gonna get the best fish sandwich we ever taste. There a old black guy workin under a green and white stripe umbrella fryin up the fish and servin up the sandwiches. He don't even look up he so busy gettin the food out to the hungry people standin in line there. The white fish has a gold fried crust on it that taste like salt and oil. It got tarter sauce with sweet pickle cut up small in it and the roll be soft and white. It got one piece of light green lettuce on there to add a little crunch. Alma get extra napkins cause she know grandma gonna yell if I get grease on my clean new top. We find a black green bench in the shade inside the park to eat on. We tell Dennis he right about that fish cause it taste real nice.

When we done lickin our lips we head up the avenue to what they call the Arsenal. It look like a big castle keepin guard on the park. The zoo right on the back side of that castle. When you go in there they got all kinds of different types of places that animals live in, in a building built in a circle. They got the jungle and they got the North Pole. Outside in the middle my favorite part. That the sea lion pool. The sea lions live in a glass pool with some big rocks like islands in the middle. Man, I could watch them all day. They slide off the island and swim back and forth, changing direction fast as you can blink. When they come out they so shiny they wet fur look like silk or satin to me. They got these pouches with whiskers in them under they nose. They black eyes bulge out like marbles and they winkin to get the water out. They so clumsy when they on the island holdin they heads up with those flippers. You wanna laugh cause they look like messed up dogs. Then pop! They in the water again movin like a bullet under there. I'm thinkin how come God make a animal that so perfect and fast in the water got to drag his clumsy ass up on land so he can breath?

When we leave the zoo we make a left and walk under a brick arch where there a man sellin balloons and Alma get me a red one. Dennis make us laugh by copyin the man cause he sound like he sayin, "Bayoons! Bayoons! Bayoons fo you baby!"

Dennis tell us we got to sit and wait cause on the top of that brick arch there a kind of cukoo clock and we got to wait till the hour change so we can hear it go off. So we sittin there on another black green bench with me in the middle waitin for the hour to change and Dennis and Alma be holdin hands behind my head. I look down at my feet and I think on how even the ground is beautiful down here. There six sided blocks under my feet that fit together side to side and top to bottom. There ain't no bumps in the road, just smooth connected blocks as far your eyes wanna look.

When the clock strike three two monkeys on the top of the arch take turns bangin on a bell. One of those old time songs start playin and then the animals under the bell start to turn around and play different instruments. There a bear with a tamborine, a hippo with a violin, a goat with some type of flute, a kangaroo with a horn, and a penguin with a drum. They turn around slow playin they song for us and it truly make me wanna cry it so pretty.

After we rest there we walk on a wide road with statues all along it. They famous people on these statues but the only one I know is Christopher Columbus. The trees there must be real old cause they so tall and wide around. There old people sittin and readin on the benches under the statues and brown skin nurses pushin rich people babies along and tourists from other places who lookin around as much as me.

Dennis take us to this little lake he call the Boat Pond. On one side a little green house with stacked sailboats that real little. People walkin around that lake sailin those boats by remote. We listen to them talkin about who got the fastest or the prettiest boat. They look like real boats from the olden days to me, zig zaggin on that bright black water. At the end of that lake there a brown metal statue of Alice in Wonderland and it so big you can climb up on the mushroom and the rabbit and the one with the hat and Alice the same size you are. Big Dennis got a lady to take our picture sittin up there on that mushroom. I still got it too. We all smilin and Big Dennis makin bunny ears behind Alma head.

CHAPTER 5

Big Dennis keep pullin us on cause he want to show us that whole damn place. He bring us to this giant fountain with another lake behind it. This one got people in row boats floatin around on it. It got a angel who got these huge wings on her back with a lily in her hand. She look like she walkin forward. Dennis say her name the Angel of the Waters. Water spillin down from under her feet into a plate below her. The plate held up by these baby angels standin on another plate that spill water into a wide stone pool under them. Alma say, "Dennis, I can't walk no more. I got to get me some rest."

So we get one of them Sabrett's hotdogs with mustard and a coke from another guy sellin food from a silver box under a green and white umbrel-la. We sit at the cool stone edge of that fountain and I dip my greasy fingers in the water to take off the food smell. There a couple there gettin they pictures taken in they weddin clothes. I think they Chinese. To me they look like what you see on top a weddin cake. He wearin a black suit and a bow tie. Her white dress off the shoulder and it poof out wide under her waist. She got a bouquet of different types of white flowers. Her hair in a fancy bun with curls and she got more flowers wound around her black hair. They do all these poses, some with her white see-through veil off her face, some with it on. They do one where they make a toast with wide glasses for champagne. I beg Alma to take a picture and she do it.

Dennis say we gonna head up town now cause we all beat. But that wasn't to be cause the best part of that day was yet to come. Behind the fountain run 72nd Street. That street go through the park with a bridge that go over where the fountain at. There a giant set of stairs under the bridge that look over the fountain. To keep in the park and head downtown you go through these three arches into a big stone room and up through these stairs. Since we headin to the train we go into there to go up those stairs. When we go through there we see there a band warmin up for a show. I whine, "Can't we just see what it's gonna be?"

Alma say, "What about you Dennis?"

Dennis say, "You know me baby!"

So we wait a little on the stairs. The band got all kinds of colored people in it. Maybe they got eight people in it all together. One guy tappin soft with his palms on some tall drums with a red and yellow triangle pattern. He got black rectangle sunglasses on and bushy dreds and a Africa shirt on with gold thread that tight across his big chest and get loose at the elbows. There three women in matchin clothes but in different colors with different types of shakers in they hands too. They all got a cloth tied around in back that just cover they breasts and wrap around skirts. They hair wrap up in thick bright scarves. They all barefoot. People start gatherin up and circlin around the stage that built up off the floor.

Me and Alma and Dennis think we can't move cause we so tired from walkin and we think we just gonna watch a little but when that beat start we just can't hold back. Dennis grab our hands and he pull us in to dance, shakin his butt to clear hisself a path. I know everybody there feelin the same thing. When that man with the drums do his thing you feel the beat in your stomach and you just start to move your shoulders and hips even if you want to stay on the sidelines and watch.

While we dancin nobody notice that the sky cloudin up and we don't smell the rain in the air. We only notice when a thunder clap hits and it start to pour down hard and heavy. Everybody laugh and keep right on dancin like fools and the band start to play louder and wilder.

Then the rain start to run down the stairs into this big giant stone room we in and it start to pool up around our ankles. Still, we keep dancin, we're splashin now to the beat, wet up to the thighs. We warm in here even though the storm crashin outside.

When we finally make our way back to Columbus Circle we could hardly pick up our feet. I think I fell asleep across Alma lap before we were out the station. I wasn't even gonna think about the look on my grandma's face when she see my clothes. For that moment I would just rest and dream of the beautiful day when I was little and we was all happy. That day that would be all mine forever.

Epilogue

I don't mind sayin that when I come before the judge I was scared shitless. The attorney they give me say me and Crystal and Tiffany and Sierra all equal in this crime. He say it don't matter who hold Bethany head under the water, we was all there with the same plan to hurt her so we all gonna go down for it together too.

When they brought me in I was thinkin that Bethany was dead so I guess it all came out the best way it could in the end. At least they let me stay at my house with my cousin Alma and her baby Little Dennis. Cause of the trouble I been in already at Binghamton the judge give me probation. He also put a order of protection on me so I don't go near Bethany or her sister, Fawn, and say I'm not allowed no contact with nobody else involved. That's o.k. cause Crystal and Tiffany over in JD in Syracuse and it happen on the last day of school so I didn't have to go back there again with nobody to hang out with. When all this mess over me and Alma goin back to NYC anyhow.

They also say I got to get a counselor for my anger issues, but since we got no insurance I got to go to the County Mental Health Clinic and the lady there can't squeeze me in till July. The counselor send me a letter though and tell me to get a notebook and write about my story to get prepared for seeing her. That's cool too since the judge make me have a electric ankle bracelet and I can't go nowhere but the county office and home without my probation officer givin permission. I got nothing to do in but sit around and smoke cigarettes and think.

Cause I'm fourteen the judge say he want me to be rehabilitated and not punish so he give me the chance. If I fuck up again he gonna charge Alma with neglect and put me in foster care.

Commentary by Patricia Leavy

1. Sensitively Portrays People, Promotes Empathy, and Promotes Empathetic Engagement

Elizabeth Bloom's ethnofiction "The Scrub Club" is a very well-written short story that engages readers in issues of social class that are often difficult to talk about. Bloom takes great care in sensitively portraying her characters, giving them multidimensionality and authenticity, and using them to share perspectives that may influence the way teachers engage with their students and the ways that students engage with their peers. Through her exquisite use of first-person narration and revealing dialogue, Bloom is able to sensitively portray the people represented by her characters in a manner that promotes empathetic engagement across differences. In doing so, she encourages both self-awareness and social reflection. This is no easy task as Bloom attempts to use appropriate expressive and vernacular language while simultaneously presenting her characters with great dignity. She also strikes a difficult balance between affording her characters agency while showing how they are shaped by institutional processes.

2. Substantive Contribution

As noted in her introduction to "The Scrub Club," Bloom set out to contribute to our understanding of how working-class and poor adolescents survive in institutional settings that blatantly privilege their middle-class counterparts and value entrée into the middle class above the other virtues. She also wanted to explore how the systems of discipline and punishment in place impact the relationships between adolescents and between adolescents and adults. Finally, Bloom aimed to explore what happens to working-class and poor adolescents when they are placed in educational environments that don't engage them or promote critical thinking. These are under-researched areas that cross disciplinary boundaries and have educational, sociological, and economic dimensions. Moreover, because social class is often perceived as difficult to talk about, particularly in complex and nuanced ways, it is often difficult to produce comprehensive research in this area. Through her skilled use of fiction, Bloom is able to significantly contribute to our knowledge in these areas. Perhaps the greatest contribution of her ethnofiction will come to fruition as the story is used in classes to promote reflection, critical thinking, and class discussion. Whereas the contribution may be intended for teacher education courses, there is clear value for using the piece in a range of social science courses as well.

Chapter 6
Visual Music

by John L. Vitale

Introduction

My experiences as a musical artist (performer and composer), music education researcher, and high-school music teacher of twelve years inform this project. I have developed an evolving interest in the relationship between music and moving images, and specifically in how music shapes the meaning of a moving image.

The purpose of this study, then, is to investigate how music changes the meaning of film. The results of this investigation are revealed through a narrative analysis. Specifically, I have written a story using an authentic film screenplay format that captures the spirit of the data generated by the participants of this study. From a theoretical perspective, this study investigates the film experience in the context of Rosenblatt's (1978) response theory, namely, the rich and diverse life experiences of each individual during film viewing/listening.

Methodologically, a film sequence of about five minutes in length was experienced by four groups of senior secondary school, non-music students (seventy-four participants in total), with each group exposed to a different musical soundtrack. The four soundtracks were selected on the basis of distinct musical styles as outlined by the Hevner adjective scale (please refer to table on the next page) for music listening (Hoffer 1973). Although a number of data sources

Fiction as Research Practice: Short Stories, Novellas, and Novels, by Patricia Leavy, 147–93.

Hevner Adjective Scale

A	B	C	D	E	F	G	H	I	J
Cheerful	Fanciful	Delicate	Dreamy	Longing	Dark	Sacred	Dramatic	Agitated	Frustrated
Gay	Light	Graceful	Leisurely	Pathetic	Depressing	Spiritual	Emphatic	Exalting	
Happy	Quaint	Lyrical	Sentimental	Plaintive	Doleful		Majestic	Exciting	
Joyous	Whimsical		Serene	Yearning	Gloomy		Triumphant	Impetuous	
Bright			Soothing		Melancholic			Vigorous	
Merry			Tender		Mournful				
Playful			Tranquil		Pathetic				
Sprightly			Quiet		Sad				
					Serious				
					Sober				
					Solemn				
					Tragic				

From Hoffer (1973).

were used (including questionnaires, interviews, and focus groups), this study exclusively addresses the final focus group session (jigsaw) that occurred at the end of the data collection process.

This jigsaw session involved at least one person from each of the four groups of students. The rationale behind this jigsaw session was that each participant ideally represented the Hevner loading (different soundtrack) that s/he was exposed to. Moreover, each participant had no prior knowledge that different musical soundtracks were employed.

The ensuing screenplay allowed me to capture many of the intricacies, nuances, and subtleties that imbued the jigsaw session discussion, which were exceedingly difficult to capture via questionnaires. Many things such as voice intonation, facial expressions, and body language of the jigsaw participants were incorporated into the screenplay. Moreover, as a qualitative researcher it is my role to "translate the text of lived actions into a meaningful account" (Glesne and Peshkin 1992, 153). The most meaningful account that I can provide is a story about an interesting and provocative discussion that transpired during the jigsaw session focus group. Although fictitious in nature, much of the text comes directly from the jigsaw participants and my life experiences as a secondary schoolteacher.

This screenplay that follows is about Mr. Ross (a high-school visual arts teacher) and his five senior students: Brandon, Jenna, Lindy, Christa, and Hasheed. Mr. Ross gives each student a DVD of a five-minute film to be viewed at home, and asks the students to paint a picture that best captures the essence of the film. Mr. Ross informs his students that they will all be watching the same film, but he does not inform them that the musical soundtracks will be different (only Lindsay and Christa experienced the same soundtrack). When the students submit their paintings, Mr. Ross examines the assignment by placing emphasis on all elements of the film (characters, plot, music, etc.—essentially the questions that were asked in the jigsaw focus session), but does not yet tell the students about the different musical soundtracks.

Just before each painting is revealed, we are taken into a time warp for each student, where significant aspects of their life experiences become evident, such as cultural background, gender, and social constructs. This is where I try to tie in the theoretical framework of my study (Rosenblatt's response theory). After each time warp sequence, the painting becomes clear and we hear the music that each student was exposed to. There is also a voice over of each student explaining what his or her painting is about. In this sequence, there are many direct quotes taken from the jigsaw session focus group.

Mr. Ross lets the cat out of the bag and informs the students that they have been exposed to the same film but heard different musical soundtracks, except for Lindy and Christa. Mr. Ross then shows the connection between each student's painting and the character of their musical soundtrack, making it very clear that the musical soundtrack of a film plays a significant role in the meaning-making process. This understanding can also be extended to other uses of music and media, such as television, video games, personal electronic devices, and online applications. Considering the media-savvy world that we live in, this study provides practical insight into daily interactions that many of us experience with music and visual images, and the relationship between these two artistic mediums.

Please note that the screenplay is written according to film industry standards. Hence, scene headings (also known as sluglines), key action words within the scene context, and character names are all capitalized.

Visual Music

FADE IN

EXT. SCHOOL GROUNDS–MORNINGSTAR SECONDARY SCHOOL

CLOSE-UP of a maple tree. We can see sap BURSTING out of its bark. The camera SLOWLY PANS OUT and we see brown and damp grass with small patches of snow. A red-bricked building SLOWLY starts to EMERGE in the distance as well as a few students RUNNING with backpacks and light jackets. We eventually see a sign that says "Morningstar Secondary School," but the CAMERA SLOWLY ZOOMS IN on a window where we START to see the inside of a classroom.

INT. ART CLASS – MORNINGSTAR SECONDARY SCHOOL

The camera COMES in THROUGH the window and we are FLYING HIGH ABOVE the classroom. DESCENDING SLOWLY, we see many objects that would typically belong in an art class (paintings, brushes, easels, paints, rags, etc.). There are four senior level students (three females and one male) CHATTING with one another as they wait for class to begin. In WALKS the art teacher MR. ROSS and WRITES the date on the blackboard: Friday March 12, 2010.

MR. ROSS
(*turns and faces the students*)
Good morning everyone! I am sure that all of us are anxious to begin our spring break after today, but we must attend to some business first.

A male student named HASHEED WALKS in the classroom.

HASHEED
(*quickly responds as he is approaching his seat*)
What kind of business?

MR. ROSS
Well, good morning, Hasheed! Nice of you to join us!

HASHEED
(*stumbles and almost trips as he takes his seat*)

Sor... Sorry I am late Sir, my lock was stuck again. Sometimes it takes a few minutes to open it.

We now SEE the rest of the students who are all SMILING and SHAKING their heads. It is evident that Hasheed's consistent tardiness is always accompanied by some lame excuse.

JENNA
(*imitating Hasheed with a child-like voice*)
My lock was stuck!

All of the students LAUGH.

MR. ROSS
(*quickly jumps in*)
Okay, folks, let's get back to business. I have an assignment for all of you to complete over the spring break.

There is a collective SIGH of MOANS and GROANS from all of the five students in the class.

JENNA
So much for our spring break!

LINSDAY
Yeah, so much for it!

BRANDON
So what is the assignment, Sir?

MR. ROSS
I am glad that you asked, Brandon.
(*pause*)
Actually, this assignment is probably a little bit different than what you are used to.

CHRISTA
(*with a puzzled look on her face*)
What do you mean, different?

MR. ROSS
Well, Christa . . .
(*takes a deep breath*)
You are all going to experience a short film—about five minutes long—and create a painting that best captures the mood, feeling, and theme of the film. The only restriction is that you must not use any human figures.

The students all LOOK at one another NODDING their heads in approval of the assignment.

BRANDON
So what exactly are you looking for, Sir? I mean, how are we going to be graded?

MR. ROSS
I will give each of you a copy of the film to take home and all I expect is that you experience the film about three or four times before you start to paint and . . .

HASHEED
(*overlapping*)
Three or four times?

MR. ROSS
Remember, folks, the film is only five minutes long!

JENNA
(*rather sarcastically, talking down to Hasheed*)
Earth to Hasheed, earth to Hasheed! He said the film was five minutes long just a few seconds ago. Duhhh!

MR. ROSS
Now, now, Jenna, no need to jump all over Hasheed.
(*pause*)
Anyway, check the film out a few times, preferably in a good environment with no noise and stuff like that, and paint me a picture that best captures the film. Your studio fees that you paid at the beginning of the semester will cover the cost of the materials.

LINDY
How large of a canvas do you want us to use?

MR. ROSS
That's a very good question, Lindy. You will all be using a two-by-four-foot canvas, already framed, which you will take home with you today.

BRANDON
What if our interpretation of the film requires a much smaller, or even larger, canvas?

MR. ROSS
Well, Brandon, my reasoning is that all of you will have your paintings exhibited in the school's main display case in the front foyer?

HASHEED
(*rather alarmed*)
What! That's not fair! Why do we have to do this?

JENNA
(*abruptly responds before Mr. Ross has a chance to answer Hasheed's question*)
Don't you ever listen, Hasheed? Mr. Ross told us several times that we would have to display our work as part of the course.

HASHEED
Whatever.

MR. ROSS
Anyway, that is the reason why I want the paintings to be the same size, so there is a sense of uniformity when they are all displayed in the front foyer.

Don't forget to sign your name in the bottom right corner of the painting. I will be waiting for you in the front foyer on the first Monday back from spring break. Try to get there a good half-hour before class begins, as it will take a bit of time to display the paintings.

BRANDON
What about marks, Sir?

MR. ROSS
There is no right or wrong here, it is simply your interpretation of the film. As far as evaluation goes, it is more a question of effort and creativity.
(*pointing to Brandon*)
If your painting is a straight line, then it will be safe to assume that you did not put much effort or creativity into the picture and you will probably fail. Sometimes the thought process behind what you paint is much longer and more arduous than the actual painting itself.

BRANDON
Sir, I . . .

JENNA
(*interrupting Brandon*)
You speak too much, Brandon. Leave Mr. Ross alone.

BRANDON
(*rather excitedly*)
I was only going to ask him to go to the washroom! When you gotta go, you gotta go!

The entire group (including Mr. Ross) CHUCKLES.

MR. ROSS
Yes, Brandon, you may go, but hurry back. We have a school assembly starting in ten minutes and I would like to hand out the film as well as the supplies you will need for the assignment before we are called down.

BRANDON
(*giving Mr. Ross a formal salute*)
Yes sir! Right away Sir!

We now see a CLOSE-UP of Brandon SCURRYING out of his seat HEADING for the bathroom. As Brandon gets closer to the door, our view SLOWLY RISES ABOVE the entire classroom. We SEE Mr. Ross

ORGANIZING art supplies and the remaining four students CHATTING.
HASHEED
I hate these stupid assemblies. All they talk about is not getting into trouble over the spring break. Give me a break.

CHRISTA
You are getting a break, guy! A spring break!

All three girls LAUGH at the joke, but the laugh is more DIRECTED at Hasheed.

HASHEED
Yeah, right. I'll be working all week. Some break!

The camera SLOWLY ZOOMS IN on one of MR. ROSS's paintings displayed in the classroom. We clearly make out the name "JAMES ROSS" in the lower right-hand corner of the painting. The painting is very abstract with a lot of colors and no recognizable form. As the picture STARTS TO FADE, we HEAR the school principal over the PA system asking all ninth-grade students to start making their way to the school cafetorium. She continues to talk but her voice FADES in perfect synchronization with the picture.

EXT. SCHOOL GROUNDS–MORNINGSTAR SECONDARY SCHOOL

CLOSE-UP of the same maple tree used at the beginning of the film. There is only a small TRICKLE of sap visible on the bark of the tree. The camera SLOWLY PANS OUT and we SEE no more patches of snow, but rather a few patches of green grass. The camera ZOOMS IN on a patch of green grass when we hear:

SCHOOL SECRETARY
(*voice over*)
Good morning, Morningstar Secondary School.

INT. MAIN OFFICE OF MORNINGSTAR SECONDARY SCHOOL
The camera now cuts to the main office of Morningstar Secondary School where we see a close-up of the SCHOOL SECRETARY. We can clearly HEAR the sounds of a very BUSY workplace. Phones are RINGING and we HEAR several people TALKING in the background.

SCHOOL SECRETARY
(*with a flustered look on her face*)
The principal is not available to take your call at this time, but if you leave me your name and number, I will have her call you back ASAP.

The camera PANS OUT and we SEE more of the main office. The camera FOLLOWS a group of teachers OUT the main door and into the hallway. We see some students HOVERING around lockers and other students MAKING their way about the school. In the distance we SEE Mr. Ross standing on a chair. His upper body is clearly inside the display place. As the camera gets CLOSER, we SEE Brandon, Jenna, Christa, and Lindy around the display case LOOKING at the paintings, but the actual paintings are not yet visible.

MR. ROSS
(*looking quite flustered*)
Well, Jenna, that does it for your painting. Has anybody seen Hasheed? First period starts in about ten minutes.

EXT. SUB-URBAN NEIGHBORHOOD

The camera ABRUPTLY CUTS to Hasheed FRANTICALLY RUNNING trying to get to school. He is being WEIGHED DOWN by a number of objects he is carrying.

INT. DISPLAY CASE IN THE MAIN FOYER OF THE SCHOOL
There is a CLOSE-UP of Jenna.

JENNA
(*rather sarcastically*)
Don't tell me that you are actually surprised about Hasheed, Sir? I'll be surprised if he even shows up today. You know him, whenever there is an assignment due, he is a lot later than usual.

MR. ROSS
Okay folks, let's get to class. There is a lot I want to talk about.

Mr. Ross CLOSES the door to the display case and locks it. As the camera PANS OUT we get our first GLIMPSE of the paintings. We notice four paintings hanging in the display case with enough room for one more—Hasheed's. It is difficult to make out any form or semblance of the paintings because of the persistent GLARE coming from the glass covering of the display case. All we see are colors with no specific shapes at this point.

The camera FOLLOWS Mr. Ross and the four students as they BEGIN WALKING toward the art class. The camera now CUTS TO Mr. Ross OPENING the Art Room door. He REACHES in his pocket and spends a few seconds searching for the right key. The door is OPENED and we are now inside the classroom watching the students and Mr. Ross COME IN.

LINDY
(*very depressed*)
What a drag! I hate coming back to school after a week off. I could hardly get up this morning.

CHRISTA
(*yawning and talking at the same time*)
I know what you mean.

MR. ROSS
(*closes the classroom door, walks toward the front of the class, claps his hands three times and looks very eager*)
Okay folks, there is a lot I want to discuss today, so let's get down to business.

We HEAR a BANGING (like someone is KICKING) at the door.

MR. ROSS
Come in, it's open

Hasheed is behind the door. We do not see him yet, but he CALLS out in a MUFFLED voice.

HASHEED
I can't open the door, my hands are full.

JENNA
(*rather surprised*)
Well, I guess Hasheed made it in after all!

MR. ROSS
(*rather sarcastically*)
Since you like Hasheed so much, Jenna, why don't you open the door for him?

All the other students laugh and Jenna has a smile on her face.

JENNA
No problem, Sir.

The camera FOLLOWS Jenna to the door. She intentionally OPENS the door VERY SLOWLY. Within a few seconds, we see Hasheed holding everything imaginable. He has a large and heavy backpack on, is holding his lunch and a few books in one hand, and his painting (framed and covered with a green garbage bag) in the other. There is an EXTREME CLOSE-UP of Jenna.

JENNA
Was your lock stuck again, Hasheed?
(*she scratches her chin with her right hand and looks very pensive*)
Wait a minute, let me guess. You couldn't find your shoes this morning? Your dog ate your painting? Your cat . . .

HASHEED
(*overlapping with a rather tired and flustered voice*)
Be quiet, Jenna, and give me a hand, would ya. I missed the bus this morning and I had to get here carrying all of this crap. My arms feel like Jell-O!

JENNA
You never learn, Hasheed!

Jenna TAKES the painting from Hasheed and BRINGS it in the classroom. As she gets UP to the front of the classroom, she begins to PULL the garbage bag OFF the painting.

HASHEED
(*rather ticked off*)
Get lost, Jenna! That's my painting. Leave it alone!

JENNA
(*stops pulling the painting out of the bag*)
What's the big deal, it should have been up in the display case already.

MR. ROSS
Okay, both of you cut it out and have a seat.

Hasheed's painting is never really exposed.

MR. ROSS
(*slowly walking toward Hasheed*)
Well, I am glad you made it in, Hasheed. I was just about to discuss the philosophy behind the assignment and this would have been the wrong class to miss.

(*taps Hasheed on the shoulder*)
I will put your painting up in the display case during lunch hour. Anyway let's get down to business.

Mr. Ross WALKS up to the blackboard and starts to DRAW a diagram. The camera PANS across the faces of the students who KEENLY LOOK at what Mr. Ross is doing. As the camera finally reaches Hasheed, he is busily RUSTLING through his knapsack LOOKING for something. Mr. Ross finishes his diagram and the camera SLOWLY ZOOMS IN on the blackboard. We see a simple diagram consisting of three boxes connected by arrows. In the first box we see the word "film," in the second box is the word "artist," and in the last box is the word "painting."

MR. ROSS
This is a flow chart, so to speak, of the assignment that you all did.
(*underlines the word film*)
You were asked to experience a film . . .
(*underlines the word artist*)
Then you were asked to interpret the film as an artist . . .
(*underlines the word painting*)
Then you were asked to paint your interpretation on a two-by-four canvas. But now I would like to look a little bit deeper into this diagram. Let's start with the film. Brandon, what do you think?

There is a CLOSE-UP of Brandon who LOOKS a little confused but also somewhat intrigued.

BRANDON
About the assignment?

The camera remains focused on Brandon but we HEAR Mr. Ross' voice.

MR. ROSS
(*voice over*)
Yes, but I am more interested in the entire process of the assignment. Let's specifically look at the film. What are the elements that make up a film?

Brandon still LOOKS a little bit confused and the camera PANS OUT so all of the students are visible. There is a moment of SILENCE.

JENNA
Story line. A film is nothing without a story to tell.

The camera now FOLLOWS Mr. Ross as he WALKS UP to the blackboard. He WRITES the word plot and CONNECTS it with an arrow to the word film.

MR. ROSS
Okay, that's great. What other elements make up a film?

BRANDON
(*quickly responds*)
Theme!

LINDY
Music!

CHRISTA
Characters!

MR. ROSS
Great, just give me a chance to write all of this down.

We see Mr. Ross FRANTICALLY WRITING on the blackboard. The Camera starts to FLY HIGH above him and ZOOMS in on a clock. The clock shows 9:20 AM; within a few seconds the clock shows 10:00 AM, forty minutes later. The camera SLOWLY COMES DOWN from the clock and ZOOMS IN on the blackboard. The once simple diagram is now an intricate and highly complicated flow chart with many words and several arrows and lines CROSSING at many points. The camera CUTS to the faces of the students. It is quite evident that Hasheed can barely keep his eyes OPEN. The camera SLOWLY PANS out to Mr. Ross.

MR. ROSS
Well, we have just analyzed the assignment to death. But if we had to summarize the core of the assignment in just a few sentences, what could we say? Hasheed?

The camera CUTS to Hasheed who is LEANING on his chair.

HASHEED
(*looks a little dazed and confused*)
What?

JENNA
Stop sleeping, Hasheed!

MR. ROSS
Let's give Hasheed a chance to answer the question.

HASHEED
(*still looking a little dazed*)
What question?

All of the students laugh.

MR. ROSS
(*still showing an exceptional amount of patience*)
Hasheed, would you please summarize the assignment in just a few sentences?

There is a moment of SILENCE and the camera now ZOOMS IN on Hasheed until there is an EXTREME CLOSE-UP of his face.

HASHEED
Well, Sir.
(*pause–the camera slowly pulls away from his face and we see all of the students*)
This assignment was a matter of input and output.

The rest of the students LOOK a little puzzled.

MR. ROSS
(*voice over*)
That's an interesting response Hasheed, would you care to explain further?

HASHEED
The film was a source of input for us, both visual
(*points to his eyes*)
and aural.
(*points to his ears*)
Our paintings, therefore, were the output, what we thought the film to be through another artistic medium. Ultimately, the output (or painting) is not only a reflection of the film, but also a reflection of the culture, gender, and life experiences of each person who experienced the film. These are the human elements that filtered the final output.

There is ABSOLUTE SILENCE in the class. The camera INDIVIDUALLY PANS ACROSS the faces of the four other students. The students are

MESMERIZED by Hasheed's articulate and highly intelligent response, particularly Jenna whose jaw has clearly DROPPED a few inches. The camera now CUTS to Mr. Ross who is SITTING on the edge of a desk with his legs CROSSED and his hand on his chin. Despite Hasheed's constant tardiness and easy come easy go attitude, Mr. Ross clearly recognizes Hasheed's intellect.

MR. ROSS
(*with a slight smile on his face*)
I could not have said it better myself, Hasheed. That is an exceptional description of what this assignment was really about.

The bell RINGS and class is over. Students GET UP out of their chairs and START TO LEAVE the classroom.

JENNA
(*patting Hasheed on the back*)
Not bad for a guy who's always late and sleeping in class.

The camera FOLLOWS the students OUT the door and DOWN the hallway. Hasheed stops at his locker and is unsuccessful at OPENING the lock. He clearly LOOKS FRUSTRATED and KICKS the lock, which then OPENS. The camera FADES OUT while Hasheed is PUTTING things away in his locker.

INT. CAFETERIA OF MORNINGSTAR SECONDARY SCHOOL

We are FLYING HIGH above several hundred students EATING lunch. There is an abundance of CLATTER and CHATTER. The camera SLOWLY ZOOMS IN on Jenna and Christa who are both DRINKING soda pops with empty plates (showing a few scraps of food) in front of them.

JENNA
Let's see if Mr. Ross put Hasheed's painting up yet. I can't wait to see it.

CHRISTA
I'll meet you there in five minutes, I just have to call my mom at work and let her know that I have a soccer practice after school today.

JENNA
Sounds good. I'll see ya there.

The camera starts to FLY HIGH ABOVE the cafeteria once again. We see Christa HEADING TOWARD one exit and Jenna toward another. The camera FADES and CUTS to the main display case in the front foyer. There are eight or nine students HOVERING around the display case, one of whom is Hasheed. We also see Mr. Ross standing to the side of the display case TALKING to Ms. Collins, the school principal. The camera ZOOMS IN on the faces of the students LOOKING at the paintings. Hasheed is the only student that we recognize. We hear some CHATTING going on and the camera VERY SLOWLY PANS across the entire glass covering the display where the five paintings very slightly come into FOCUS within about ten seconds. The glass covering the display case, however, still creates a persistent GLARE so we do not get a clear view of the pictures. The camera starts to SLOWLY ZOOM IN on the first picture to the left, which was created by Brandon. As we finally get beyond the GLARE of the glass, the painting is still UNCLEAR because we are now ENTERING a tunnel—a time warp of Brandon's life. There are many special effects (both visual and aural) that imitate the MOVEMENT of time through the tunnel.

BRANDON
(*voice over*)
Hello, my name is Brandon Chan. I am eighteen years old and I was born in Hong Kong.

Slightly abstract images of Hong Kong are evident as we are PASSING THROUGH the tunnel and we can HEAR music in the background with an Oriental tonal structure.

BRANDON
(*voice over*)
I came to Canada when I was only four years old.

Brandon's immigration to Canada causes the tunnel to make a very SHARP and RIGID 180-degree TURN to the right, accentuated with more intense aural and visual special effects. During the TURN, a slightly abstract image of an airplane LANDING also becomes apparent.

BRANDON
(*voice over*)
I grew up in the east end of Toronto with my parents and my younger sister. Although my sister and I got along, we were interested in different activities.

The tunnel makes another SHARP TURN with more accentuated special effects. We can now SEE a suburban house.

BRANDON
(*voice over*)
I was more interested in the arts, especially music, but my sister was more interested in playing sports.

We see slightly abstract images of Brandon playing the piano while his sister is RUNNING and KICKING a soccer ball.

BRANDON
(*voice over*)
My love for the arts continued throughout high school. It is hard to believe that I am in my last year of high school already.

We are MOVING FASTER through the tunnel and an image of Brandon PLAYING the saxophone in the school band is barely visible.

BRANDON
(*voice over*)
This is my painting.
(*pause*)

The tunnel MOVES at warp speed and the aural special effects are getting LOUDER and LOUDER. Within a few seconds, there is a sudden STOP of movement and there is complete SILENCE. All we SEE are blurred colors. Very happy and lyrical music STARTS TO PLAY and the colors START to take shape. Within a few seconds, the painting is completely CLEAR, FOCUSED, and UNOBSTRUCTED. It becomes evident that the painting is relatively LIGHT in texture, form, and color.

BRANDON
(*voice over*)
I called my painting "Mind Games."

We SEE a painting with five distinct shapes (triangles, circles, squares, hexagons, and rectangles) that manifest themselves several times throughout the painting. There is no one color or size associated with a specific shape. Sometimes the circles are large and red, and sometimes they are small and green. The same is true for the other shapes. In general, the shapes themselves are MOVING in some sort of pattern.

BRANDON
(*voice over*)
These five shapes represent the five characters in the film moving from one location to another. As the shapes move from one location to another, they change colors and size. This represents how each character changes and evolves throughout the course of the film. The shapes eventually find themselves outdoors in a sun-filled sky.

Although the painting as a whole is relatively light in color, there is a noticeable difference between the bottom and top half. The bottom half (where the pattern of shapes begin) is slightly DARKER than the top half where the pattern of shapes finish in a bright and robust BURST of colors, almost like fireworks EXPLODING in the sky. We start to FAINTLY HEAR the SOUNDS of the time-warp tunnel, which get LOUDER and LOUDER. The painting STARTS to LOSE FOCUS and we now ENTER Brandon's tunnel once more but we are TRAVELING BACK to the direction that we started. We MOVE BACK through the entire tunnel in about five seconds, with all the same images that we had seen before PLAYING BACKWARDS. We COME OUT of the time warp tunnel and find ourselves outside of the display case. The GLARE coming from the glass significantly OBSTRUCTS Brandon's painting. The camera STARTS to SHIFT to Jenna's painting, the next one to the right, but again the GLARE of the glass IMPEDES our view. The camera starts to SLOWLY ZOOM IN and we are now ENTERING a time-warp tunnel of Jenna's life with many of the same special effects (both visual and aural) that imitated the MOVEMENT of time through Brandon's tunnel.

JENNA
(*voice over*)
Hello, my name is Jenna. I am nineteen years old and I was born in Bucharest, Romania.

Slightly abstract images of Romania are evident as we are PASSING THROUGH the tunnel and we can HEAR classical music in the background with a very European tonal structure.

JENNA
(*voice over*)
I came to Canada only five years ago when I was fourteen years old. I was not far behind in school because I studied English back in Romania since grade school.

Jenna's immigration to Canada causes the tunnel to make a very SHARP and RIGID 180-degree TURN to the left, accentuated with more intense aural and visual special effects. During the TURN, we SEE a slightly abstract map of Europe SLOWLY TURNING into a map of North America.

JENNA
(*voice over*)
I have a brother two years younger than me and both of us enjoyed playing together as children. It was difficult growing up in Romania, though, as our family lived on a farm and we did not have a lot of money.

The tunnel makes another SHARP TURN with more accentuated special effects. We can now SEE a young boy and girl RUNNING together in a rural area.

JENNA
(*voice over*)
My life really changed when our family moved to Canada. There is so much to do in this country, especially here at school. I love acting.

We are MOVING FASTER THROUGH the tunnel and an image of Jenna with a lavish stage costume is visible.

JENNA
(*voice over*)
This is my painting.
(*pause*)

The tunnel MOVES at warp speed and the aural special effects are getting LOUDER and LOUDER. Within a few seconds, there is a sudden STOP of movement and there is complete SILENCE. All we SEE are blurred colors. Very TRANQUIL and LONGING music STARTS TO PLAY and the picture SLOWLY comes into FOCUS. It becomes quickly evident that this painting is very different from Brandon's. It is not abstract at all, but rather the type of picture you would see hanging in someone's house. The colors are somewhat dark, but there is a certain softness and delicate touch to the painting.

JENNA
(*voice over*)
I called my painting "Silent Choice."

We SEE a painting that shows the top half of the sun (more orange than yellow) setting over a large body of water. The remaining trickles of sunlight GENTLY SHIMMER along the surface of the water. There is a GENTLE sliver of a moon that is present in the top left-hand corner of the painting, REFLECTING the SOFEST FLICKER of light on the water's surface. There are also a few stars present on the painting's top edge. This night sky gently blends into the soft orange light of the sunset. On the water are five sailboats, each TRAVELING in different directions.

JENNA
(*voice over*)
These five sailboats represent the five characters in the film. These characters do not really cooperate with one another, so I have painted each ship sailing in a different direction. Despite this lack of cooperation and rather dark ambience, the film had a certain serene and tranquil quality to it.

We start to FAINTLY HEAR the SOUNDS of the time-warp tunnel once more, which get LOUDER and LOUDER. The painting STARTS TO LOSE FOCUS and we now enter Jenna's tunnel once more but we are traveling back to the direction that we started. We MOVE back through the entire tunnel in about five seconds, with all the same images that we had seen before playing backwards. We come out of the time-warp tunnel and find ourselves OUTSIDE of the display case. The GLARE coming from the glass significantly OBSTRUCTS Jenna's painting. The camera starts to SHIFT to Lindy's painting, the next one to the right, but again the GLARE of the glass IMPEDES our view. The camera STARTS TO SLOWLY ZOOM IN and we are now ENTERING a time-warp tunnel of Lindy's life with many of the same special effects (both visual and aural) that imitated the MOVEMENT of time in the previous two examples.

LINDY
(*voice over*)
Hello, my name is LINDY. I am eighteen years old and I was born and raised here in Toronto.

Slightly abstract images of the Toronto skyline are evident as we are PASSING THROUGH the tunnel and we can HEAR moderate rock music in the background.

LINDY
(*voice over*)
I have not really traveled much growing up, but I did enjoy my childhood, especially playing in the snow during the winter.

As the tunnel keeps MOVING in a straight direction, we begin to SEE a slightly abstract image of Lindy MAKING snow angels.

LINDY
(*voice over*)
I have a much older sister who always played with me. But ever since she went to college and moved out of the house, I do not see her that much anymore.

The tunnel makes its first SHARP TURN to the right with more accentuated special effects. We can now SEE an image of Lindy's sister WALKING with a cap and graduation gown on.

LINDY
(voice over)
Although I have enjoyed high school, I am glad that this is my last year. I hated doing homework.

We are MOVING FASTER through the tunnel and an image of Lindy WORKING at a desk with a mountain of books beside her is visible.

LINDY
(*voice over*)
This is my painting.
(*pause*)

The tunnel MOVES at warp speed and the aural special effects are getting LOUDER and LOUDER. Within a few seconds, there is a sudden STOP of movement and there is complete SILENCE. Although it takes a few seconds to come into FOCUS, we can readily discern that this painting lacks a lot of color. A very SOLEMN SOUNDING, LOW-PITCHED DRONE is audible which almost has a spiritual quality to it. Although the painting is very concrete in form (like Jenna's), the subject matter of the painting is quite different. The colors are very DEPRESSING and GLOOMY, and there is a COLD and METALLIC feel to the painting.

LINDY
(voice over)
I called my painting "The Escape."

We SEE a painting that shows a large room covered in metal. A vast majority of the painting relies on two to three shades of metallic gray, with some elements of black and a few tiny dashes of other colors. A closer examination gives the impression that we are INSIDE a spaceship of some sort. PRESENT in this room are three doors that are SLIGHTLY AJAR. We cannot SEE beyond the doors, but there are very dim sources of light (of varying degrees) COMING OUT of each door.

LINDY
(voice over)
This is the inside of a spaceship many years from now. It is actually a prison within a spaceship, just like the film. Prisons of the future are very different because they offer a variety of cells for the prisoners to choose, kind of like a maze. Some doors lead to freedom and some lead to adversity, possibly death. Or one may simply choose to stay put. Ultimately, humans have that natural instinct to escape bondage if possible.

We start to FAINTLY HEAR the SOUNDS of the time-warp tunnel once more, which get LOUDER and LOUDER. The painting STARTS TO LOSE FOCUS and we now ENTER Lindy's tunnel once more but we are TRAVELING back to the direction that we started. We MOVE back through the entire tunnel in about five seconds, with all the same images that we had seen before playing backwards. We come out of the time-warp tunnel and find ourselves OUTSIDE of the display case. The GLARE coming from the glass significantly OBSTRUCTS Lindy's painting. The camera STARTS TO SHIFT to Christa's painting, the next one to the right, but again the GLARE of the glass IMPEDES our view. The camera starts to SLOWLY ZOOM IN and we are now ENTERING a time-warp tunnel of Christa's life with many of the same special effects (both visual and aural) that imitated the MOVEMENT of time in the previous three examples.

CHRISTA
(voice over)
Hello, my name is CHRISTA. I am eighteen years old and I was born and raised in the Greater Toronto Area.

Slightly abstract images of Toronto (slightly different than those used for Lindy) are evident as we are PASSING THROUGH the tunnel and we HEAR the same moderate rock music in the background that was used for Lindy's time-warp tunnel.

CHRISTA
(*voice over*)
Although I always lived in and around Toronto, I have lived in many different homes.

The tunnel MAKES several sporadic right and left TURNS within a few seconds. During this time, we SEE slightly abstract images of various residential abodes (houses, town homes, and apartments).

CHRISTA
(*voice over*)
My parents got divorced when I was very young and I was constantly being shipped off between my father's and my mother's home. This was a very difficult time with me. Now that I am eighteen, I have chosen to live with my dad.

The tunnel continues to MAKE SEVERAL SHARP and SPORADIC TURNS with more accentuated special effects. We can now SEE an image of an older man and woman PLAYING tennis with a very large ball.

CHRISTA
(*voice over*)
I have enjoyed high school very much, particularly the extra-curricular programs after school. I really liked playing on the school soccer team.

We are MOVING FASTER THROUGH the tunnel and an image of Christa PLAYING soccer is visible. Christa is a goaltender and she is making a save.

CHRISTA
(*voice over*)
This is my painting.
(*pause*)

The tunnel MOVES at warp speed and the aural special effects are getting LOUDER and LOUDER. Within a few seconds, there is a SUDDEN STOP of movement and there is complete SILENCE. Although it takes a few seconds to come into FOCUS, we can readily discern that there are two very large objects that dominate this painting. As with Lindy, the same SOLEMN SOUNDING, LOW-PITCHED DRONE is audible. Although the picture is DIFFERENT than Lindy's, there are STRIKING similarities. The painting is very dark and gloomy, and also has a cold and metallic feel to it. The theme of a spaceship and outer space is also evident.

CHRISTA
(*voice over*)
I called my painting "Stellar Conflict."

We SEE a painting that SHOWS two large spaceships on course for a HEAD-ON COLLISION at warp speed. Although the two spaceships are different in appearance, they are the same size and both are of a metallic grey color. The remainder of the picture is also very dark. We are clearly in outer space, with small FLICKERS of stars and planets providing the backdrop for the painting.

CHRISTA
(*voice over*)
My painting is an illustration of how wars will be fought in the future. Entire civilizations will live in travelling spaceships. These spaceships will have other spaceships who are allies, and others who are enemies. Enemies will engage in war with one another. In this example, the five characters in the film represent one civilization in conflict with another. Past, present, or future, humans have had and always will have a natural instinct to engage in war.

We start to FAINTLY HEAR the SOUNDS of the time-warp tunnel once more, which get LOUDER and LOUDER. The painting STARTS TO LOSE FOCUS and we now ENTER Christa's tunnel once more but we are TRAVELING back to the direction that we started. We MOVE back through the entire tunnel in about five seconds, with all the same images that we had seen before PLAYING backwards. We COME OUT of the time-warp tunnel and find ourselves OUTSIDE of the display case. The GLARE coming from the glass significantly OBSTRUCTS Christa's painting. The camera SLOWLY FLYS ABOVE, where we SEE several students LOOKING at the display case. The camera now ZOOMS IN on Hasheed, where we SEE an EXTREME CLOSE-UP of his face. A soft light STARTS TO SHINE on Hasheed's face. The light SLOWLY gets DARKER and a very quick TICKING sound of an alarm clock SLOWLY FADES in.

After a few seconds, there is music SLIGHTLY AUDIBLE in the background, which SLOWLY gets LOUDER and LOUDER. As the music gets LOUDER, we notice that the rhythmic PULSE of the music is in perfect synchronization with the TICKING sound of the alarm clock. Eventually the music becomes so loud that the TICKING sound of the alarm clock is no longer AUDIBLE. We now ENTER the time-warp tunnel of Hasheed's life with many of the same special effects (both visual and aural) that imitated the MOVEMENT of time for the previous four students.

HASHEED
(*voice over*)
Hello, my name is HASHEED. I am seventeen years old and I was born in Africa.

Slightly abstract images of Africa are evident as we are PASSING THROUGH the tunnel and we HEAR African drums BEATING in a very distinct rhythmical PATTERN with tribal CHANT on top.

HASHEED
(*voice over*)
I came to Toronto when I was nine years old. Although I am not fond of the weather here in Toronto, it is still a great place to live.

The tunnel makes a SHARP and SPORADIC TURN to the left. We now SEE a tropical natural environment FADE into a rather cold and snowy natural environment.

HASHEED
(*voice over*)
Although I have made a lot of good friends here in Toronto, I miss a lot of my extended family that still live in Africa. I have since been back to Africa only one time in the eight years that I have been in Canada.

The tunnel MAKES SEVERAL SHARP and SPORADIC TURNS with more accentuated special effects. We can now SEE an image of Hasheed nostalgically LOOKING THROUGH a photo album and simultaneously TALKING on the telephone.

HASHEED
(*voice over*)
My father makes me work at a part-time job. He says it is important for a man to learn how to be responsible and work hard. Although I make a lot of extra money, I am always very tired.

We are MOVING FASTER THROUGH the tunnel and an image of Hasheed WORKING at a grocery store is visible. The camera ABRUPTLY CUTS to a CLOSE-UP of Hasheed's face.

HASHEED
This is my painting.
(*pause*)

Hasheed's face SLOWLY FADES OUT and his painting SLOWLY FADES IN. As Hasheed's painting is COMING INTO FOCUS, we HEAR DRAMATIC and VIGOROUS MUSIC with a QUICK PULSATING RHYTHMICAL PATTERN. When the picture completely COMES INTO FOCUS, it becomes difficult to detect the overall theme and motif of the painting. The painting seems quite VIBRANT and ANIMATED, yet it is paradoxically dark in overall color scheme. An initial look reveals five alarm clocks that Hasheed has discreetly designed to LOOK like human faces.

HASHEED
(*voice over*)
I called my painting "Hidden."

A closer examination reveals that the ANIMATED FEEL to each of the clocks represent rather DARK HUMAN EMOTIONS. Some clocks look FRIGHTENED, some look STARTLED, and some look EVIL. Furthermore, each clock is not quite INTACT. Some are MISSING hands, and those that have hands are MISSING numbers. Each clock APPEARS to be ENCASED in some sort of compartment that SEPARATES each clock from one another.

HASHEED
(*voice over*)
My painting is an illustration of how the characters in the film are hidden. None of them knows where they are or what time it is. Since there is very little dialogue in the film, the characters are unable to effectively communicate. This puts a significant barrier between them, essentially leaving five characters that are alone with certain death facing most of them.

There are a few seconds of SILENCE with the camera still FOCUSING on Hasheed's painting. There is a SHARP CUT to an EXTREME CLOSE-UP of a large clock SHOWING one o'clock sharp in the main office of the school. As we SEE the clock, we simultaneously HEAR the school bell RINGING EXTREMELY LOUD, indicating that lunch is over. The camera DROPS DOWN to ground level and STARTS TO PAN ACROSS the office.

OFFICE WORKER #1 (MALE)
(*talking on a phone*)
I'll make sure he gets the message.

The camera continues to PAN.

OFFICE WORKER #2 (FEMALE)
(*working on a computer and talking to a man hovering over her shoulder*)
According to my records, Frances Stiles has missed twenty-two days of school this semester.

The camera continues to PAN where we see Mr. Ross and the school principal Ms. Collins STANDING UP and having a CHAT. The camera ZOOMS in on their conversation.

MS. COLLINS
And that painting by Hasheed! Wow! What a talented young man.

MR. ROSS
Hasheed is a bit different than most students. He is a little rough around the edges, but what an intellect.

MS. COLLINS
Actually, all of the paintings were great. I could not believe how different they all were, except for the two spaceship paintings. It's amazing that most of the students had such a different vision of the film.

MR. ROSS
Well, I conducted a little experiment with the students. They all experienced the same film, but each of them had a different musical soundtrack, except for Lindy and Christa, the two girls who painted the spaceship pictures. They both had the same musical soundtrack.

MS. COLLINS
Do the students know this?

MR. ROSS
Not yet.

MS. COLLINS
Oh James, it would be really unfair if you did not tell them.

MR. ROSS
Of course I will. I think the students will be intrigued with the whole concept. We already had a great discussion about the philosophy of the assignment where we slightly touched upon the film's soundtrack, but I didn't let the cat out of the bag. Tomorrow I will tell them and see how they react. I would like to know, if possible, how the changing musical soundtracks affected their perception of the film. Since there was very little dialogue in the film, I think that the music played a vital role.

MS. COLLINS
Well, I think you could be on to something, since all of the paintings were different except . . .
(*Ms. Collins is tapped on the shoulder by another teacher*)
I'll be right with you, Sue. Sorry, James. What was I saying? Oh yes, the two girls who painted the spaceship pictures. They both listened to the same soundtrack, right?

MR. ROSS
Yes, that's right.

MS. COLLINS
Great stuff, James!
(*glances over at Sue Roberts, the teacher who just tapped her on the shoulder, who looks a little on edge and nervous*)
Let me know how the students react.

Mr. Ross catches on that Sue Roberts needs to URGENTLY talk to Ms. Collins.

MR. ROSS
Thanks, Janet. Talk to you later.

The camera FOLLOWS Ms. Collins as she PUTS her hand on Sue Roberts's shoulder. They both begin WALKING into Ms. Collins's office. The camera TURNS BACK to Mr. Ross who is now CHECKING his mail slot. He PULLS OUT several papers and envelopes, and SLOWLY STARTS WALKING toward the door, simultaneously RUMMAGING through his mail. The screen GENTLY FADES OUT as Mr. Ross WALKS out the main office door.

INT. ART CLASSROOM

It is 9:00 a.m. the next day and we SEE Mr. Ross sitting at his desk READING a book and SIPPING a coffee, WAITING for class to begin. We HEAR the CHATTER of the students but we do not see them yet. The bell RINGS and "O Canada" STARTS TO PLAY. Mr. Ross STANDS UP and the camera now TURNS to the students who are SLUGGISHLY GETTING UP to STAND for the national anthem. The camera PANS ACROSS the faces of the students and they are very FIDGETY and RESTLESS. We also NOTICE that Hasheed is not there. The anthem finishes and the students SIT. The camera now GOES BEHIND the students. We SEE the back of the students' heads and we have a relatively CLEAR VIEW of Mr. Ross, who GETS UP OUT of his chair and SITS on the corner of his desk FACING the students.

MR. ROSS
(*has a bit of a smile on his face*)
When was the last time you heard "O Canada"?

The camera CUTS TO the front of the students and we SEE all of their faces. They all seem a little STUNNED and SURPRISED.

JENNA
Yeah, like, Sir, about five seconds ago.

CHRISTA
Yeah, Sir, what's up?

There is a KNOCK at the door. Mr. Ross STARTS WALKING TOWARDS the door.

MR. ROSS
(*with a very serious tone of voice*)
Yeah, but when was the last time you truly heard it?

He OPENS the door, and in comes Hasheed who looks very TIRED as usual. His tardiness is so commonplace that he TAKES his seat without being noticed. Although Jenna briefly LOOKS at him, she remains SILENT. The camera now stands BEHIND Mr. Ross, but we can still SEE all of the students.

LINDY
What exactly do you mean, Sir?

MR. ROSS
(*voice over*)
Well . . .
(*pause*)
You hear "O Canada" every morning here at school. You have probably heard it thousands of times in your life. But when was the last time you noticed it and truly listened to it for the sake of the music?

The camera CUTS TO Jenna.

JENNA
(*with a slightly sour look on her face*)
Sir, that song sucks. No offence to Canada, but it's not a great song.

The camera CUTS TO Mr. Ross.

MR. ROSS
So you are saying that you would truly and honestly listen to "O Canada" if it was a great piece of music.

The camera CUTS TO a PROFILE of Jenna. We can make out the rest of the students as well as Mr. Ross.

JENNA
Yeah, I guess so. But I would probably get bored of the same song playing every day, even if the song was amazing. So I guess I would not truly listen to it every day.

MR. ROSS
What do you think, Brandon? You are a musician.

The camera CUTS TO Brandon and SLOWLY PANS OUT so we SEE all of the students but Mr. Ross is not visible.

BRANDON
Well, I guess I kind of agree with Jenna. But I think it depends on the situation.

MR. ROSS
(*voice over*)
Give me an example, Brandon. What do you mean by situation?

BRANDON
Uhh . . . if you are at a sporting event, like the Blue Jays or something, "O Canada" is listened to a bit more seriously. It's like a major part of the

game. Sometimes they even have big stars singing the anthem. But here at school, the anthem is more like a background thing. Even though we stand up and stuff, no one really pays attention as much.

The camera CUTS TO a side PROFILE of the class where Mr. Ross and the five students are all visible.

MR. ROSS
So then, Brandon, I am assuming you are talking about the difference between music being more of a background thing versus a mindful activity that requires undivided attention and concentration.

BRANDON
I guess.

CHRISTA
There is a lot of background music out there, like, ummm, like music that is playing in an elevator or a shopping mall. You notice it, but you don't really listen to it.

MR. ROSS
Ahh . . . So what is the purpose of this background music, then. If we are really not listening to it, then why are we exposed to it?

LINDY
Our sublinimal, sublinimal, blahhh . . .
(*sighs, takes a deep breath and significantly slows her speech down*)
Our sub-lim-i-nal mind. The music can make us do things.

MR. ROSS
Yeah, yeah, give me an example, Lindy.

LINDY
Like when you are put on hold on the telephone and they play music. The music is supposed to make you forget that you are actually on hold.

MR. ROSS
Good example, Lindy. Can anyone else think of another example?

BRANDON
I guess elevator music is the same kind of thing. You hear music to make the ride more enjoyable.

JENNA
What does any of this have to do with art class?

HASHEED
Duhh, Jenna! It has to do with the film assignment. How the film's soundtrack influenced our painting.

The camera ZOOMS IN on Jenna. She is taken aback by Hasheed's sudden and uncharacteristic VERBAL ATTACK.

JENNA
Take it easy Hasheed, I was only asking a question!

The camera is now BEHIND the students. We can SEE the back of their heads and we have a good VIEW of Mr. Ross.

MR. ROSS
Well, Jenna, that was a very good question, and Hasheed has stolen my thunder. Yes, my intention was to steer the discussion toward the film assignment and how the musical soundtrack affected your paintings. Let's first talk about the concept of film music. Why do the vast majority of films use music?

The camera REVERTS BACK to a PROFILE VIEW of the students and Mr. Ross.

JENNA
(*quickly and nervously answers*)
M-M-Music makes us better understand the film. You know, a scary film will have scary music to go along with it.

Before Mr. Ross has a chance to answer, the voice of Ms. Collins is HEARD over the school PA system.

MS. COLLINS
(*voice over*)
Pardon for the interruption, but I have a very important announcement to make. We are doing a test on the school's fire alarm this morning. If the alarm goes off, please ignore it and continue with your regularly scheduled class. I apologize for any inconvenience.

MR. ROSS
Well, this announcement is right on topic. When we hear a fire alarm, we are conditioned to leave the building right away. If we hear one this morn-

ing, we will have to ignore it, which will not be an easy thing to do based on our conditioning. Anyway, Jenna, you are right, scary films usually have scary music. The music helps us better understand what is going on. But let's turn the tables a bit. What if a really scary, horror type of film had happy and comical music? Would that change your perception of the film?

JENNA
Do you mean, like, merry-go-round music playing while someone is getting their throat slashed?

MR. ROSS
(*chuckles*)
I guess that's a good example.

CHRISTA
(*quickly responds*)
It's a dark comedy!

LINDY
What's a dark comedy?

CHRISTA
A film that makes death seem funny.

There is a moment of SILENCE in the classroom.

MR. ROSS
Let's think about that for a second. "A film that makes death seem funny." Can death even be funny?

HASHEED
Of course it can, Sir, especially if the right kind of props, actors, lines, music, etc. are used.

MR. ROSS
What about just music, Hasheed? What if only the music was funny and everything else–characters, lines, props–were rather serious?

HASHEED
Well, I guess there would be a mixed message, which would make the film very hard to understand.

MR. ROSS
What then, does that say about musical soundtracks and their role in the film viewing experience?

There is another moment of SILENCE. The camera CUTS TO an AERIAL VIEW of the entire classroom and then SLOWLY ZOOMS IN on Brandon.

BRANDON
I guess the musical soundtrack can change the meaning of a film, or at the very least influence the meaning.

The camera CUTS TO a front VIEW of all five students when we HEAR the fire alarm of the school, an extremely LOUD and INTENSE buzzer. Christa and Jenna make the MOTION to GET OUT of their seats but QUICKLY remember that it is only a test. All of the students are PLUGGING their ears. After about five seconds the alarm STOPS.

BRANDON
Wow that alarm is loud! My ears are killing me!

The camera CUTS TO a PROFILE of the class where we SEE all five students and Mr. Ross.

MR. ROSS
(*pointing to Christa and Jenna*)
Do you see how hard it is to ignore that sound? We are consciously conditioned to bolt for an exit whenever that darn alarm goes off. With film music, however, we are subconsciously conditioned. Film directors know that the musical soundtrack will manipulate our minds to believe whatever is happening on screen. It is no coincidence that a bad film usually has a bad or mismatched soundtrack.

HASHEED
But, Sir, there are other factors that make a film good or bad.

MR. ROSS
Of course, Hasheed. The musical soundtrack is just one component within the entire film viewing experience. There are many other factors as well. Do you remember our conversation the other day about the philosophy of the assignment? Sometimes what we get out of a film has more to do with our own personalities and life experiences. Anyway, what I want you to do this evening is experience the film again. This time I specifically want you to listen to the music and try to consciously notice how that music is being used to generate and influence meaning.

JENNA
Why can't we just watch it in class together?

CHRISTA
Yeah, Sir. Let's watch it in class.

MR. ROSS
That sounds like a good plan, but I would prefer if you experience the film–not watch it–one more time at home and make notes on the following . . .

The bell RINGS and first period is officially over. The camera FOLLOWS Mr. Ross to the blackboard.

MR. ROSS
(*writes the word "orchestration"*)
What type of instruments are being used?
(*writes the word "tempo"*)
Is the music fast, slow, or somewhere in between?

JENNA
(*voice over*)
Hurry up, Sir. I have gym next period and Ms. Campbell takes off marks if we are late.

MR. ROSS
Hang in there, just a few more seconds.
(*writes "musical mood & characteristics"*)
Listen for things like melody, harmony, loudness, softness, etc.
(*writes down the word "synchronization"*)
Ask yourself if the music matches the visual content. Have a good day.

The camera CUTS TO the students who are all FRANTICALLY WRITING DOWN the information on the blackboard except for Hasheed who is just SITTING rather MOTIONLESS. Jenna BOLTS OUT of her seat and HEADS OUT the door. The other students START PACKING their things and the camera ZOOMS IN ON Hasheed who looks like he is FALLING ASLEEP.

MR. ROSS
(*voice over*)
Put it in high gear Hasheed, or you will be late for second period.

HASHEED
Okay, Sir. I am just a little bagged out.

The camera FOLLOWS Hasheed OUT the door. Just before he exits, the classroom door TURNS into the employee entrance door at the local supermarket where Hasheed works. Hasheed WALKS through the door and we FOLLOW him inside

INT. EMPLOYEE QUARTERS AT BUSYBODY GROCERY STORE

It is a fairly busy back room and we SEE three other employees all WEARING the same uniform. Hasheed TAKES OFF his jacket and is also SPORTING the same uniform. We now SEE him get his time card from a board sporting about thirty other cards. He TAKES a few STEPS TOWARDS the punch clock. As he is doing this, we SEE a large man (the store manager) HOVERING over Hasheed's shoulder.

STORE MANAGER
(*in a very stern voice*)
I need you in the dairy aisle tonight, Hasheed. That loser Mitchell has called in sick again. That guy is nothing but problems.

HASHEED
No problem, Mr. Singer.

MR. SINGER
We need more people like you around here, Hasheed. You're never late and have never called in sick once in over two years. Remember, we have a full-time job waiting for you as soon as you finish high school.

Mr. Singer WALKS away. We now SEE Hasheed PLACE his time card into the punch clock. The camera ZOOMS IN ON the punch clock and we notice that it is 3:55 p.m. As we hear the LOUD and reverb LADEN THUD made by the punch clock, the picture FREEZES and FADES OUT.

INT. HALLWAY OF MORNINGSTAR SECONDARY SCHOOL

It is the next morning and we SEE Jenna APPROACHING the art classroom with a knapsack over her shoulders and SIPPING a cup of coffee. We also notice Brandon and Christa SITTING on the floor in front of the door.

JENNA
What's up? Is Ross away today?

CHRISTA
There's a note on the door saying that he is going to be a few minutes late. But, he wants us to wait here.

JENNA
Cool, I have time to finish my science lab.

Jenna SITS down and TAKES OUT some notes and a pen from her knapsack. Lindy SHOWS UP at the door.

JENNA
(*talking to Lindy but still remaining focused on her work*)
Have a seat, Ross will be here shortly.

Lindy NOTICES the note on the door and MOVES a little closer to READ it. She SITS down and there is a slight PAUSE. We now HEAR "O' Canada" PLAYING over the school PA system. The students LOOK at each other and notice that no one is STANDING. They all CHUCKLE a bit and remain SEATED feeling as if they are getting away with something.

LINDY
(*with a slight look of guilt on her face*)
Come on you guys, let's stand. It's only for a few seconds.

All four students SLUGGISHLY GET UP and LEAN AGAINST the wall. It LOOKS like they are half SITTING and half STANDING.

JENNA
(*imitating Mr. Ross*)
When was the last time you truly listened to O Canada?

Everybody CHUCKLES a bit. The anthem FINISHES and the students SLIDE DOWN the wall and are fully SITTING on the floor. Hasheed now ENTERS the picture.

JENNA
(*sincerely*)
Working again last night, Hasheed?

HASHEED
Of course. My father makes me do it. If it were up to me, I would work only on weekends. The night shifts are tough, especially when I get home

and still have homework to do. Some nights I don't get to bed until one or two in the morning.

BRANDON
Did you watch the film again last night? Or should I say "experience" the film last night?

HASHEED
Yeah, I watched, I mean, "experienced" the film with a set of headphones so I could really listen to the music and not be interrupted by any other noises. Where's Mr. Ross?

MR. ROSS
(*voice over*)
Sorry I'm late, folks. I was having some car problems this morning.

Mr. Ross ENTERS the picture. He RUSTLES THROUGH his keys and OPENS the door. We SEE all five students GO INTO the classroom FOLLOWED by Mr. Ross. The camera now CUTS TO the inside of the classroom where we SEE the students SITTING and Mr. Ross COMING IN the classroom CLOSING the door behind him. Mr. Ross ASSUMES his usual post on the corner of his desk FACING the students.

MR. ROSS
Before we get started, I want to quickly remind you that the deadline for submitting your term research paper for this course is two weeks from today. Please make sure you are on top of it. I would hate to see you lose marks for a late submission. Anyway, the film soundtrack. Brandon, what did you think of the soundtrack?

BRANDON
The soundtrack was a lot of classical music. I think there was solo piano and violin

MR. ROSS
Lindy?

LINDY
It didn't really sound classical. It was more New Age, or maybe a mixture of both.

CHRISTA
The music was definitely not classical, but I do agree that it was New Age sort of, like something I've never really heard before.

MR. ROSS
What about you, Hasheed?

HASHEED
It was hard to categorize the overall sound. I did find it to be very piano-based but definitely no violin as Brandon has suggested. This music was also very scary to me all the way through. I also heard a very loud, metal-like dinging sound. You know, those steel triangles.

JENNA
Triangle! I didn't hear a triangle sound!

MR. ROSS
What did you hear, Jenna?

JENNA
I found the music to be very calming and nice, music that is slow and relaxes you. The movement of the characters were slow, and so was the music. It worked well together.

MR. ROSS
Yes, that was another aspect that I asked you to look at, the relationship between the musical and the visual. Hasheed, what do you think?

HASHEED
The overall color and tone of the film matched the music to create a thriller- or action-like type of film.

MR. ROSS
Wow, that's very different from Jenna who thought the film and the music were slow. Brandon, what about you?

BRANDON
I sort of agree with Jenna that the music was more of a feeling and thinking film, not an action or thriller. I mean, an alien is not going to pop out or anything.

HASHEED
There seems to be a lot of different opinions here about the music and the overall feel of the film.

MR. ROSS
Absolutely. So let's get to the real issue here. How did the musical soundtrack affect your paintings?

There is a moment of SILENCE.

MR. ROSS
All of us have seen the paintings several times over. Which one comes across as the scariest?

There is a unanimous and QUICK RESPONSE.

JENNA, CHRISTA, LINDY, AND BRANDON
Hasheed's!

MR. ROSS
Okay, we have some agreement here. Hasheed also said that he found to the music to be scary all the way through the film. Is there any relationship then between Hasheed's painting and his interpretation of the music? Hasheed?

HASHEED
Of course, there wasn't that much speech in total so you had to listen to the music in a sense.

MR. ROSS
What about the most attractive and charming painting?

LINDY
That would have to be Jenna's. I mean, after all, she painted a sunset over calm water with sailboats.

MR. ROSS
Okay, so Jenna painted a rather slow moving and tranquil painting. She also found the soundtrack to be very calming, relaxing, and nice. Is there a relationship here? Jenna?

JENNA
Well, as I said, the slow and calming music worked well with the slow movement of the characters, who themselves were very quiet. I guess that's why I named my painting "Silent Choice."

MR. ROSS
Brandon, your painting was very colorful, with a lot of different shapes. Although your painting was a little more abstract than Jenna's, do you notice any similarities?

BRANDON
Well, uhh, as I said, the film was more of a feeling and thinking film. Especially when I hear the classical music, it makes me think more for some reason. I also used a lot of bright colors because the music was very happy, especially toward the end of the film—it gives you kind of like a foreshadowing or something like that, that something good is going to happen.

MR. ROSS
Christa and Lindy, both of you mentioned the term New Age when discussing the musical soundtrack. Your two paintings were by far the most comparable of the five. Both paintings dealt with spaceships sometime in the future, in some sort of new age. Is this a coincidence?

HASHEED
Sir, what's up? It sounds like you are leading to something.

MR. ROSS
Well, I guess it is time to let the cat out of the bag.

JENNA
(*with a puzzled look on her face*)
Cat out of the what?

CHRISTA
Cat out of the bag! It's an expression, Jenna. It means that Mr. Ross has been keeping something from us, and now he is going to tell us.

There is a KNOCK at the door.

MR. ROSS
Jenna, could you please answer that?

We SEE Jenna GET OUT of her seat and OPEN the door. We SEE Ms. Collins, the school principal, STANDING IN the doorway.

MS. COLLINS
Hello, Mr. Ross. I was just wondering if I could speak to Hasheed for a few seconds.

LINDY
(*chuckles*)
Been a bad boy again, Hasheed?

CHIRS
Yeah, Hasheed. What have you done now?

Hasheed WALKS TOWARD the door and STEPS OUTSIDE IN the hallway to SPEAK with Ms. Collins while Jenna is simultaneously WALKING back to her seat. We SEE a PROFILE of the entire class, with the four students to the left, Mr. Ross to the right, and Hasheed and Ms. Collins through the doorway COMMUNICATING to each other in the hallway.

JENNA
So, where's the cat, Sir?

MR. ROSS
As soon as Hasheed is done.

There is a moment of SILENCE and then Hasheed WALKS in the door with Ms. Collins.

MS. COLLINS
Sorry for interrupting your class, Mr. Ross.

MR. ROSS
Actually, you are more than welcome to stay, Ms. Collins. I was just about to tell the students about the assignment, you know. . .

MS. COLLINS
Sure, I'd love to stay and hear all about it.

Ms. Collins COMES IN the class and TAKES a seat a little FAR REMOVED from the students and Mr. Ross as to be as unobtrusive as possible. The students LOOK at each other and wonder what exactly is going on. Mr. Ross NOTICES how CONCERNED the students APPEAR to be.

MR. ROSS
There is nothing to be worried about, folks. Honestly. There is something about your assignment that I would like to share with you–if you have not figured it out already–that Ms. Collins already knows about. She probably wants to see, or better yet, hear your reaction.

JENNA
Get on with it, Sir.

MR. ROSS
Well, uhh. First let me say that I was very impressed with all of your paintings. Many teachers in the school also noticed the paintings and commented on how great they were.

CHRISTA
Oh well, that's really good to know.

JENNA
Yeah!

MR. ROSS
This assignment was also a bit of an experiment for me. You were all asked to create a painting that best represented the film. There was one important catch, however, that neither of you knew about.

There is a SLIGHT PASUE and the camera PANS ACROSS the face of the students. The TENSION is BUILDING and we HEAR suspenseful music get LOUDER. We also SEE the camera BRIEFLY CUT TO Ms. Collins, who LOOKS very INTRIGUED. We now CUT BACK TO Mr. Ross and the rest of the class.

MR. ROSS
You all experienced the same film, but each of you were exposed to a different musical soundtrack, except for Lindy and Christa who had the exact same musical soundtrack, which seems to have been reflected in their paintings that were somewhat similar.

The camera CUTS TO the faces of the five students. We hear a lot of SIGHS and the students' faces LOOK a little BEWILDERED, except for Hasheed who looks more PENSIVE.

JENNA
That's smart!

BRANDON
That's really cool, Sir.

HASHEED
That's why!

MR. ROSS
What is it, Hasheed?

HASHEED
At the end of the film, that lady says "sunshine" and she looked like she was happy and the background, it was like–how the music was wrong!

MR. ROSS
Well, it is very difficult to accurately measure how much the changing musical soundtracks actually influenced your paintings. But I would say that the soundtracks played an important role in the meanings you all generated based on the differences in your paintings–or the similarities, for that matter, between Christa's and Lindy's.

MS. COLLINS
(*stands up and comes to the front of the class*)
I just wanted to congratulate all of you for creating such wonderful paintings. I think this assignment was very worthwhile not only for the finished products, but for what you have all learned along the way. Great stuff, Mr. Ross. Have a good day everyone.

Ms. Collins STARTS TO WALK out the door.

HASHEED
Sir, since the film is only five minutes long, can we watch, or rather experience, all four versions? You know, all of the different soundtracks.

JENNA
Yeah, great idea!

MR. ROSS
Well, we won't have time today, but if you all bring in your videotapes, maybe we can do that in the next couple of days.

BRANDON
What about tomorrow, Sir?

MR. ROSS
Well, Brandon. I have some other aspects of the assignment that I would like to discuss.

JENNA
Are you going to let another cat out of the bag, Sir?

LINDY
Yeah, Sir. No more surprises.

MR. ROSS
(*waving his right hand back and forth*)
I promise, no more surprises! Anyway, I am interested in the personal perspectives that you incorporated into your paintings.

BRANDON
What do you mean, Sir?

The camera starts to FLY HIGH ABOVE the classroom. As the camera gets HIGHER, the picture SLOWLY STARTS to FADE OUT, although Mr. Ross' voice is still AUDIBLE.

MR. ROSS
You know, your own life experiences. How has what happened in your life, your knowledge, culture, gender, etc. affected your interpretation of the film? So, I want you to experience the film yet again, and see if you can make any personal connections with the film–you know, characters, story line, etc.

Once the FADE OUT is completed, we CUT TO a CLOSE-UP of Brandon's painting and HEAR the musical soundtrack that he was exposed to for about ten seconds. We do the same for each of the other paintings, with the only exception being that Christa's and Lindy's paintings are showed simultaneously. As the final painting (Hasheed's) BEGINS to FADE, the scary musical soundtrack CONTINUES TO PLAY over a dark background where the film's credits ROLL. After the last credit ROLLS off, the screen is completely black and the scary music COMES TO an ABRUPT and SUDDEN ending that ECHOES and LINGERS for a few seconds more.

Commentary by Patricia Leavy

1. Form, Structure and Narrative Coherence

John Vitale's fictional screenplay "Visual Music" is based on a traditional research project that seeks to investigate how music changes the meaning of a film. Methodologically, the study involved exposing four groups of high-school students to different musical soundtracks and then conducting a focus group session (referred to as a jigsaw) in order to explore how music impacts cinematic content. Vitale then turned to a fiction-based approach to making sense of and presenting the intricate themes that emerged from the focus group session. Given the subject matter, Vitale decided to write the story using a screenplay format. This is an outstanding example of linking form and content in a piece of fiction-based research. The structural design underscores the content. The coherence between form and content, including attention to details (writing the screenplay according to film industry standards), aids in the delivery of the content. Moreover, the narrative itself is well constructed.

2. Audience

Vitale's screenplay hits on all of the major "audience" areas. First, by using the screenplay format, portraying characters (students and teachers) in resonant ways, and writing at a level that anyone can understand (appropriately including high-school students who were the participants in the study), Vitale has maximized his ability to tap relevant audiences. Second, the detailed introduction to the piece discloses significant details about the study as well as Vitale's decision to use the fictional format. Third, in the spirit of participatory research, Vitale engaged high-school students in this study and then, through the fictionalizing process, represented those participants as well as himself through the construction of characters. Moreover, the piece is written so that the participants can engage with the resulting screenplay to stimulate further discussion and learning.

Novella

Chapter 7
The Wrong Shoe

by Elizabeth de Freitas

Introduction

The novella *The Wrong Shoe* follows an educational researcher named Martha West as she relentlessly interrogates her research intentions while completing an ethnographic study of a private girls school. Through continuous self-scrutiny, Martha West emerges as a conflicted witness to the often cruel and always complex power relations of school culture. The roots of Martha West's dilemma lie in the humanist tradition of the moral agent. She longs to serve the researched community, as though doing so were a straightforward matter of finding and then following through with the correct intentions. The focus on research intentions foregrounds the politics of writing research. Martha dwells on her ethnographic intentions, naming the constraints that regulate her voice, questioning the process of re-inscription in the school archives, and tracing the path of power relations across the school terrain. The novella depicts a form of self-disturbing sustained reflection—a "rigorous disorientation" (St. Pierre 2004)—that functions to disperse the good intentions of

Fiction as Research Practice: Short Stories, Novellas, and Novels, by Patricia Leavy, 195–210.

the main character. As Martha encounters various other characters at the school—Agnes Fu (a new teacher), Red (a student), and Elizabeth Bain (a veteran administrator)—and attempts to tell their story, these characters shift and alter the terrain, forcing Martha to confront her desires.

The novella explores this dilemma through the use of third-person narration. The third person voice locates the narrator outside the story. The outsider status is compounded when the narrator focalizes on the private thoughts of the characters within the story world. In *The Rhetoric of Fiction*, Wayne Booth suggests that access to the inside of another is perhaps a key characteristic of fiction: "The most important single privilege is that of obtaining an inside view of another character, because of the rhetorical power that such a privilege conveys upon a narrator" (1961, 160–61). In the case of Martha West, this deliberate doubling of outsider privilege (both hers as a researcher and that of the third-person narrator) is meant to stir the reader's suspicion. The question as to who is telling this story complicates the critical questions that Martha asks of herself: Whose voice is heard, and who is silenced?

I chose not to write in the first person, reluctant to deploy the seemingly authentic "I" because of the way it would legitimate the reader's access to Martha's reflexive self. The reader tends to assume the narrator's complicity when the first-person voice is employed. This story, in contrast, is meant to trouble the reader's sense of insider access precisely because it is written in a third-person voice. The narrator trespasses into the mind of the character, performing a rhetorical practice common in fiction, but considered highly problematic in reflexive inquiry. It is precisely because this is a work of fiction that I am able to more fully address the issue of voice and the limits of facticity and personal reflection. The third-person narration addresses the limits of facticity exactly because of its invasive power. My aim was to craft a multilayered text in which the third-person voice of the narrator would be interrupted by the voice of an "other" within the fiction. I did this using two strategies, both of which are common in contemporary fiction: indirect discourse and unreliable narration.

The third-person narration used in *The Wrong Shoe* is a form of *free indirect discourse* that conjures an amorphous dislocated space as the narrator's point of view. Free indirect discourse is a literary form (found in Kafka's *Metamorphosis* or Woolf's *The Waves*) by which the collective nature of language is disclosed; the boundary between author, narrator, and character is troubled through the grounded (and often unreliable) nuance of the narrator's third-person voice. The voice is not embodied, and yet the voice embodies particular idiomatic observations and evaluates and speculates on the meaning of the incidents recounted.

Once free indirect style frees language from its ownership by any subject of enunciation, we can see the flow of language itself, its production of sense and nonsense, its virtual and creative power (Colebrook 2002, 114).

Free indirect discourse often merges with stream of consciousness, as in the case of Woolf, whereby language pulses through the character, who is then constituted through the flow of affects and sensations. The pronouns shift as the narrator moves in and out of the story world. That which the character perceives and feels is intertwined and made indistinguishable with that which is perceived by another character; in some cases, it becomes impossible to determine who is feeling what and to whom the feelings are attributable. Free indirect discourse allows for a more disorienting style of narrative, as it underscores how language is disowned and dispersed, while undermining the assumption that the "I" is the origin of meaning.

The narrative of Martha West is an attempt to open up toward the object of research through the disorientation of the Self. The story resists closure as a story; the characters find little solace in their actions; the narrator is unreliable. Together these facets form a fiction that sustains a somewhat uncomfortable space where stasis and position are put into play. The work refuses to settle its meaning, and also refuses to prescribe a proper reading, although it sufficiently abides by the rules of narrative to name itself within the genre.

The writing was inspired by the risk involved in pursuing this form of deconstruction. My aim was to write a research story depicting the turmoil of a researcher who disrupts the border between inside and outside and yet insists on the structural non-knowing of the other. The resulting fiction is strangely melancholic, as though the character Martha West knew all along that her intentions were always already traces of yet other traces, indeed as though she was aware of this impossible situation even before I was. The dissymmetry between her paltry intervention and the fullness of her desire, despite or perhaps because of the delusional aspect of the latter, creates a space of contested ideology. The reader may sense the gaping incongruity between Martha's hopes and her actions and become more aware of the coercive discursive practices operating within the school. Martha demonstrates how our best intentions are already traces of the invisible or tacit structural forces operating through our longing to engage the other. The reader is invited to identify with Martha's struggle and empathize with her frustration at how each of her utterances is always implicated in the very power struggles she hopes to resolve. In this effort, I hope to have created a research text that attends to one goal of post-positivist social science research, as identified by Stronach and Maclure in *Educational Research Undone* (1997), whereby ambivalence is in the foreground and the text declaims its own textual politics.

The following selection is chapters 2 through 4 of the novella.

The Wrong Shoe

Tight Fit

The fit and style of the shoe is a peculiar fetish fostered by the school. Pictures of both acceptable and unacceptable sorts of shoes are sent home early in the summer. Faculty are informed of the fine line between frowned-upon buckles and tolerable straps. Suede is out of the question, heels are taboo, and anything other than black is prohibited. The wrong shoe is a serious uniform infraction. Those who try to make do with shoes that satisfy only some of the criteria are quickly dealt with. Ensuring proper footwear is an obsession, as though it defined the very character of a Charlton girl. The wrong shoe severs the girl from all good fortune, her future and her birthright revoked by any breach concerning this small but essential wardrobe item. No other violation seems so subversive. No other infraction so treacherous. Only the shoe can show the real quality of character. Only the shoe can measure true nobility. And when the shoe fails to measure up, and the girl fails to fit the mould, she is discretely asked to leave. The euphemism for expulsion, heard in the hallways and over lunch, is the always blameless "It wasn't a good fit." The crest motto, *steadfast on the good path*, seems a maxim for those who tread too far afield without the proper footwear.

The war against foot-crime is the first item on the September agenda. Vice-Principal Elizabeth Bain, herself immaculately groomed, has devised a means of disciplining the wrongdoers. Upon their discovery, she explains at the staff meeting, they are to be sent to the office where the unmentionable is to be removed from the bearer, the transgression documented in a black book, and the girl forced to wear little Asian slippers throughout the rest of the day. Mrs. Bain, like the rest of the veteran faculty, takes perverse pleasure in this punishment. Not only does it undermine the offender's sense of fashion, but it also reduces their self-image to that of an immigrant servant, like the many Filipino maids in their parents' pay. And in doing so, she hopes that it maddens the deep-seated sense of pride and privilege that wealth has bestowed upon all her little ladies. This, she feels, will surely be sufficient penalty to discourage any deviance from the uniform.

"Send them to me if they seem recalcitrant," she says to all present, meeting the eye of one or two teachers who seem to be dozing off. "The next item is graduation photos. We're moving to a slightly different format: the usual profile to the right, chin up, pleasant smile, but this year we want to incorporate a forward tilt." She pauses and consults her notes, "of the head." Another pause before she raises her own head to address the crowd. "I'm finding it difficult to envision, but apparently all the independent schools are moving to this new format."

Elizabeth Bain has been at Charlton Academy for nineteen years. She feels as though time was grimly excising all the alternative paths she might have taken. At night, when alone in the all too familiar hallway outside her office, she shudders at the sight of the shrinking walls and the unrelenting rows of framed graduate photos. It is these photos, perhaps more than anything else, that bear witness to her years of service. Frame after frame announces another year passed and another set of faces marching onward. Ageless and eager faces whose eyes look inward and barely see the life of Elizabeth Bain. Each year a document to a place left behind, the place that contains her. She never imagined that she would stay so long, nor rise to such a powerful administrative position. And yet she strove to establish herself with what some would say was almost ruthless ambition. She transformed her talent for organization into the corporate skill called *people management*. With time, her renowned equanimity turned to stock and rigid behaviour; she dismissed the shudders and the doubts, and focused on the task at hand.

"Letters will go home informing the girls of the new graduate photo configuration. Perhaps a sample portrait should be included, if one can be found. I suggest that you rehearse the pose in class during the preceding week. No harm in that. A properly tilted head draws more light onto the face. It's an attempt to reduce unseemly shadows."

As a young white Bajan, Elizabeth spent hours in the umbrella shade of her parents' walled garden, drinking fruit punches and devouring novels, big fat nineteenth-century novels with tragic heroines that consumed her adolescent mind. She hid beneath giant sun hats and linen umbrellas, stretched out on the chaise longue among the striped amaryllis and vibrant hyacinth. A full-time gardener worked on the grounds that would otherwise grow wild at a moment's neglect. This constant battle against the damp verdant nature annoyed Elizabeth who believed that the cloying growth of the tropics had been the underlying cause of slavery. If it weren't for the jungle, she would often complain, the blacks would never have become enslaved. She was polite to all three servants who walked the four miles up the hill from the bus stop every morning, but she cringed whenever they called her "sweet Lizzie" and tweaked her cheek with maternal affection. She promised herself that she would never become a racist as it was a sign of parochial perspective. She found island culture suffocating and tried to escape through reading and immersing her imagination in other worlds, and thus she slowly erected another wall between her and the island, an imaginary wall that buttressed the thick racial barriers. She prayed for an end to summer holidays and the speedy return to the school in England she attended. The more enamoured she became with the imagined world of novels, the less tolerant she grew of Bajan culture. Every element stirred feelings of disgust: the small white enclave, the heat and humidity, the looming darkness of the impoverished black community, and the righteousness of the growing middle class who saw the Bains and other old Bajan families as a species of white dinosaur. At night when the lizards slithered into her bedroom and climbed the walls, when the bat-sized moths flew through the house and crashed into her bed lamp, when the centipedes curled up in her sandals, she wished she was in England, in a small well-kept room lined with wallpaper and book shelves.

In her final year at school she won the English prize and went on to study nineteenth- and twentieth-century literature at Cambridge. Her accent soon lost all traces of the Caribbean colony, and became instead subtly English and authoritarian. She became a trim and frigid young woman, who was known for her eloquence and her matchless manners. She often sat in the garden courtyard at her residence, sipping her tea and reading a journal, and marvelling at herself for being so perfectly English. She knew that each turned page, each well-loved book, each rich character, removed her more and more each day from the everyday. She knew intimately the nature of unrivalled love, for no one and no thing had ever moved her more than a well-written story. Elizabeth began to fear the waking world, and it was this fear that would later haunt her. As her fear mounted, she sought even greater solace in her books. Others moved on to "productive" paths, but Elizabeth was reluctant to plan for a concrete future, certain that it would pale miserably beside the depth of feeling she already experienced through fiction. After so many years of surrendering to a good story, she seemed to have no future of her own. She had spent so much time dissolving her life history into what she imagined was a better one, so much time denying her past, and later her body, and even her mind, that suddenly the obliteration felt utterly complete, her desires all but identified with the current character, her experiences profoundly mediated through fiction. She became a chameleon, bathing herself in the warmth of others' actions, and then sluggish and dulled in the cold interstices between stories. She was all potential, capable of everything, except, perhaps, integrity. Her days began and ended like structured novels, her entire perception projected into the current narrative, her face on those pages, her pain felt deeply as the drama unfolded. Decisions and choices were all mediated through the labyrinth of accumulated literary references. In this vein, and for no reason she might have identified as her own, she became an English teacher.

Elizabeth soon discovered that teaching was far messier than reading books. The small daily disruptions that tampered with her immaculate lesson plans became a constant source of annoyance. Student written and oral responses were never quite what she hoped for. At first she enjoyed their charming and inelegant essays, their shallow interpretation of symbols, their dramatic unfounded conclusions, and their general naïveté. She was fascinated by the way they juggled half-truths and emotional upheavals. She grew to admire their complex social networks and their cruel secret schemes of exclusion. They vied for power and control in the classroom, like a typical mob in revolt. It was this, their attempts to wrestle the reigns from her hands, that most intrigued her. On the one hand, she detested the pettiness of this conflict and believed that power should remain firmly with the granted authority and not be shared through a democratic process. On the other hand, she was aware of a burgeoning sense of satisfaction in the struggle for power, for it seemed to finally establish that she did possess something of value. After ten years of a successful but didactic teaching career, and a growing satisfaction with authority and discipline, she started exploring various administrative portfolios, and eventually landed in the vice-principal office.

"Are there any questions?" she asks, hoping there aren't.

Censored Signature

The office door is shut. The walls are creamy soft white. Above the couch hangs a framed poster from a touring musical production. The sound of the two women breathing is lost to the noise of air pumped and circulated through the ceiling vents. The scent of Elizabeth Bain is expensive and exhaustive, her entire surface emitting the fragrance of olfactory privilege. The pores of her skin are tightly shut and indiscernible, as though she was made of plaster. Her eyes survey the borders around her seated body. Martha West readjusts herself, inching away from this elaborately invented creature. She presses her thigh against the arm of the linen-covered coach, and imagines herself tucked in behind the pillow, like a crumb. Lint clings statically to her black clothes, in striking contrast to the magnetic-free Elizabeth.

"I often miss teaching," says Elizabeth Bain, having rewritten her own story, "I'm always dreaming up ways to visit classrooms and to feel that warmth again." She smiles and glances at the blipping red light on her phone. Martha West scribbles away as Elizabeth continues. "Teaching is such a . . . fulfilling vocation. I consider myself extremely fortunate to be a part of the support staff." She rises, walks to the phone, reads the call display, and shunts the caller into her voice box. Martha nods as she attempts to transcribe Elizabeth's words. She is using her own personal shorthand, which often degenerates into chaos, especially when the speaker is obviously lying, as Elizabeth is now. There is something in Elizabeth's voice that makes her deceit self-evident to Martha, whose hand censors itself, and refuses, as though by its own accord, to reproduce the lies. The page on her lap has become blotted with odd ink insignia meaningful only in Martha's unconsciousness. She is listening intently, as she always does, but she hears so much noise within Elizabeth's spoken words and so much scarring around the meaning of those words that transcribing them becomes too problematic. Her pen traces arcs and dotted spirals in an attempt to capture the meaning of her phrases. She is not sure herself of what the script denotes. There seems to be no decoding key that might unlock the cryptographs. Her desk is covered in similarly cyphered pages, all of which begin in standard English but quickly lapse into something else. Her intention to accurately portray Elizabeth and the others leads always to this difficult terrain where direction is obscured. Their spoken words never gel into seamless positions, their voices in conflict with the words they use. Martha finds that every response obscures its own meaning. There is a kind of seamlessness to this, the way the ocean is both one body and an unbound system of tumult and friction, but this is not the sort she is there to document. Martha is supposed to tell their story the way they want it told. Implicit in her research is the assumption that she will respect their desire to be portrayed accurately and fairly. Contracts have been signed ensuring everyone's good intentions on this account.

Martha West has been commissioned by the board of directors to produce a popular history of the school, to be published at the end of the year celebrating the school's centenary. The board wants a book that will sell the school to potential customers, and remind alumnae that endowments are welcome. They chose Martha West upon the recommendation of Vice-Principal Elizabeth Bain, who knew her sister at Cambridge and owed her a longstanding favour. Martha has no qualifications for the assignment, and no experience writing popular history, but she does have experience working as an educational researcher for a private management organization. She quit the job six months ago, unable to stomach the flow charts and consumer targets. She was tired of stuffing people into envelopes, tired of the formulaic diagnoses, and tired of cognitive theories that left her cold. She published a slim volume on school bullying which is considered an excellent source for detailed case studies. But looking back at her efforts, she feels disappointed at how overly descriptive and prescriptive the portraits seem. She left her job suddenly, after a Christmas staff party. She is still surprised that the upper-crust Charlton Academy was willing to hire her. Perhaps it was her low fee. Her sister said she had no recollection of the supposed longstanding favour.

Favours are common currency amongst associates and alumnae at Charlton. They are never offered in the spirit of generosity, but with the understanding that an eventual payback is expected. Martha hasn't yet asked for any favours, but as she sits with Elizabeth in her office she cannot help but imagine Elizabeth's merciless extraction of paybacks. She imagines her doling out favours and documenting the names and whereabouts of all the grateful. She tries to stamp out the cynicism and listen to Elizabeth, but her need to imagine the moment differently, her need to recreate the so-called facts, is precisely what now defines Martha as a writer. She watches the world from an invisible vanishing point, investigating the minor incidents she witnesses as though she were privy to the personal lives of others. She engages the world only insofar as she is able to recreate it. Every mundane experience is given an altered life through her retelling, every moment is invested with meaning and made bearable. Her creative impulse imposes difference on what she observes, difference from her own self so as to justify the retelling. Elizabeth and she are as different as night and day. The way the one puts an end to the other is the way her mind is mindful of Elizabeth. As much as she needs to write the commissioned book, she cannot yet find a syntax that will accommodate both Elizabeth and herself.

But to tell the story is to tell it differently. Each person makes each story her own distinct odyssey. She remembers as a teenager learning that there were only seven plots possible, most of which involved a boy meeting a girl. She remembers contemplating the moral consequences around such a categorical statement, remembers her decision that plot would play a minor role in all her stories. Causal connections became a weak point in all her thinking. She excelled at lateral associations and obscure references but often failed to make the most rudimentary deductions. Her arguments developed into beautifully circular associations, too slippery for judgments and conclusions to be drawn. She had strong opinions, each of which rested on a complex network of reasons, but none fit the rhetorical mold for logical justification. She could never succeed at representing her thoughts within the linear confines of traditional academic writing. In high school she always chose to write stories instead of essays, and what history she knew came from novels and plays. In university she developed anorexia while training her mind to write introductory paragraphs and footnotes. It always felt hugely unnatural to write herself out of her own essays, but the institution demanded she express herself in this anonymous form. She learned to heel her intellect like a dog, to keep it on a tight leash, nose to the ground, an obedient and loyal companion. Her words achieved validity through their anonymity, like folk tales and moral claims and all the master narratives of science and culture. Her articles gained a certain lawfulness amongst designated readers. Her writing became void of authenticity as she aped after the objective judgment, stumbled after the verifiable facts, and choked herself dry in a vacuum. She longed to dip the page in water so as to blur her argument and make visible the invisible ink signature, that rolling and playfully extravagant signature that announced her authorship. She knew it was deeply wrong to write in such a censored form, a form that had become so ossified it could barely function as a medium for communication, and she knew that someday her hand would become so stiff she would be unable to write. The interviews at Charlton Academy and the strange notes on her desk were proof enough.

The *true* story is another issue altogether. She imagines it lurking behind the inoffensive facts and assertions, ready at a moment's notice to sabotage reality's surface and then slink away despite all her attempts to substantiate it. Martha believes that truth itself is playful, that a willful trickster embodies all validity and that no individual can both grasp and communicate its content. She sometimes glimpses the shameless double-dealer grinning behind some spurious scenario that the rest mistake as dormant fact. Elizabeth's highly contrived persona is almost an antidote to Martha's assumptions. For if nothing else, the synthetic Elizabeth proves that deception is the premise of all signification. In the midst of Elizabeth's interview Martha finds herself scribbling a quote from Shakespeare, "The truest poetry is the most feigned." Perhaps this nonsense she has been writing for days is a kind of poetry capable of weaving her and Elizabeth together as no other form could. Perhaps there is no authentic voice for this encounter save the soundless unknown alphabet that emerges on the page like automatic writing. She wonders if her notes would qualify as images instead of words as they have no spoken equivalent and no defined meaning. Truth would then be subtended by aesthetic criteria and audiences would judge the beauty of her words. Her eyes rest on the only readable line on the page, "The truest poetry is the most feigned." The expression confirms all her suspicions. To feign is to be deceptive, deceitful, and counterfeit, and in the very least, invented. Perhaps Elizabeth's lies are all that matters. Perhaps her words are all in code. Euphemisms seem to spread across the school like a thin layer of marmalade on toast. Every comment is layered with coded meaning. Martha looks down at her red running shoes, remembers her credit debt and how badly she needs the commission.

"Do the school archives contain all previous principals' papers?" she asks.

Elizabeth pauses longer than usual. She rubs the thumb of one hand into the palm of the other and then touches the band of her diamond ring. Her hands move with dry precision, as though everything she touched turned to rank and ordered custom. She begins to reply, and then stops herself. Martha is shocked by what appears to be an authentic faltering. Could it be that Elizabeth has pushed aside the pat answer and is about to say something real? Martha chastises herself for imposing her own ranking of reality. Just because her own benchmarks are physiological necessities such as food and shelter doesn't exclude others from having far more cultivated frames of reference. She is being too judgmental of Elizabeth. She smiles and waits patiently for her response.

Pure Document

Brown accordion folders filled with black ledger books filled with columns filled with numbers. Numbers followed by other numbers. Multi-digit and decimal, summed and divided, the tally continuing page after page. A nameless slanting scrawl, the plight of a secretary or treasurer, pencilling the numerical rhythm of daily expenses. This, thinks Martha West, is a document. No other archival entry is so factual and meaningless. No other page can say so little and yet be so perversely detailed. She smudges a number with her finger and wonders what future worlds will be altered by her intervention. She skims the pages, in search of some direction or development, but the progress of numbers is modest and unassuming. The books say so little; the books in fact refrain from all judgement. They contain only the concrete traces of commercial exchange, or so she is meant to believe. They are offered as an antidote to the many stories told on any given day. Someone in the past hoped these numbers might escape the narrative flush of time. And yet she knows that some future generation will base their objective accounts on these figures; stories will be squeezed out from them, like blood from a stone. Perhaps the most persuasive stories. This is the refrain of the righteous researcher. Meek numerical documents have a certain vengeance to them when they break free from the lives that composed them. Martha begins speculating on the truth-value of the black ledger books. Her eyes flit across each page, her brain firing away questions that no one can hear: How can truth be broken off from time? How can her story already be a part of these fifty-year-old ledger books? Where is she named on these pages? Why does she feel as though she was always already scripted into future accounts? Where does that feeling come from? Martha's mind shakes off the feeling. She is in the habit of shaking off feelings. It is the only way she can have a good look at them. All too often her feelings vanish under scrutiny. Martha, alone, her mind free of feelings, knows that numbers cannot lie. They have no intentional propensity. Numbers are the perfect existential being. They bring on nausea, our sickness unto death. Now, thinks Martha, here is a feeling. Nausea is visceral.

She wishes she could eat the numbers up and swallow them whole and feel that gut-wrenching nausea. She finds the last entry in one of the black books, selects a finely sharpened pencil from the jar, and begins scratching numbers down. She is unaware of how long she stays there, and how many pages of sabotage numbers she enters. She is unconscious of the time passing. She wonders if her actions are arresting time. Could it be that she has become the timekeeper? Can everything be so easily upset? She looks now at her hand holding the pencil, and immediately time re-enters. She compares her random numbers to the previous pages, and perceives how little has changed. Good, she thinks, I won't bother erasing it.

She settles down in front of a filing cabinet, and is astounded by the wealth of archival resources. Each principal has left her papers. Copies of speeches and notes have been carefully retained, as though the school anticipated a future of educational researchers. Martha grabs a file with the name of the founding principal. Despite the freedom from religious affiliation, the woman's notes are replete with biblical references. On a New Year's Day speech in 1910, she tells the story of Abraham. She tells it again in her 1911 speech.

Martha begins taking notes. The kind of notes she was trained to take. Obsequious parasitic notes that confirm the original document. Dates, names, forthright intentions, and safe interpretations. An avid note-taker acquiesces to the text. Martha's critical eye ferrets out the hidden meanings, but even these have a turgid presence, bound as they are to the surface. She unpacks the occasional sentence to show how it is saying the opposite of what it claims to say. The well-trained critical eye sees evidence of the contrary; it is no less formulaic than the closed grammar on the page. She looks for what is commonly withheld–a list of cultural baggage claims that come in and out of circulation. She finds exactly what she is looking for. Principal after principal proves her point. They speak about leadership, about integrity and honour, about role models and respect. But in their arguments every reference to these ethical principles is driven from authority. Honour and integrity are in the service of tradition and compliance. All the jargon of citizenship is bandied about in order that the school might retain its identity. Two flag poles carved with the mottoes–honour, tradition, purity–stand in a corner of the archives, a generous gift from a retiring member of the board of directors. "Defiance of the rules is bad in and of itself," states Principal Quinn, 1961. "Respect and honour the customs at Charlton Academy. They help define who we are," claims Principal Darcy, 1974. "Each of you has received the Code of Conduct and has agreed to abide by its guidelines. Proper uniform is expected of everyone, especially our prefects and school leaders," announces Principal Darmit, 2004. Poor creatures, desperate to stamp out any defiance. Their documents tell at least two stories: a story of a normative institution, and a second subdued story that exposes the hunger beneath each document. They dress up their authority in moral garb, and hope that no one dares doubt or question moral goodness.

Martha cannot bear this phony appeal to virtue. She agrees with Nietzsche–women are such suckers for virtue. It enslaves them. They become compliant virtuous martyrs patiently accommodating the current tyrant, until they rebel, and betray him. She reads a speech from a long-standing male president of the board of directors. He praises the notion of purity. Martha feels nauseous. She drinks from her water bottle and then closes the filing cabinet. She walks over to another cabinet labeled *photographs*. She opens a drawer and discovers reams of graduating class photos. To her horror, each year's photo shows approximately one hundred girls in white dresses. The hems go up and down, the corsages change colour, but the dresses remain white, a pure virginal white. Graduation is like a mass wedding. Coiffed hair-dos reveal delicate ribbon and flower woven into the braids. Cheeks are matted with make-up, lips glossy with lipstick. Row after row of straightened teeth beam at the camera. Each smile so unaware of how they capitulate and contribute to the legacy of white dress after white dress.

Martha wonders how she will write about this purity. She wonders which set of administrative ladies decided on white, and why the decision was never revised. In photos taken as early as the mid-1930s, the girls are paraded in and out of St. Thomas's cathedral in their white gowns. Passers-by must wonder whether it is indeed a mass wedding, or perhaps a late group christening. Martha has always had a psychological loathing for white clothing. She is certain that others have related reactions; she can't be the only one. She can make sense of white wedding dresses that represent the sexual purity of the bride, but a white graduation dress? Is it meant to represent the intellectual purity of the graduate? Is it almost an apology for having educated the young girl and jeopardized her purity? Is it meant to assure all parents and potential grooms that she remains a potential bride, first and foremost, despite her education? Graduation marks a journey made, but the white dress seems to suggest that the journey is a cloistered path. Martha scans the faces of the one hundred nineteen-year-old girls in their white dresses on the church steps. Why, she wonders, would they be willing and keen to participate? Where is the defiance? Where are the ones who refused to conform? She opens another drawer and finds informal photos at the garden party following graduation. More recent photos from the previous few years reveal tight and seamless white dresses. The girls are all wearing thongs and drinking beer. They cling to each other arm-in-arm, forever friends. Martha stares as though looking at some alien creature she cannot comprehend. Purity, she decides, should not be cultivated at a girls school. The concept is dangerous.

She knows that her research method is actually a counter-method. She explores the archives with shameless curiosity, poking about in places, skimming files, and examining that which draws her attention. The volunteer alumnae who have organized everything would shudder to see Martha scatter her thoughts about the carefully structured room. She moves from document to document, her personal feelings driving her motives. She disrupts the chronologies of fact and the paths of least resistance, constructing an entirely new narrative that more consciously honours her own unconscious. She hopes there is a validity in what she does. She hopes her work will act catalytically in the service of some needed social transformation. Martha does not want to create documents that validate the status quo. She rebels against all formulaic production, and longs for a place of freedom where her unique aesthetic instincts can playfully question the flatness of master narratives. She has always found herself within the walls of repressive and conservative institutions, engaged in tedious, stultifying acts of submission. Each new commitment, no matter how passionately begun, ends trapped by coercive rules. She wonders if her life history will simply be a testament to resistance, or if there is another valid point to be made through her research. Is it that she simply refuses to serve anyone? Is she despairingly without cause? Every cause, she reflects, always turns sour and pigheaded. And yet she knows that no cause is pure. She knows that persons of all positions are invested in obtaining specific outcomes. She knows that bias and judgment and desire are human traits to be celebrated and not regretted, but she hates the severe disappointment of abandoning ideals. She hates the thought that she too may be simply serving her own interests while pretending to fight for a greater cause. What if her underdog is just another less apparently greedy projection of herself? She realizes that she must remain humble. She must undermine her authority at every step, without retreating into the safety of supposed neutrality. She must collaborate with those she hopes to serve, and in solidarity struggle against the forces of silence. Her subversive acts of resistance must become more communal, more public, more given to improving the lives of the oppressed. She sits amongst the groomed Charlton archives and wonders how her current assignment might serve the lives of the oppressed. It seems rather unlikely. Who at Charlton, she wonders, is in need of liberation?

Commentary by Patricia Leavy

1. Aesthetics

Elizabeth de Freitas is a gifted writer and clearly takes great care during the writing process. She draws on her previous experience writing fiction in order to craft *The Wrong Shoe*. Her careful attention to the craft of literary writing draws readers into the narrative. She skillfully employs literary tools such as description, detail, and expressive language as she weaves her narrative. Even in the brief excerpt presented, readers are drawn into the story through her careful character construction. Moreover, through her mastery of literary tools de Freitas offers readers great aesthetic pleasure even as she tackles a complex subject matter.

2. Personal Signature

As an experienced writer in both fiction and nonfiction formats, de Freitas has developed a style that is unmistakably her own. De Freitas's personal writing style comes through both in her use of literary tools and in her content-based choices. Beginning with the former, de Freitas uses language beautifully, combining words and phrases in original ways and constructing sentences that bear her fingerprint. Specifically, she details particulars in ways that bring the reader into the story. She also subtly weaves humor and irony into the narrative. With respect to her content-based choices, de Freitas has written extensively about the character Martha West. For readers who come to this text having read her earlier work there is great pleasure in continuing to explore this recognizable and relatable character. Further, de Freitas's ongoing commitment to exploring the nature of reflexively researching and writing underscores her fiction and makes it uniquely her own.

Novels

Chapter 8

Waiting Room

by Cheryl Dellasega

Introduction

Although evidence of human ability to tell stories is as ancient as the earliest paintings on cave walls, it is less clear *why* we do so. Is there a primal drive that prompts us to express feelings and events in writing, or do we merely strive to create an ongoing historical record of the species? Do poems, letters, journal entries, screenplays, memoirs, essays, blogs, and stories all tap into the same domain, or do different motives inspire each?

Many years ago, when online teaching was in its infancy, I took a course from the New School titled Writing as Therapy. One of our assignments was to ponder this very question, prompted by the instructor: "Why do we write?" My answer was a bold one: "We write to satisfy some unresolved issue churning around at either a conscious or unconscious level in our brain."

A lively written debate followed, with one student in particular disagreeing.

"Look at Stephen King," she posted. "You can't tell me he's ever experienced the things he writes about, so there's no way he's trying to resolve anything."

Still, I politely agreed to disagree. A few months after that exchange, Mr. King wrote his compelling autobiography, *On Writing* (2002). In it, he described a lifelong fascination with the struggle between good and evil. I rest my case.

Still, a writer is not a writer is not a writer, especially in the fiction genre. Coming from a background in medical humanities, I was fascinated to learn about a genre my colleague Anne Hunsaker Hawkins labeled "pathography." In *Reconstructing Illness: Studies in Pathography* (1999, 1), she introduces us to this concept, defining it as "the personal narrative concerning illness, treatment and sometimes death."

In part as a consequence of Dr. Hawkins's work, people suffering from terminal and chronic illness were recognized as legitimate authors of their own stories. They were empowered to share their experiences and all they had to teach us. A new wave of "medical memoirs" about painful situations previously cloaked in the guise of fiction was evidenced by books such as Lisa Roney's *Sweet Invisible Body: Reflections on a Life with Diabetes* (2000), Paula Kamen's *All in My Head* (2006), a chronicle of her painful headaches, the heartbreaking *Autobiography of a Face* (2003) by Anne Patchett's pal Lucy Grealy, and Elizabeth Wurtzel's movie-spawning diary, *Prozac Nation* (2002).

Waiting Room is a novel that deals with the slow unraveling of a "perfect" family confronted with the mental illness of a child. Agents and publishers have suggested it is another spin on the nonfiction book I wrote titled *Surviving Ophelia* (2001a), and although I think it is not, the novel is uniquely mine. My professional and parental experience of many of the same issues I write about shaped the writing in a way that would be hard to replicate.

For example, the nurse practitioner/counselor part of me understands the clinical treatment of eating disorders: the battery of medical and psychological therapies required, the nature of inpatient treatment, and how parents are often blamed and shamed by healthcare providers for the condition of their child. Indeed, when I went on to write *The Starving Family* (2007), another self-help book based on interviews with dozens of mothers and fathers whose sons and daughters had anorexia and/or bulimia, many of the feelings and situations experienced by Laura, the protagonist of *Waiting Room*, and her family, were experienced in real life by the parents I spoke with.

At the same time, I mothered a young woman who struggled tremendously during the teen years. Her diagnosis of anorexia connected me with many other parents who were persevering through similar situations. Conversations with women whose daughters were in treatment with my own led me to wonder, what happens in real life when a scenario like Joyce Carol Oates's *We Were the Mulvaneys* (1997) occurs?

Fragments of two particular stories stayed with me. In both, a father/physician had a demanding but very successful career and was employed in a hospital where his daughter received psychiatric treatment. In addition, both mothers were attractive and well spoken, having soft-pedaled their own careers to stay at home during the active child-rearing years. Both families lived in small communities where they were "high profile" for various reasons. None of these descriptors was true for me, but they were essential to the story of *Waiting Room*.

However, many of Laura, David, and Mark's responses to traumatic situations *were* familiar to me: I had both lived them and worked professionally with families going through them. Therefore, putting those emotions into words that both validated and permitted them was therapeutic for me. As a novelist, writing, editing, and rewriting the story allowed me to create what Dr. Jamie Pennebaker, psychologist and author of *The Healing Power of Expressing Emotions* (1997), calls a "cogent narrative."

Perhaps that's why I'm so enthusiastic about revision—when presented with feedback from early readers, or in setting the manuscript aside and revisiting it later, the chance to recraft the story is as exciting as originally birthing the idea and capturing it on paper. (Not all critique evokes this response, however. Well-intentioned attendees of conferences and workshops who focused on craft to the exclusion of veracity helped me identify what *didn't* need to be changed.)

As a professional who is also a health educator, *Waiting Room* was also an opportunity for me to entertain, engage, inform, and, in some cases, support readers, although that was not my primary focus. I "vetted" medical content and read numerous scholarly articles to make sure the snippets of information on anorexia, bulimia, and other eating disorders were correct, even though this was a novel.

It's picky, I know, but fiction readers who are experts in a particular area become, unfortunately, derailed by a descriptive detail, behavior, or scenario that doesn't line up with the truth. Who among us has never heard the comment: "Oh, that could never happen in real life"? One writing instructor wisely advised me: "Even though you know [it] *could* happen in 'real life,' it doesn't matter. The fact that a reader believes it couldn't means you need to either get rid of it or present it differently."

Although *Waiting Room* was originally developed with a first-person point of view, my writing skills at the time made me stray into the many potholes such an approach can present. Somewhere in my computer files is a version of the manuscript from a third-person perspective. This may even be the version a literary agent fell in love with and labeled "an Oprah book," but during one of my many rereads, the sense of urgency that Laura's voice added to the story seemed lost. It took months, but the change back to first person was one of those necessary revisions a reader suggested.

Whether intentional or not, social fictions offer readers a different experience than fictions by "outsiders" telling a similar story. Sometimes, such an author can visit our world and capture the intimate details of our professional lives and it's stunning. For me, Chris Bohjalian has captured both female and professional voices in his books on midwives, transgenderism, mental illness, and post-traumatic stress, but he is a rare exception.

Just as the line between fiction and nonfiction can be blurry (think historical fiction, comics, and autobiographies, to name a few), the complete separation of our professional and fictional selves is rarely possible. We feel a moral imperative to be true to what we know professionally, even when writing to entertain. And, I would argue, in the end readers are the better off for it.

Waiting Room

Chapter One

The day when my life began to change was innocent enough. It was mid-September, and a chill pressed in against the warmth of afternoon as I headed toward the high school soccer field. Already, a few bright leaves that looked like red paper snowflakes dotted the ground, stirred by the crisp breeze.

"Laura! Wait up!"

The sound of my best friend's voice stopped me from a quick trip back home to retrieve the sweater I realized was hanging on a kitchen chair. When she caught up to me, Hillary pulled me close for a quick hug, and then tipped her head back and took a deep breath.

"What a glorious day. They're cooking."

I inhaled chocolate too, which wasn't unusual since our small town was home to a factory that produced candy bars of every size and flavor imaginable. Most afternoons, the same delicious scent, part brownies baking in an oven and part rich hot cocoa steaming from a mug, floated through the air like a gentle breeze.

"Sometimes I really miss living here," she told me as we crossed the parking lot and made our way to the bleachers.

After her divorce, Hillary moved to a condominium ten miles away, where the streetlights weren't shaped like foil-wrapped candy kisses and there was neither a Cocoa Bean Museum nor a store that sold huge plastic bags of brightly wrapped chocolate to eager tourists. In absentia, these things, along with the smell, charmed her in the same way they did the droves of visitors from around the world.

"I still haven't figured out if smelling the stuff makes me want to eat more or less," I said, trying to rub away the goose bumps on my arms as we climbed up the bleachers.

"More! I'd kill for some right now."

While she unpacked her equipment, I settled onto my plastic padded seat (with the team emblem printed on each side), arranged my binoculars and water bottle nearby, and offered to get her a snack from the fundraising table of treats situated on the sideline.

Before I could, my daughter's team surged onto the field and we were instantly immersed in a ritual that marked the beginning of each sports season. Hillary, a professional photographer, came to my children's opening games as often as she could to take pictures. That meant I was free to watch the twins compete, knowing she would capture the highlights on film and deliver them to me later. If our house ever caught on fire, the first thing I would rescue was the miniature gallery of their lives she created over the last decade.

Our opponents that day were longtime rivals from the nearby city, so there was excitement from the first kick, with a narrow lead that alternated every few minutes. The sun rallied with a glare that made the long shadows of soccer players dance like crazy cartoon characters on the field, and everywhere was a dazzle of color–bright green grass tipped with gold, a sky condensed into pure blue, and the swirling, rainbow colors of slick uniforms.

"Com'on, Meg! Show 'em what it's all about!" Hillary shrieked at one point, clamoring down to stalk the sidelines with her camera. The previous year, Megan scored the most goals for her team, just as she'd set a record for home runs in softball that summer.

With only seconds left on the clock and a tied score, someone kicked the ball to Megan with a hard *thunk* I could hear from the stands. My daughter took it and weaved her way to the goal line in a deft half-polka, stopping short when she was almost there, as if confused. A slight movement of her head made the wiry girl guarding the goal shift left; in that millisecond, Megan booted the ball, hard, into the right pocket of the net.

"That's our girl!" The wooden bleachers swayed as Hillary sprinted up to grab me, shrieking.

The match ended with a shrill of the referee's whistle, and, as if a gate had opened, Megan's teammates swarmed onto the field and surrounded her.

"It's a sign, Laura. She's going to have a great year." My friend, a devout believer in premonitions, gave me a knowing look.

A tiny smile pulled at my mouth as I let out the breath I'd been holding deep in my lungs. Megan had looked really good on the field, running fast and managing to control the ball in impossible situations. So far, her classes were going well, and she was on the verge of getting a boyfriend, all good things.

"What a game! I feel like I played it myself."

"I got some gems this time." Hillary patted her camera with the same type of gesture I once used on the heads of my children.

"How about coming over for dinner?"

"David working late again?"

She knew I wouldn't have invited her if my husband had been there. David, usually mild-mannered, blamed Hillary for the breakup of her marriage to his best friend, Spence Tate.

"She always picked fights with him," my normally mild-mannered husband told me when the two of us had gone out to eat on one of our rare Friday night "dates."

I took a bite of my salad and chewed carefully. "You know, David, Spence has been a good friend to you since med school, but don't you think he's a little . . . intense at times? It isn't surprising he's a surgeon."

"I'm a surgeon, too, you know."

"Yes, but you're different. You have children to balance your life out. Spence didn't want kids, and I know that was hard for Hillary."

His eyebrows lifted into the triangle shape I knew well. "That's not the story I heard."

We moved on to a different subject, but without Spence at her side, Hillary and David seemed to rub against each other like sandpaper. She would never criticize him openly, but the way her voice dropped when she said his name told me all I needed to know.

"Six o'clock isn't 'late' any more. He's supervising residents now, so getting home at seven is just a normal day. Anyway, how about it? I made lasagna."

Hillary considered the offer, twisting her mouth sideways in a familiar gesture, then shrugged her shoulders. "What the hell? My diet can wait 'til tomorrow. I bought a gallon of protein powder this morning, but then I had some for lunch and it tasted like liquid paste. How do people live on that stuff? Only a little piece for me, though. I promised myself I'd lose twenty pounds by the end of the month."

"You don't need to lose weight," I protested, thinking a smaller Hillary just wouldn't be the same.

Eyes still scanning the field, she threw empty film containers, a water bottle, the soccer program, and an apple core into her suitcase-sized purse, then said: "Wait a minute."

Below us, Megan was suspended between two of her teammates, arms draped over their shoulders. The girls around her danced with joy, some slapping hands in midair and others spraying their water bottles straight up, so the last rays of sun sparkled on the drops. Without moving her eyes from the scene, Hillary felt for her camera case, opened it, and reached for a zoom lens. Anchoring one sturdy leg on the bleacher in front of us, she attached it and then rested her forearm on her knee, and played with the camera settings. After another round of rapid-fire pictures, she held the camera to her heart.

"Perfect. You know, maybe I ought to be a sports photographer. Athletes in action, the thrill of the game... guys in locker rooms. I like that idea."

I laughed at the thought of her advancing on naked men with her camera. As we moved through the crowd of spectators, other mothers congratulated me as if I had scored the winning goal myself. Just being the mother of twins was enough to make me a celebrity, but Megan and Mark attracted attention for other things as well: both were pleasant-looking, stars on different sports teams, and diligent students.

"I have to pick Mark up at the library. Want to wait for Megan while she showers and then the two of you can meet us at home?"

"Oh, come on, let me get Mark. Everyone will think I'm dating a younger man."

"Hillary! That's my son you're talking about!"

"What better person to take him under her wing than your best friend?" She gave me a lock of mock innocence, then pouted. "Okay, spoilsport, Meg and I'll meet you in half an hour."

As I fished in my purse for my keys, Hillary joined the other spectators clustered around various soccer players. Her caftan top fluttered in the breeze, a bright blue and pink patterned flag streaming out from her body, with camera equipment balanced on either generous hip saddlebag-style. Among the mothers, she stood out like a sunflower in a patch of daisies.

To pick up Mark, I followed the same route Hillary and Spence used when they gave David and me a tour of the community several years ago. David had just finished his fellowship and was job-hunting; they were trying to lure us to their small town where a sprawling academic medical center was flanked at each corner by a large community center, modern library, and several new schools.

"This place is perfect!" David glowed as we drove home from the interview. "What do you think? Did you see those streetlamps and smell that chocolate?"

"It's cute," I agreed. "Hillary seems to think it's a great place to raise kids, even though they don't have any."

"Spence says there's no comparison between this and private practice. He looked pretty happy, didn't he?"

"He did, and so do you. Is your mind made up?"

David pulled the car off to the shoulder of the road quickly and took my hand. "We have to agree about this. I won't mention it again if you aren't one hundred percent in favor of moving there."

"It's not that I didn't like what I saw . . ." My voice drifted off because he didn't know that small towns in rural areas reminded me of my childhood. He did know I loved the city where he was completing his fellowship, despite the lack of career opportunities there for me.

"Take a few days and think about it," he urged, kissing my forehead before pulling back onto the road. "And don't forget—we're a team." "It looks great."

I acquiesced after two days, cheered not only by his enthusiasm, but the prospect of a real job with regular hours and a permanent position for him. Had anyone warned me he would soon be working even longer hours than during his training, I wouldn't have believed it.

After we moved in, we socialized sporadically with Spence and Hillary, but for a long time she and I hadn't been close, even though I accepted her offer to photograph the children's activities. Our husbands saw a lot of each other at the hospital, but my time had been consumed with the children and all the things their lives involved until one day when we happened to run into each other at a medical supply store.

"Never thought I'd go shopping for a potty chair," Hillary cracked, her lips slanted in a wry frown.

"That's what I'm here for, too," I said. "My mother is living with me. She has . . . cancer."

"Mine too. Breast cancer. Metastasized."

"My mom has that, too." "Chemo?"

"Awhile ago. The doctor says there's no reason to keep on now."

"Me, too. I mean, my mom, too."

During the weeks that followed that chance meeting, we talked on the phone daily, discovering more similarities. She was a real photographer, just as I had once hoped to be, and we'd grown up in the Midwest. When our mothers died within weeks of each other, we grieved together.

Since then, we'd been the sisters to each other that neither of us really had, even after she and Spence divorced bitterly and her lifestyle became even more flamboyant and carefree. We were quite a pair: her with flame red hair, outrageous clothes, and imposing height, next to me, a person people passed on the street without turning their heads to look closer. At times I envied her, wishing I was the one jumping in a 1998 Chrysler convertible and taking off for a week or two of photography assignments.

"You're late!" Mark informed me when I reached the library, climbing in the car and raising his eyebrows at me in a junior version of David.

"Sorry. The game ran a little late. But we're celebrating tonight." He wasn't listening because he was too busy nodding through the window at a shapely girl waving to him from the double doorway of the library. "Megan made a last minute goal."

"Huh? What?"

I repeated myself.

"Really? Good for Mushy. Too bad I missed it. Got a big paper due tomorrow." He wedged his backpack underneath his legs and drummed his fingers on his knees. "I'm starved."

He was "Mucky," the male version of "Mushy," a mirror image of Megan with fine dark hair that flopped on his forehead, fair skin that freckled in the summer, and restless cat-green eyes. In the last two years, his body had grown taller and more muscular than hers, but they were still clearly twins.

For a long time, David and I thought we would be childless, despite vigorous efforts to conceive. After four miscarriages we nearly gave up, but then I discovered myself pregnant with twins. The anxiety that was a constant from the day the test was positive exploded into panic when premature labor required me to be on bed rest for six weeks. At eight months, my labor was agonizing but Megan and Mark were born healthy. I was thrilled to finally be a mother, but knew they were the only children I wanted to have.

"They're more than enough," David crooned when I said as much to him. He was holding one baby in either arm, a look of total joy on his face. Although there are no pictures of that particular moment, the look on his face is still vivid in my mind.

"Who's your friend?" I asked Mark innocently, focusing on the fifteen-year-old version of those infants who now sat in the passenger seat of my minivan. When he looked blankly at me, I nodded my head back toward the library.

"Just a friend, Mom."

His tone of voice told me to end that line of conversation. When we reached our red brick bi-level, he bounded out of the car as soon as I pulled in the driveway.

"Gotta make a phone call before we eat."

Three of my favorite flowered placemats were already on the kitchen table, along with a vase of roses from our garden, which were most likely the last full blooms of the season. Adding another place setting, I hummed a tune from the radio station the twins usually turned on in the car and moved around the kitchen, preparing food.

"Why'd you put dressing on the salad?" Megan came through the door and bee lined for the table. Her cheeks were still flushed, and the hair pulled back into a ponytail high on her head was damp.

Looking at the basket of rolls, she continued. "You know coach told us to watch our fat intake. I'm in training!"

"Aren't you going to tell Mark about your great game?" I pretended not to notice her shoving her salad bowl aside as I centered the casserole of lasagna on a trivet. "Or should I?"

"Suffice it to say your sister was the superstar of the game," Hillary assured Mark, who slid into a chair and pulled his plate closer.

Megan ignored both of us, busy scraping the top layer off her lasagna. "You put too much cheese on this."

"Meg, I always put that much cheese on, and you always like it." I paused with the serving spoon in my hand. "Listen, just because you're a soccer star doesn't mean you can take charge of my kitchen."

"Maybe I should just shovel my food in like Mark," she snapped.

Mark looked at her, a piece of garlic bread in one hand. "You mean like this?" He rolled the butter-soaked slice into a tube and shoved the entire thing in his mouth, grinning.

"Mark!" I scolded, but he was beaming at Hillary, cheeks bulging, while she pretended to hide her laughter behind a napkin.

When Hillary said she needed to use the bathroom, Megan scowled at Mark.

"How can you pretend she's so funny? If I had a rear end like hers I sure wouldn't eat two pieces of lasagna and garlic bread."

"That's enough!" I said. "Both of you stop it, right now."

To avert an all-out battle, I was about to offer ice cream for dessert when Hillary returned with a pack of cigarettes in one hand.

"I can't stand secondhand smoke," Megan sniffed, stalking off to her bedroom.

"Hey, I was going out to the porch!" Hillary protested, a cigarette half-way to her mouth. "She knows I never smoke in your house. What's up with her?"

I wondered, too. Normally, Megan couldn't get enough of Hillary, insisting she was a better clothes-shopper and more appreciative movie-watcher than me.

"That's Mushy. It happens every season. Remember this summer when she threw her spaghetti in the garbage without taking a bite?" Mark shrugged. "What's for dessert?"

Much later, when I went up to say good night, she cleared a space for me on her bed and patted it invitingly. "Sit. Talk."

"Okay."

"Guess who Franny has a crush on?"

Franny was Megan's oldest and dearest friend, so the news must be significant. I tried to look puzzled. "Who?"

"Mucky." She shook her head in amazement, watching for my reaction.

"What's wrong with Mark? I happen to think he's a pretty great kid!"

"Did you see what he's been wearing to school this year?"

I tried to think of anything unusual but knew he wouldn't have made it out the front door without me noticing, since I got up in time to wake both of them every morning. "I give up again. What's he been wearing?"

"His bedroom slippers. He's started this whole goofy trend with everyone wearing plaid bedroom slippers to school just because he is." She rolled her eyes and burrowed down under her covers, yawning and then giving a dramatic sigh. "Sometimes it's such a challenge to be his sister."

"I'm sure he feels the same way about you–sometimes." I waited for an explanation of her earlier behavior, but got none. "It's a good thing some people find your brother more appealing than you do. What are the chances he and Franny will get together?"

"Oh, I don't know. If a certain someone," her eyes met mine, "decides to talk to a certain someone else, there might be a pretty good chance."

"Well, I hope that certain someone gets a good night's sleep, so that certain someone isn't so grouchy about that certain someone's mother's best friend again," I said, standing up and giving her a kiss on the forehead.

Her lower lip thrust out in a stubborn sign I recognized, and for a moment she seemed ready to insult Hillary again. Then something in her relaxed and she held out her arms for a hug.

"Good night mom."

Long after I'd said good night to Mark, reheated some food for David when he arrived home, and cleaned up the kitchen, I couldn't sleep. Standing in front of the bay window that looked out over the rose bushes planted in honor of the twins' birth, it was hard to pinpoint why Megan's behavior seemed unusual. Mark was right about her taking the "training diet" suggested by coaches more seriously than he did, but normally, after doing well in any kind of sports event, she would be boisterous and unflappable, refusing to rise to even the worst of his taunts.

Maybe she was just premenstrual: I'd heard plenty of horror stories about the days right before a daughter's period. Standing there in the pool of moonlight that turned my skin and nightgown silver, I thought of what I'd been like at fifteen, then shook the memories off before they could settle.

Worrying about Megan's behavior wasn't going to help the situation–if there was even one to be helped. I padded back to the bedroom where David was already collapsed in sleep, and eventually managed to drift off into a restless half-awake slumber. Fragments of dreams replayed over and over, leading to a night full of my daughter, disgusted and sarcastic as she stared after Hillary.

Chapter Two

A week after the soccer game, a loud horn honking from my driveway summoned me outside. Hillary, car top down, handed me a packet of pictures.

"Can't talk–I'm catching the last plane out and I'm already late. This is the Canadian job I was telling you about. It'll be cold and long," she said, pointing her thumb over her shoulder at two suitcases in the back seat of her car "But the number where I can be reached if my cell doesn't work is on that envelope. Or at least they tell me I can be reached there."

All too often, Hillary traveled to remote places for photo shoots, so we'd lose contact for the duration of her trip. This one was at a barren stretch of mountains in northern Canada, which took away any glamour I might have associated with being a freelance photographer.

Walking back to the house while flipping through the pictures, a feeling of bewilderment returned. There was one of Megan running up the field, face wrinkled with concentration; in another, she dribbled the ball with her arm outstretched, poses I'd seen at least a hundred times over the last ten years. What was different?

"She looks fine to me," David said when I showed them to him that night, then glanced back at the ten o'clock news. His long surgeon fingers rested lightly on the remote control, ready to switch channels in a second. "Didn't you say she played a great game that day?"

I agreed, but knew that until the TV was off we wouldn't have any kind of meaningful conversation, not that there was more to say. Upstairs, I found Megan in the usual place: curled in bed with a thick comforter pulled up to her chest, a stack of school books on the floor next to her, and the phone within ready reach.

"Cold?" I asked, sitting down next to her. She marked a page in her science book and saw the picture envelope in my hand.

"Me?" She snatched them, holding the top one close, then far away. "Yuck."

"I think they're good. It's great to have actual pictures on paper to look at and save, don't you think?" I smoothed out the covers, trying not to be too obvious in my search for signs of problems. The Megan in front of me looked pretty much the same as the one in the photographs: not sick, but somehow changed. "So how are things? You and Benny getting along okay?"

Benny happened to be the object of her affection, as well as her brother's best friend. I hadn't pointed out to either of them the irony of twins possibly pairing up with each other's best friends.

Megan sat up and threw the pictures at me, scattering them on the bed and floor.

"He's a jerk. I hate him!"

"You might hate Benny, but that's no reason to throw things at me."

Her eyes narrowed and she pressed her lips into a thin line. "Why do you care about Benny and me?"

Slowly, I gathered up the pictures and returned them to the envelope.

"You told me Franny was going to ask Mark to the King Bruin dance and you were going to ask Benny."

"Well now I'm not. I don't want to talk about it." She picked at her blanket, avoiding my eyes.

I plunged on. "Meg, are you feeling okay?"

"Okay? What do you mean?"

"I mean, do you feel sick at all?"

She snorted. "Mom, I feel fine. Look at me—do I look sick? Why are you asking?"

"I don't know. Mother's intuition? You just seem different lately."

My eyes shifted away from her face, which suddenly looked more pale and drawn than it had the day before.

"I need a haircut, that's all. Maybe you can take me on Saturday, and then we can go shopping."

"That's a good idea. I need a trim, too."

"Goody. It'll be a mommy-daughter day."

She turned back to her book, satisfied; thus dismissed, I went into the extra bedroom we had converted into a study, opened the closet, and slid open the top drawer of the file cabinet inside. Stacked in the drawer were sets of scrapbooks embellished with locks of hair, crayon drawings, report cards, award ribbons, certificates, and other memorabilia, with my neat script recording the details of every milestone.

Some afternoons I spent hours in the study, lost in a happy glow as I browsed through the books, smiling at the sweetness of their infant and toddler years. While I had long ago discarded things that would remind me of my childhood, I wanted Megan and Mark to have plenty of happy times to reflect back on.

Easing out an album from the bottom of the drawer, I paged through it, smiling to myself. There were dozens of pictures, some taken on the same day: Mark with a bottle in one hand and blanket in the other Megan with the stuffed rabbit she'd slept with since the day she'd come home from the hospital, and their initial attempts to walk were documented, with Megan mastering the challenge first.

There were carefully preserved shots of them climbing onto the bus for their first day of kindergarten. There was even the shot I'd taken of them side by side on swings at the park that won first prize in a local contest.

"Reminiscing again?" David asked, peering over my shoulder before depositing some mail on his desk. "Those were great days, weren't they? You know, you should take more pictures. You're just as good as Hillary."

It was his attempt at a compliment, but far from the truth. Over the years, my energies had shifted away from photography and toward a career he jokingly called "home management." Although every now and then I snapped a few rolls of film, Hillary provided me with plenty of vicarious pleasure with her professional success.

"You know I'd rather look at pictures than take them."

"You mean you'd rather reminisce," he repeated, beginning to sort through bills. "But Megan and Mark will be out of here before long. Maybe you'll go back to it then."

The bottom file drawer was filled with the remnants of my short-lived photography career. A black leather camera case sat on top, carefully stocked with spare film and clasped shut, unlike Hillary's bags, which were made of nylon and stuffed so full the Velcro straps threatened to give way.

It had been months since I'd shot any pictures, but I closed the scrapbook and took my camera out, relishing its feel in the curve of my palm. After college, I had hoped to become a freelance photographer, but ended up in the portrait department of Sears to help put David through medical school. A few of our friends hired me for their weddings, and every now and then a classmate had wanted pictures of his or her children, but for the most part, I was little more than a hired hand, trying to persuade customers to purchase the most expensive packages Sears offered.

I returned my camera to its case and centered it back in the drawer, sorting through my collection of empty frames, purchased on sale. Finding one with four slots, I eased the best pictures of Megan in place and wiped the glass clean with the edge of my shirt.

David's beeper went off, which led to a murmured phone conversation. "They're flying in a sick kiddo. I'll probably end up sleeping at the hospital."

At one time, I would have sighed loudly and brushed away the quick peck he gave my cheek, but now, I squeezed his arm. "Do that. You need to take care of yourself, too. And don't forget to eat some breakfast!"

He left, and the house was quiet. Zorro followed me to the family room, where I placed the newest picture and stood back to survey the panorama of my children.

David was right. In two years they would be off to college and I would be "unemployed," more or less. My heart hesitated for a second at that thought, but then Zorro whined to go out and I turned away from the pictures, each one as precious to me as the medals and ribbons my children won at their various competitions.

The following weekend David was on call Friday night and Saturday; the medical center was full and the little boy he'd operated on during the week was doing badly, which meant he was there continuously. I woke to an empty house Saturday morning, padding through the upstairs in search of the twins just as the front door opened.

"Pancakes, pancakes!" they chanted, hands clutched into fists.

I peered over the banister. "Since when do you two get up early to go running on a Saturday?"

"Since Short-stuff woke me up and challenged me to keep up with her for five miles," Mark jeered, tugging at his sister's ponytail.

"So how much did she beat you by?"

"I went slow just so she could keep up."

"You did not!" Megan protested, swatting at him. "You're a sprinter. You faded after the first mile, and I had to slow down for you."

They followed me to the kitchen, shedding their sweatshirts and sneakers as they did so. Megan turned her attention to me. "Are you taking me to get a haircut today?"

I cracked eggs into a bowl, sizzled butter on a frying pan, and poured myself a cup of coffee. "This afternoon."

She nodded in satisfaction, but her mood turned sour several hours later when we were on our way to the mall.

"Can we shop after my haircut?"

"Oh Megan, I don't think so. We shopped all day last week, and I've got to work on the auxiliary budget this afternoon."

"Come on. No one cares how a bunch of frumpy old doctors' wives spend their money."

"I care. It's money for a good cause. We work hard to raise it. And I doubt there's one woman there who would feel kindly about being called 'frumpy' or 'old.'"

"Then why don't you all go out and get real jobs and do something that really matters?"

I glanced over at her when we reached a stoplight. "What's up with you all of a sudden?"

She sniffed, her attack silenced until we reached the beauty shop.

"Instead of standing over my shoulder, why don't you get them to do something with your hair? It's a mess," she commented when I came to stand next to her chair after my cut was finished. The stylist, who was still scissoring Megan's hair into a shoulder-length bob, rolled her eyes at me in the mirror.

"She sounds just like I used to with my mom," she told me.

After her hair was done I relented a bit and agreed to stop in just one store. Before I knew what was happening, Megan headed to the dressing room with an armful of clothes.

"I just bought you three new pairs of jeans for school," I reasoned, standing in the doorway of her changing room as she modeled the pants.

"Please mom, just one pair!"

"Megan, I made it clear when I bought you hundreds of dollars of back-to-school clothes that you have to buy anything extra with your own money."

"But why?" She stamped her foot. "The jeans you bought me don't fit right anymore. Just because you wear your old clothes so baggy doesn't mean I have to, too."

"What is this–'Dump on Mom' day?"

"Just because you don't care what you look like, it doesn't mean I have to wear ugly clothes." She hurtled the hanger in her hand in my direction, then picked up her old jeans from the floor and yanked on them so hard the zipper broke. "There. Now you have to buy me new jeans."

"That's it. I'll meet you in the car," I snapped, jerking the curtain shut and marching off.

Sitting in the driver's seat, waiting for her, I fumed. She had certainly voiced her opinions about my failure to use makeup, my out-of-shape figure, and lack of fashion sense in the past, but in a less hurtful way. Still, our drive home was wordless until I pulled in the driveway and Megan hopped out of the car, slamming the door shut harder than she needed to.

"Tell Mark I'll be home in a bit. I'm going over to check on Oscar," I called after her, but she gave no sign that she heard me.

Hillary's apartment, the upper floor of an old Victorian-style house along the main street of her small town, was like a portrait of her personality. There were vases of real peacock feathers, exotic silk scarves draped over the lamps, and walls hung with empty gilt frames that were waiting for pictures. Books and magazines spilled off of mismatched antique end tables, and an entire wall was devoted to her photographs, mounted collage style and with an occasional comment inked in.

There was a shot of a much younger me and David with a blue heart she had drawn in one corner, while images of Megan and Mark were checkered through the rest of the space with words like "Wow!" "Top Dog!" and "Whiz Kid!" scrawled on them. Hillary *had* wanted children with Spence–desperately. His refusal to take on the role of father was just one of their many problems, but I sometimes wondered what might have happened if they had been parents. After the divorce, Hillary talked about adopting from time to time, but as her career required more frequent and distant travel, the comments dwindled.

I sank down on the red leather sofa in her living room and wished I could stay there for the rest of the day. After the sparks that had flown between Megan and me, the silence was like a tranquilizer. I'd never had a place I could decorate the way I wanted and call completely my own. Before meeting David, my residence had been dormitories or furnished rooms; now our house was more functional than decorative.

Was that my problem as well? Was I too functional? I looked at the picture again, realizing my appearance hadn't changed much over the years. My black hair was cropped in a straight line at chin length, too thick to fuss with, and my brown eyes were nothing more than ordinary. The pants and shirt I wore back then were still a regular part of my wardrobe, but I was in better shape: the photograph had been taken before a major cartilage tear sidelined my daily runs.

Still brooding, I punched Hillary's number into my phone.

"What's up?" she asked as soon as she heard my voice.

"Am I a frump? Be honest."

"Hey, just because you could be a poster person for Middle Class Moms of America, doesn't mean you're a frump," she joked, but then changed her tone when I didn't laugh in response. "What, is Megan giving you a hard time?"

"She told me I never do anything different with my hair and that my clothes are ugly." "Laura, you look just fine. You wouldn't be you if you looked any different."

"What does that mean?"

"It means you are perfectly fine. Sure, I'd love to see you streak your hair blue or purple and start wearing really wild clothes, but then you wouldn't be Laura Carson anymore. You're a khaki kind of person." She paused, waiting for me to comment, then went on. "Megan will complain no matter how you look. That's what teenaged girls do."

"Maybe. You're not making me feel a whole lot better, though. What's a 'khaki kind of person'?"

She was in a public place of some sort; there was muted music in the background, and before answering, she covered the phone and spoke to someone. Maybe she was out with someone: it was the weekend and that's what single people did.

"A 'khaki kind of person' is someone you can depend on and know what she's all about. Listen, if she has you really stressed out, use that spa certificate I got you for your birthday and treat yourself to a day away."

The subject was dropped, and after we chatted for a few minutes about the shoot she was on, the people she was working with, and the man she had met at a local camera store, I returned home to what seemed like an all-out war between Megan and Mark.

Taking a deep breath, I went in the front door. "What is going on, Megan? I could hear you screaming as soon as I got out of the car."

"He's feeding pizza crust to Zorro. I wanted the pizza crust!"

Megan was holding a glass of water in one hand and an empty pizza box in the other, her face flushed. Mark sat on the sofa, casually rubbing the special spot behind Zorro's ears and flipping through channels on the television. Hearing his name, Zorro hopped down and trotted over to her, his tail wagging hopefully, but she shoved him away with her foot. On the sofa, Mark continued to aim the remote at the television.

"I told you I wanted to watch a movie, shit head! You've had the remote for the last hour." With one angry jerk, she threw her water, dousing his hair and shirt. He sprang up, grabbed her arm, and poured the can of soda he'd been drinking on her, then glared at me. "She deserved it," he said, marching upstairs.

"Mom, aren't you going to do something?" Megan wailed.

"I just did. I watched you two act like babies. Now go change and let him alone."

"But . . ."

"Megan. Don't push me. Mark has been feeding that dog pizza crusts since he was a puppy, and until now you've never had a problem with it. Go get cleaned up, and I'll order another pizza."

"You always take his side! Forget it, I don't even want pizza anymore." In a flash, she stomped upstairs.

That night, in bed, I sat up and faced David, my legs crossed. "Tell me the truth. Do you ever wish I looked different?"

He wrinkled his forehead and laid the book on pediatric anesthesia he was reading across his chest. "No, I can't say that I have. Why?"

"Oh, Megan made some comment about what a frump I was today, and it made me wonder. Do you ever wish I would cut my hair short, or wear makeup?"

"Laura, you look just the way you did when we got married. If I liked the way you looked then, why would I feel any different now?" He sighed and tilted his book back up. "If that's the worst thing Megan ever says about you, we're in pretty good shape, don't you think?"

"Probably."

The sting of her comment stayed. Instead of brushing my teeth in the bathroom that night, I did nothing but stare at myself in the mirror. David, Megan, and Hillary were all right: nothing about me changed—ever.

But was that a good or a bad thing?

Commentary by Patricia Leavy

1. The Creation of Virtual Reality

Waiting Room centers on the unraveling of the "perfect" family due to a daughter's eating disorder. It becomes important from the outset for Cheryl Dellasega to present this family clearly, realistically, and resonantly. As soon as we enter into the pages of *Waiting Room*, we are presented with a highly relatable "family" engaged in the "typical activities" expected of a middle-class American family. Readers watch and listen as activities and interactions unfold before them in highly resonant ways. Dellasega effortlessly creates a virtual reality for readers to step into. Through her use of resonant experiences, details and particulars, authentic character portrayals (including realistic dialogue), and rich descriptions of seemingly mundane activities, she has captured verisimilitude.

2. Substantive Contribution

Dellasega brings a range of personal and professional experiences to bear on her writing of *Waiting Room*. She has experience as a nurse practitioner/counselor, researcher, and mother of a young woman who struggled with an eating disorder. In her nonfiction work she has written extensively about how eating disorders impact entire families. Her aim in writing *Waiting Room* was to provide health education to a broad audience through an engaging and entertaining novel. *Waiting Room* makes a substantial contribution to our understanding of how eating disorders/mental illness impacts family units and individual family members in complicated ways (an under-researched area in the eating disorder literature). Through writing in the fictional format, Dellasega also contributes to public scholarship on a topic that affects many.

Chapter 9
Low-Fat Love

by Patricia Leavy

Introduction

As I wrote in the preface to this book, I didn't initially sit down with the intention of writing a novel.

I spent more than a decade teaching undergraduate courses about gender, sexuality, intimacy, and popular culture. Those courses sparked wonderful conversations with students that taught and inspired me. However, I always left those classes with ample frustration too—so many of my female students seemed to settle in their romantic relationships, to suffer from poor body image, and were willing to accept less in love and life than they really wanted. What's worse, there were clear patterns of behaviors with accompanying rationales that emerged over and over again. As a professor I could never fully express myself, which would have involved shaking some of these students and loudly asking, "Why are you doing this?"

I also spent a decade conducting interview research with women (and at times men) about their relationships, gender and sexual identities, body images, and pop culture consumption. I experienced many realizations as well as the same frustrations in my role as interviewer.

Fiction as Research Practice: Short Stories, Novellas, and Novels, by Patricia Leavy, 233–56. Extract from *Low-Fat Love* (2011) reprinted with permission from Sense Publishers, Rotterdam, The Netherlands.

It's not appropriate to reach across the tape recorder, shake someone by the shoulders and say, "You don't have bad luck; get reflexive and make better choices. You deserve more."

I also had personal experiences from which I learned many lessons. I made my own share of relationship mistakes, settling for less than I really wanted and mistaking drama for passion. Through a reflexive process I came to see my choices were the result of poor self-esteem. I worked on myself and ultimately transformed my life. I felt I had something to share with others.

When I started writing *Low-Fat Love* I quickly realized that my teaching, research, and personal experiences were guiding me. How could they not? They had shaped me. I also feel a deep commitment to feminism, so a belief in people's ability and right to self-actualize underscores all of my work. I determined that there were a few themes I had learned about over the years—areas where I felt I had something to share—and that these would become the basis of the novel.

The concept of "low-fat love" refers to settling for less than we want and trying to convince ourselves that it is better than it is. I believe people can't really fool themselves, not for long, without dire consequences, from general discontent to depression to rage. Life is simply too short.

Thematically, *Low-Fat Love* explores low self-esteem, the psychology of negative relationships, women's identity building in the context of their relationships with men, and the social construction of femininity in pop culture and how that impacts women's psyches. One of the first things I wrote about my atypical heroine, Prilly Greene, was: "Prilly lives in between who she is and who she longs to be." This concept of living in the gap between our lives as we imagine them and our lives as they are—and how we can face our own demons to cross that bridge—is a major theme of the book.

As I began writing, I quickly realized that the novel format was the only form that would allow me to fully explore the thematic content I was interested in, while reaching my intended audience. The novel format allows for rich characterization that is central to *Low-Fat Love*, which in some ways is really a character study. I drew on common character types and stereotypes in order to subvert them, challenge readers to reflect on their own lives, and offer a feminist rewriting of commonly held assumptions about gender identity and heterosexual relationships. I also relied on readers' empathetic engagement with the text, which was dependent on their connection to characters. The length of a standard novel allows for a plot to develop based on the interweaving of numerous storylines, allowing themes to be crystallized in complex ways. I decided that *Low-Fat Love* would unfold the way that life does, without a grand ending. Rather, characters would go on, hopefully having learned from their experiences, which is the most any of us can hope for.

Low-Fat Love suggests that we each find our voice and do not stray from it. I hope the book encourages young women and men to reflect on their lives in ways that promote the development of positive self-concepts and healthy relationships. I believe my turn to fiction-based research, and the novel genre, was the most effective (if not the only) way to achieve my goals. This approach allowed me to liberate myself from the confines of the professor-researcher roles. Due to the pleasure to be found in reading fiction, I am hopeful that this approach will also cultivate an empowering reflexive process in readers.

Low-Fat Love

I

"'Casey bombed into town with her daily organizer.' It's the worst first line I've ever heard! I mean, you're left with this organizer, just sitting there, for no reason. You never mention something so irrelevant right in the beginning. It's awful. Nowadays everyone thinks they can write. There are no real writers anymore," he said, flinging the manuscript on Prilly's desk.

"Just real editors, right Stuart?"

"Ah, you're just soft Prilly. You can't coddle them. There's no point."

With a friendly roll of the eyes she agreed to the inevitable. "I know, I know," she said shaking her head. "I'll tell him we can't go forward with publication."

"Good. We've got to start streamlining our list. Bad writing that sells millions of copies is one thing, but unsuccessful bad writing is an embarrassment. And I don't have to remind you that we can't afford the drain."

Prilly smiled, thinking his remark about unsuccessful bad writing was dead-on. "Got it. I'll take care of it."

Stuart left her small drab office, inadvertently knocking a teetering stack of mail off the corner of her desk. The piles on her desk taunted her. She desperately desired to have everything organized and in its place, but she just couldn't manage it for more than a couple of days at a time. She had seen an episode of Oprah where an expert said that clutter in one's office or home meant clutter in one's emotional and spiritual life. As she wondered whether that was true, she reread the beginning of the manuscript. Was it really such a bad opening line?

That night when Prilly entered her apartment she immediately kicked off her comfort heels and slipped on her at-home uniform: Old Navy black pajama pants and worn-out Ugg boots. She poured a glass of Beaujolais and lay on the couch. Remote in hand, she flipped between her usual stations and landed on "Access Hollywood." They were featuring a story about Brad Pitt and Angelina Jolie. She always bought tabloids when they were on the cover. Although she despised the idea that they were mostly adored for their good looks, she too was fascinated. Sometimes she would fantasize about what Angelina's life was like. Of all the celebrities, Angelina seemed to have it all. She was ridiculously gorgeous, the kind of beauty that doesn't seem to go out of style, or to age. She had lived a wild life, and now she had a massive multicultural family (that she probably never had to take care of with all her nannies, assistants, and so forth), a fabulous partner who undoubtedly worshipped her, and an amazing career. Somehow she had managed to be both an artist and a commercial success, or at least she could reasonably claim to be both. People admired her. People like Prilly. As Prilly watched the story she felt a familiar storm cloud of envy, longing, and self-loathing.

"Access Hollywood" was just the prelude to whatever "movie of the week" she could find. Tonight she was watching a Lifetime movie about a woman who worked as a newspaper reporter and, while reporting on a local crime, became the next target of a psychopath. As she picked up each forkful of the vegetable stir-fry she made during the commercials, she couldn't help but think that in some ways the reporter was lucky. At least her life was exciting.

Prilly lived in between who she was and who she wanted to be. She had moved to Manhattan from Boston in search of a *big life*. She had always felt she was meant to have a *big life*. To date, she had barely had a small life. Although she was an atheist, like many other atheists she blamed God for all her problems (at least when she wasn't blaming her parents). She thought it all came down to looks, to genetics. She was convinced that beautiful people have a much greater shot at a big life. Ugly people have no shot. People somewhere in the middle, which is where she was firmly located, had to work hard for it, but it *was* possible. So ever since Prilly was about seven years old and she figured out that she was regular looking at best, she blamed God and her parents for her lot in life. As a teenager she admired the beautiful, popular girls. To her, they had been graced with the best gift of all, the gift of possibility. When you were beautiful, all you had to do was add on to that to get what you wanted, to be who you wanted to be. When you weren't beautiful, you spent your life making up for it, filling in what was lacking. Compensating. At times Prilly even envied the ugly girls. If you were ugly and knew it, there was no hope of a big life and so ultimately that would be very freeing. You could focus on being content with your life as it was. Ugly girls didn't have to waste time or money with makeup, hair care, exercise, beauty treatments, and fashion. What was the point? No one fabulous would ever get close enough to reject them, so they must be free from disappointment too, she thought—at least once they accepted their situation. The ones who had it the worst were those in the middle; the girls who with enough work could be considered pretty, but never beautiful. Those girls had it the worst because they could taste the big life, they could see it close enough to want it, to reach for it. Prilly was in the middle.

Peter Rice had just picked up the latest Neil Gaiman book and planned to spend the next several hours reading it while drinking dark roast coffee. He loved the smell of coffee brewing. It was his favorite smell.

As Pete waited for the coffee to brew, he replayed the scene of Rachel storming out of his apartment the night before. He decided not to call her; he didn't care. He had a theory about women. If they loved you, you could control them. But if they loved you too much, disaster. He had had disasters. (There was Alice who showed up to a party at his friend's house, plastered, shouting that he had an STD. He didn't. Then there was the catalogue model, Georgia, who slashed his vintage T-shirt collection and trashed his apartment. This, of course, brings to mind Sophie, who upon catching him in bed with Georgia, used his dirty clothes to make a bonfire on the fire escape outside of his apartment. Worst of all was Sadie, who would stake out his usual haunts—a local teahouse, a sandwich shop, a pub—waiting to see him arm-and-arm with another woman, which would cause her to scream publicly as if the world was burning and only she could see it. Interestingly, this would cause the woman currently with Pete, in her guiltiest of thoughts, to want him all the more.)

Pete's days depended primarily on three factors: whether or not he was screwing someone steadily (steadily for him being a long series of intense relationships that lasted about two months each), whether or not he had been out all night (he had a penchant for dance clubs, though at thirty-eight he was nearly two decades older than everyone else there), and whether or not he was working (although he resisted any kind of long-term commitment or "career" that would interfere with his art, he did take very occasional part-time jobs ranging from telemarketing to working in a one-hour photo shop, which also never lasted for more than two months). He also vacillated between feeling invincible (he had an "unknown genius" complex, one that was imprinted with the arrogance of a guy who was better looking than behaved) and feeling utterly depressed. That day Pete had expected to be alone.

His studio apartment consisted of one small room that served as his bedroom and workspace, a kitchenette with a cutout wall that looked into the bedroom, and a small hallway that led to the bathroom and front door. The main room had two large windows, one of which led out to a small fire escape that he used as a teeny tiny porch. Sometimes he grew pot out there, but it was usually stolen by his neighbors.

He used an old queen-size mattress and box spring, but no bed frame, so his bed was low down on the floor. Gaiman book in hand, he propped up two pillows against the white stucco wall and sat down wearing his black and white checkered boxers and an old David Bowie T-shirt. He placed his oversized "I Love NY" mug on the cinderblock to the right of his bed, and opened the book. He always read the dedication first. He felt you could learn everything about the soul of an author by reading the dedication page and, thus, the soul of the book. Books without dedications always disappointed him. Just as he flipped to the first page there was a knock on his front door.

He walked to the door and shouted, "Who is it?"

"Melville."

Pete opened the door. Neither said a word, and Pete just walked back down his narrow hallway to his bedroom while pulling at a wedgie. Melville locked the door and followed. Pete plopped down on his mattress and picked up his coffee. Melville pulled out the rolling computer chair tucked under the desk opposite the bed. He turned it to face Pete and sat down. Then he stood up and took off his jacket and sat down again, placing the orange garment across his lap.

"So what's up?"

"Oh, nothing, I was downtown visiting my cousin so I thought I'd stop in. I thought maybe we could get some coffee or something. What are you doing?"

"Nothing. I got the new Gaiman book and I was just going to start it."

"I could have gotten you a deal on that. I hope you didn't pay full price, not for the hardcover. I know a store where you can get hardcovers half off, even new ones. If you get 'em used you can get them for a few bucks. Hardcovers are a rip-off anyway."

As Melville was talking, slowly as ever, Pete wished that he would shut up. He was the cheapest person he had ever met. He had holes in his sweaters and had sported the same worn-out ugly orange windbreaker for the whole time Pete had known him—more than a decade. Pete hated going out to eat with him because Melville would refuse to tip appropriately. He would leave spare change, usually about a four percent tip at the most. Pete was cheap too, but only privately. In public he intentionally gave the impression of being generous, but in private he would often screw friends who loaned him money or haggle with the landlord over the rent if there was any minor repair needed in the apartment (real or imagined), and while he always had money for expensive restaurants, liquor, books, art supplies, and all things entertainment, he never seemed to have money for anything else. For example, he had no health, dental, or life insurance. Nor did he have any property (beyond the books and odds and ends in his tiny rented apartment). He routinely bought an overpriced cappuccino from the café down the street, only to drink a sip and then put it to the side where he would forget about it, but he couldn't manage to pay his utilities on time and consistently ended up paying late fees and even reinstallation charges. As the flaws in others are always much more apparent than those in ourselves, Pete was oblivious. He wished that Melville wasn't so cheap or at least that he'd have the sense to shut up about it. The truth was, he was embarrassed to be friends with Melville. Pete prided himself on chasing the muse, being in tune with the zeitgeist, and living in the moment. To Pete, Melville was the embodiment of all that he disdained. Pete decided that Melville lived one beat outside the moment. That was why he was so slow relaying the simplest of information and why, at the age of thirty-six, Pete suspected he may still be a virgin. Yet despite his harsh evaluation of Melville, he remained the only reliable presence in Pete's life.

Totally ignoring Melville's inane hardcover commentary, Pete shot back with, "Yeah, ok, let's go grab a bite. I need to shower. You can make yourself some coffee if you want. I'm out of filters but there's paper toweling there. Flip through that book, or look in that folder over there," he said, pointing to a pile of papers on the desk behind Melville. "I've expanded the carnival part of the story and I'd like to know what you think. No one's read it yet. You're in for a treat."

"I'll be out in a jiff," Pete hollered as he walked into the bathroom, coffee mug in hand.

Forty-five minutes later they were sitting down in a diner three blocks away. Pete was an inconsistent regular. He would go through spurts of eating there nearly every day, sometimes more than once a day, and other times he wouldn't go for months at a time. Just as any given waitress was getting to know him, he'd take a hiatus and she'd forget him by the time he returned. When the waitress came to take their order, Pete couldn't help but notice how unusual looking she was. He had a knack for noticing atypical faces, and this face intrigued him. It was fairly old but probably appeared older than its biological age. It had very long features and a strong nose. After further examination he determined that the nose was in fact so ugly that he actually found it quite wonderful. He expected an interesting accent to match the face, but when she said, "What'll it be?" it was with the same New York accent he had come to tire of in the last five of the fifteen years he had been in the States.

"I'll have two eggs over easy with wheat toast. I'd like marmalade on the side, not jam. And coffee, with cream."

"And you?" she asked looking at Melville who was still staring directly into the oversized plastic laminated menu.

"Um, what does the special egg sandwich come with?"

"Homefries."

"Does it come with a drink?"

"No, just homefries."

"Um, ok, I'll have that."

"Something to drink?"

"Just water."

Pete, growing tired of these uncomfortable exchanges, had occupied himself by doodling in the small notepad he always carried with him. By the time Melville looked up from his menu, Pete was in another world.

"So I read the new pages."

"Yeah, and?" Pete asked both eager to hear the response and annoyed that he had to coax it out of him.

"They're good but you're missing some commas in a couple of places. I can show you where." (Melville had been an English major in college, until he dropped out sophomore year.)

"Commas? Fucking commas? This is your insight? I don't give a fuck about commas! I hate fucking commas. Do you have anything useful to contribute or are you just taking up space?"

Although hurt by Pete's patronizing rant, Melville ignored it as he was accustomed to doing. Wanting to show Pete he had more to offer, that he wasn't just "taking up space," he quickly retorted, "Well I don't get where you are going with the main character. The writing is good but there's nowhere to take it."

"Ha! You should stick to commas," Pete said through hearty laughter.

Melville shrugged, looking down. Although Pete had never noticed, Melville never looked him in the eyes. Never. He normally looked down and sometimes to the side.

"You'll get it when it's all there. That's your problem, you need it all spelled out. Can't feeeeel where it's headin'. But don't worry, it'll all be there and you'll get it."

With that the waitress brought breakfast. Melville ate swiftly, looking down at his food the entire time. Pete spent a few minutes dunking the corner of his toast into his egg yolks before eating.

At the end of the meal there was some typical squabbling about the bill. Melville left his usual four percent tip. Anyone else would have just thrown some extra money down but Pete, being secretly cheap himself, guilted Melville into putting down a couple of dollars. Pete either didn't realize or care that when Melville gave in it was just to get Pete to shut up. He couldn't stand the sound of his voice. Although Melville envied him, particularly with women, he also found Pete laborious. Walking out, Pete noticed a flyer in the entrance of the diner. It announced a book reading by Jeanette Winterson that Saturday afternoon at a local bookstore. He ripped down the flyer and said, "We should go to this. It would be good for you to hear a real writer. No one uses metaphor quite like Winterson. She's good."

Not acknowledging the condemnation, Melville simply replied, "Yeah, ok."

On the train Melville Wicket sat still and silent. Only weeks before he had moved into his younger brother Jacob's apartment in Brooklyn, which he shared with a manic-depressive named Jeremy.

Melville was a telemarketer for a medical insurance company. He only worked twenty-eight hours a week so his employer could get away without paying him benefits, like medical insurance. With hardly enough income to live, Melville had been staying in a small basement room in a rooming house for the past three years. He paid month-to-month. Some residents had week-to-week deals. The room was half above ground and half below. There were two small rectangular windows high on the right wall, nearly touching the ceiling, with rusty iron bars. Underneath there was a small refrigerator, the kind you would expect to find in a college dorm room, a microwave, and an electric Crock-Pot that violated building codes. Across from the windows there was a twin-size bed with old off-white sheets, one flattened pillow, and a worn-out queen-sized down comforter with a few holes. Sometimes when Melville woke up in the morning, there would be feathers in his hair. In his mind he called them chicken feathers. To the left of the bed was a small unfinished wood desk and brown leather chair. On the desk, a stack of library books, a few pieces of old mail, notebooks and pens, an old word processor from 1995, and a small alarm clock with a CD player. On the floor beneath, stacks of CDs. To the right, a tall halogen lamp. There was a shared bathroom in the hallway. Melville was allotted one shelf in the medicine cabinet for his personal items, which he used, although he didn't feel good about it.

Melville would have stayed there forever, but he had been asked to leave at the end of the previous month. One of the female residents complained to the Super that Melville had been peeping on her while she was in the bathroom. She claimed that she saw him through the slit of the barely opened door, a door she claimed to have closed, that he must have pushed ever so slightly open. Two years earlier another woman had made a similar complaint. Melville had denied it, in his usual quiet manner. The Super took pity on him and let him stay, but now with a second complaint, he was out. When he told Pete what happened Pete said, "Spying, you were spying on the girls? Ha!" Melville insisted he hadn't done it, and Pete rolled his eyes but didn't say anything else. He always assumed that

Melville was guilty but not because he was a pervert, just because he was shy, and awkward, and terribly lonely.

Jacob hadn't wanted Melville to move in with him, but what could he do, the guy was basically homeless, and he *was* his brother. Besides, he could get money for rent and utilities, leaving more money for pot and the occasional celebratory mushroom. Jacob was twenty-four and worked in what he called a "vintage music store" in the Village, near Washington Square Park. It was a store that sold rare vinyl and also used CDs, dealing largely in trade. Melville wondered how in the age of eBay and iTunes a store like that could stay in business. When he once asked Jacob about it, Jacob told him to "shut the fuck up." Melville never mentioned it again. Melville didn't know what Jeremy did for a living. Most days he would be in his room all day, sleeping, Melville assumed. But every Tuesday he was up and out of the house by 8:00 am and didn't return until after 6:00 pm. Melville didn't ask questions.

After spending the morning with Pete, Melville returned to his apartment at 3:00 pm. He went straight into his small bedroom. In actuality it was a two-bedroom apartment, with a small living room and kitchenette combo room, and one tiny bathroom with a stall shower. The apartment also had a very small sunroom that Jacob turned into a makeshift bedroom for his brother. With no room for a bed, Melville slept on a small couch. The room was very drafty, and Melville was worried about winter. He thought about it all the time. On that day, as most, he entered his room, took off his sneakers, and put on a Puccini CD. He lay on his couch with his jacket still on, listening.

Prilly's search for a big life hadn't amounted to much. She was in her office from 8:00 am until 6:30 pm every weekday. By the time she got back to her apartment, it was time for "Access Hollywood" and a healthy dinner, followed by a bad junk-food binge with a side of guilt and a movie about women who steal other women's babies or who murder their young repairmen lovers. Although she had been in New York for several years, she hadn't managed to make more than a couple of friends. And she didn't really like them. Much like the fat girl in high school whom she befriended, this, for now, was the best she could do. The single women at work routinely went to local bars together, and, although they always invited her, she never once went. She didn't feel comfortable and thought it would be awful. After a while she also noticed that they didn't so much invite her, but rather state, "We're heading to Maxwells." She assumed she was welcome to join them; else why would they bother to announce where they were going. But she wasn't sure.

She did take one stab at Internet dating. The Internet appealed to her for two main reasons. First, no one had to know about it. So if it didn't work out she wouldn't have to explain it to anyone. Second, she could screen the men on the basis of income, education, looks, and interests. She wanted a man who earned more money than she did, not because she had any intention of becoming dependent on a man, but because it would be hard to have a big life in Manhattan without more money, and a lot of it. She also really wanted to get out of her mounting credit card debt which weighed on her, particularly on the nights she drank a lot. She hoped to meet someone interested in the arts, who could take her to the best shows. Although she wanted to be with a good-looking man, which she felt made a so-so-looking woman seem much more attractive, she didn't want to be with a man that was too good-looking. Men like that always eventually left average women. It was hard to fool them into thinking you were prettier than you actually were. If she managed to get a decent man and turn it into a steady thing, she didn't want to have to do it all over again someday. She also feared being a part of a couple that made other women look and wonder: "What is he doing with her?" The Internet dating ended up costing her $199.00, a weekend's worth of screening time, one terrible evening, and an untold sum of shame. She had made a date with Henry. He seemed promising. He was an accountant who owned his own apartment and claimed to see every foreign film that came out. They were to meet at a Spanish tapas restaurant a few blocks from where she worked for a drink and quick bite. She thought about the date incessantly for five days. She got a manicure, bikini wax, and bought two new outfits (neither of which she wore; she decided one was weird and the other looked too "datey"). The night they were supposed to meet she got to the restaurant, stood outside for a minute panicking, walked around the block, and then decided that if he had seen her walk around the block he would already think she was a freak. She went home, drank nearly a bottle of wine, and watched four hours of a nine-hour "Murder She Wrote" marathon on the Hallmark channel. Henry sent her an email the next morning asking what had happened and if she was ok. She never responded and took her profile off of Match.com immediately. She felt guilty for months, thinking of Henry often.

Without many friends to go out with, and no real effort at dating, her life had become fairly lonely. She decided to invest energy into her weekend routine. Convinced that if you lead an interesting life you will meet interesting people, Prilly made being interesting her full-time weekend occupation. For her, there was nothing more interesting than the arts. Had she been braver, she might have been some sort of artist, or at least a journalist. She took to surrounding herself with the products of others' bliss. The monotony of the workweek was soon juxtaposed to weekends of ballet, theater, concerts, gallery openings, craft markets, spoken word performances, independent films, museums, and poetry readings. It was exhausting.

"Well I wanted to tell you in person. I know it's difficult but please don't take it personally. We're a mid-sized press and we need to be very careful about what books to publish, particularly for our trade market. Usually we don't even consider unsolicited works."

"But you've sold fifteen thousand copies of my last book. That should count for something. That's why I came to you first. I just don't understand this. Isn't there anything I can do?"

"Yes, I understand how you must feel," Prilly responded in a hushed tone, "but that was an introductory geography textbook, it was an academic printing with a built-in audience we could market to. If you talk with Marcy I'm sure she can explain it to you. The trade market is very different and we publish very few new fiction authors each year. I'm sorry but we can't go with this and I don't want to waste your time. I encourage you to submit it elsewhere."

After a moment of silence in which Prilly could hear her own breath, Charles matter-of-factly said, "Well I'm very disappointed. Very disappointed."

With that the large, pear-shaped man got up, outstretched his arm over Prilly's desk for a sweaty handshake, and left.

Prilly felt awful. Normally she would just send rejection emails or letters. She never had to see the person she was rejecting, but because Charles was already published with the house, Stuart had suggested she do it in person next time Charles stopped by to see Marcy, the geography editor.

Just before Prilly could regroup from that experience, Janice popped her head in her door, left ajar by Charles. Just the sight of Janice made Prilly crave Advil.

Janice was a long-time acquisitions editor with the press and Prilly had been her assistant for nine months before being promoted to editor. It was the longest nine months of her life. At first she thought she was incredibly lucky. She was told that there were very few women in publishing who had made it to Janice's level, with her list of accomplishments. After ten years of working in their geography division Janice was given a new list to build, history, a market the press had never ventured into before. With a degree in history, Janice had purportedly been thrilled. She had introduced herself to Prilly as a feminist. She boldly said, "Prilly, this is a male-dominated industry. It's not easy. But it can be done and we have to support each other." She also prided herself on including women's history and Black history in her line, books she swore other editors would pass by.

Prilly soon found out that feminism was more of a conceptual with Janice. She really enjoyed talking about supporting "women's issues," but she didn't support *actual women*. In fact, over time Prilly learned that Janice was particularly harsh on the women she worked with out of some irrational fear that they would become more successful than her, and what's worse, that they wouldn't have to work as hard to do it. Janice had to work for everything she had, and unlike the "anorexic bitches" she went to college with, she scraped for everything she got, including her education. As a result Janice only liked women beneath her, those that she could easily manipulate and therefore control.

Janice had liked Prilly well enough at first but, when she realized that Prilly wouldn't be content being an assistant forever, she began to grow weary. This weariness led to a quiet resentment. During those days Prilly would often find herself working outrageously long hours that mostly consisted of doing secretarial work for Janice, which was not in Prilly's job description. Assigning these kinds of tasks helped Janice on two levels. First, it made it clear to Prilly and anyone else paying attention that she was in charge, she was Prilly's boss. Second, and even more importantly, it prevented Prilly from doing the kind of work that the publishers would notice, the kind of work that would get Prilly promoted. What Janice failed to recognize was that the publishers had always intended Prilly for an editorial position. They just made her an assistant first so the others wouldn't complain that there was too much rank jumping. When Prilly was promoted she immediately went to Janice, hoping to avoid future unpleasantness, and said, "Thank you so much. Without your mentorship this never would have happened." To this Janice replied in her usual quiet and monotone voice, "Well, actually I did put in a good word for you too. I had to push for this. I had to make this happen. But you deserve it." Prilly thanked her although she knew it wasn't true. In fact she suspected that Janice secretly gave her mediocre performance reviews so that she would remain her assistant indefinitely. Ever since, Janice went out of her way to be nice to Prilly, so much so that it alarmed her. But once in a while, Janice would find a way to say something cutting, under the guise of being helpful, like the knock about having to convince the bosses to promote her. It was no wonder that the mere sight of Janice at her door caused a sharp pain in her spine.

"Hi Prilly. What was that about? Charles Pruit looked pretty upset when he left. He used to be one of my authors you know."

Prilly relaxed a bit, hoping Janice was just nosing around for gossip as she was prone to do, and didn't in fact want anything from her beyond chitchat.

"Oh, that's right. He's one of Marcy's now. Same old, same old: he's an academic who thinks he can also be a novelist. I had to tell him that his manuscript isn't for us. He took it pretty hard but . . . what can you do, you know."

At this Janice shimmied her way into the doorway, allowing her back to gently tap the door closed as if unintentionally. "Oh great," Prilly thought, "There's more."

"Do you want to come in and sit down?" Prilly asked entirely out of obligation.

"Oh sure, just for a minute."

Prilly noticed how Janice always had a way of making things seem like they were someone else's idea, and like *she* was doing *you* a favor.

"Prilly, I wanted to run something by you."

"Sure, what's up?"

"I want to build a list of memoirs, focusing mostly on unknown female authors."

"That sounds great Janice, you should give Stuart a proposal."

"Well I did actually, and that's where you come in. Stuart said that memoirs would fall under your list, that they're sold as trade books and since we don't publish nonfiction trade, they'd have to be a part of our current trade list. He thought it would make sense for someone in your division to partner up with me."

"Hmmm."

"So I suggested that you and I work on it together. We could do it as a book series, instead of a line, at least as a sort of pilot test. If we solicit authors who have already drafted manuscripts we could premier at Trade Launch this spring. You and I could serve as coeditors-in-chief for the series, with my name listed first. If it does well, we could eventually build a full line. I think this would be an excellent opportunity for you."

"Yeah, I bet you do," Prilly thought to herself. She had learned long ago that Janice only cared about opportunities for herself. Anytime she framed something as an opportunity for someone else, Prilly thought that poor soul should run like the wind. In Prilly's case, there was a part of her that actually liked Janice, despite all the obvious reasons not to. At times Prilly even thought that her fondness for Janice grew in direct proportion to Janice's manipulative behavior. Although she was very different from Janice, deep down she knew that there was a part of them that was the same. A part of each of them that had been shafted and was clawing their way out the best way they knew how; it was just that Janice's claws were sharper. She also wanted to believe in Janice's tale of great feminist heroism in publishing, even though she knew it was a lie. If Janice would just be more forthright, Prilly could even be friends with her. She kept this thought to herself.

"Well it does sound interesting. Why don't you give me your proposal and I'll look over it and we can talk more. I'm really swamped as it is, but I'll definitely look over what you have."

"I'm telling you, this is a great opportunity for you. In fact, Stuart didn't think you were up for it yet, but with my convincing, he's willing to give you a shot."

"Well I appreciate that," Prilly said, the way a child thanks their parents when they're given socks for Christmas. "It sounds like a great opportunity but I'd like to look over the specifics and think about it."

Janice couldn't conceal her irritation as she fiddled with her pin-straight light brown hair, but she played along. "Ok, I'll email you the proposal and Stu's notes; we can talk about it early next week."

"Ok, great, thanks Janice."

And with that, Janice left her office, shutting the door behind her. Prilly took four Advil immediately.

The weekend couldn't come fast enough for Prilly. She spent Friday night at home with half a bottle of red wine and Chinese takeout. (She always ate right out of the container with the disposable chopsticks. She thought it was more sophisticated even though no one was there to see it, and even though she had no idea how to use chopsticks properly so food invariably dribbled on her couch. This also prevented her from ordering the veggie fried rice she liked, she couldn't possibly eat rice with chopsticks.) Saturday she woke up late with a wine-MSG headache and took two Advil.

With no plans until Sunday (when she was meeting an old friend for a several times rescheduled lunch) she supped her French roast while perusing one of her favorite New York websites, which listed things of interest. Jeanette Winterson was doing a book reading and signing at 4:00 pm. The bookstore was near the shoe repair store where she had left her silver shoes for heel reinforcement. Pully liked to multitask, plus she thought there were sure to be interesting people at the book reading.

2

"Hang on a minute. Fuck, Melville's banging on the damn door. No, we're going to a book reading. I'm not even dressed so I better get movin. I'll call you later. Hang in there. Bye."

When Pete hung up the phone he stammered down his hallway and opened the door. He turned around and walked back to the kitchenette without saying a word. Melville shut the door and followed.

"Fuck, I was on the phone. Can't you wait a minute?" Pete asked with a tone that made it clear he was not looking for an answer. "I'm making coffee, do you want some?"

"No thanks," Melville said as he grabbed a comic book off of Pete's desk and sat in the chair, flipping through its pages. Melville didn't care for comic books; he thought they were juvenile and beneath him, but, like so many other thoughts, he kept this to himself.

"I just need to throw my clothes on. I'll bring the coffee to go."

"Ok," Melville said as he started to read a random page in the middle of the comic book.

The bookstore was crowded and by the time Pete and Melville got there, fifteen minutes late (though Winterson hadn't begun her reading yet), there weren't any seats left. Melville was secretly annoyed that Pete, per usual, hadn't been ready on time. They stood in the back, leaning against a wall. Pete, burnt out from a sleepless night, sipped his coffee steadily.

CHAPTER 9

When Winterson appeared, everyone stood up and began clapping ferociously. She began by talking about her new work, from which she read several passages. She then took questions from the audience about her first novel *Oranges Are Not the Only Fruit* and fan favorites like *Sexing the Cherry*. Prilly, sitting in the corner of the back row, hadn't read any of Winterson's books, although she owned several. They were amidst the collection of "important artistic works" she thought everyone should own... and someday even read.

At the end of the question period, there was a book signing. The mob scurried to the front forming a swerving line through the store. Prilly detested standing in lines. Also, she hadn't brought any books with her and wasn't committed to buying the new book. She picked up her unmarked brown paper bag that contained her newly repaired shoes and turned to head out. The bag didn't have a handle and was thus cumbersome. She had to stick it under one of her arms and throw her handbag on her opposite shoulder. She fumbled a bit as she made her way past the rows of arranged chairs towards the door. Melville, still leaning against the wall with Pete, noticed her immediately. She was lovely, he thought. It was his irrepressible staring that made Pete aware of her. As Prilly walked by, Pete said, "You're not getting a book?"

"I'm sorry; did you say something to me?" Prilly asked, catching a glimpse of Pete for the first time. He had striking teal eyes framed with a few soft lines that made her think he had "really lived."

"I just asked if you were getting a book; everyone else seems to be."

"Oh," noticing how sexy his voice was. "The line is too long."

"My friend and I were going to go get a coffee, to talk about the reading. Would you like to join us?"

Stunned by the invitation from a tall, dark-haired man whose name she didn't yet know, Prilly stammered. Pete quickly responded, "It's ok, no worries, but if you're not busy come along."

With that, Pete walked in front of Prilly, opened the door, and let her pass through. He then stepped outside with Melville following. He turned to Prilly, who was now shocked by both the unexpected invitation and the willingness with which this man would let her just leave. "Well, have a good evening," he said as he turned and started walking down the street.

Prilly watched as he and Melville went into a café only half a block down. She turned to walk in the other direction but as if in slow motion stopped mid-movement and turned back towards the café. She would hate herself if she didn't check this out. When she walked into the café Pete was sitting on a long red velvet couch. He smiled and said, "Well, you changed your mind."

"I thought I'd just come for a quick coffee."

"Great." With that he jumped up and got in line next to Melville, cutting in front of several people who didn't seem to mind.

Prilly placed her brown bag on the couch and sat on a wooden chair opposite where Pete had been sitting. "What'll ya have," he hollered. "Oh, a cappuccino. A non-fat cappuccino please."

Soon the two men joined Prilly. "Thank you," she said as Pete handed her a drink. "My name is Pete, and this is Melville, my editor," Pete said with a smirk as he plopped down on the couch.

"I'm Prilly. Prilly Greene." Turning to Melville who was sitting in the chair to her right, she then said, "You're an editor? Me too, that's so funny. I'm at WISE. What house are you with?"

Pete started laughing and said, "The house of Jacob."

Melville stuttered a bit and Prilly, not knowing what was so funny, turned to Pete. "Are you a writer?" she asked.

"Yes. Graphic novels mostly, but I do a little of everything."

Prilly was disproportionately impressed by him, considering they had just met. He was very sexy, too sexy for her really, but he seemed interested. She loved his British accent though she was embarrassed by her own trite thinking. He immediately reminded her of the lead singer from the '80s band A-ha. She had always loved the video for their song "Take on Me" in which the singer is transformed into a cartoon illustration who falls in love with a plain-looking diner waitress. Every time she saw that video she wondered why they didn't get a more glamorous woman to play the love interest, but she cherished the video because it gave her hope. That was exactly how she felt with Pete.

After talking about the book reading for quite a while (although clearly a bit full of himself, Pete was well read and Prilly was enamored), they decided to go out for dinner. Prilly said that she wanted to stop at her apartment first to drop off the bag with her shoes. She actually wanted to freshen up and throw a toothbrush and some makeup in her pocketbook just in case she didn't make it home that night. Although she had no intention of sleeping with him, this was the most exciting thing that had happened to Prilly in a long time and she wanted to be prepared for spontaneity. Suddenly worried that she just invited two total strangers into her

apartment, she felt a mix of trepidation and exhilaration as she clumsily turned the key in the lock. “I’ll just be a couple of minutes, feel free to look at those books,” she said pointing to her bookshelf as she darted into her bedroom. She returned ten minutes later with a larger handbag and without the brown paper bag that had become a source of gags on the way to her apartment. “Are you ready to go?” she asked.
“I’m going to go home. I forgot that I promised my brother I’d watch a movie with him tonight,” Melville said. “He already rented it.”

“Oh, ok,” Prilly responded, not knowing if it was true or if Pete had asked him to make himself scarce so they could be alone. Though she was hoping the latter was true, that thought also made her stomach knot. She had never been with someone so good-looking before.

The three walked out together and Melville headed left while Pete and Prilly headed right.

When Melville entered his apartment, Jacob was sitting on the couch with three guys that Melville had seen there before but had never been introduced to. They were passing around a joint and listening to some god-awful reggae music. Melville walked over to the refrigerator and took out a small bottle of Orangina and a Tupperware with leftover macaroni with meat sauce that he had made a few days earlier. He popped the Tupperware into the microwave. The ninety-second cooking time felt like forever as Melville awkwardly stood waiting for it to beep. “Hey, I thought you were hanging with Pete tonight. Did he ditch you?” Jacob hollered from the couch. Suddenly there were four sets of bloodshot eyes peering over at him. “He met a girl. Wanted to be alone with her. She’s beautiful,” Melville quietly said, embarrassed that in fact he had again been ditched. With that Jacob and his friends refocused on their joint and Melville took his dinner into his room where he ate while listening to a Stravinsky CD and thinking of Prilly.

“‘Casey bombed into town with her daily organizer.’ Ha! That’s terrible,” Pete said as his voice became higher and his laughter morphed into a cackle.

“Really? You think so? It’s not Pulitzer material but I don’t think it’s so bad. You should have seen the guy. He looked... he looked like he was trying to pretend he wasn’t shattered. He’s already one of our authors; I felt really badly for him.”

"You've got to be kidding. It's dreadful. That could be an example in a book about how not to write. Maybe you could use it for that," Pete said, again punctuating his suggestion with laughter.

Even though Pete was getting close to hurting her feelings, and he was definitely arrogant, she let it slide and just said, "Yeah, I guess it's pretty bad" (even though she still didn't understand why).

After a two-hour dinner sitting at the bar of a pub that Pete recommended (where they had gone Dutch), Prilly was in Pete's apartment sharing a bottle of red wine they picked up on the way there (which Prilly had paid for because Pete suddenly became fascinated looking at plastic lighters when it was their turn at the register). Normally Prilly would have been put off by such a scruffy little apartment, but on that night she saw the simplicity differently. He was living like a real artist, she thought.

With only one chair in the apartment, Pete invited her to sit on the bed. When she hesitated he said, "Don't worry, you don't have to sleep with me or anything," followed by a short burst of laughter which she was beginning to realize was a regular part of his communication. "Oh, I know," she said uncomfortably as she went to sit on the bed being careful not to spill her wine.

Wanting to quickly start up the conversation Prilly asked, "What have you written? You said something about graphic novels. I don't know much about that genre, but would I know your work?"

"Oh no. No, you wouldn't know my work. I haven't been ready to publish. Haven't sent it out anywhere. But soon."

As an editor Prilly didn't know what to make of this. She dealt with writers every day who were desperate to publish, who wanted it more than anything else. "When you say you're not ready to publish, do you mean that you haven't completed a work or are you one of those perfectionists who wants to get it all just so before you hand it over? Because you'd be amazed how useful copyeditors can be."

"Well I'll put it to you this way, if I were a gardener I would have the most beautiful, unusual flowers in the most unexpected and glorious colors. Everywhere the eye darted it would be unimaginable wonder. However, I wouldn't remember to water them and they would all die." He started laughing. "Besides, Melville does my copyediting."

"Ah," Prilly said, choosing to ignore the warning the universe might be sending her. She also chose not to ask how he earned a living (days later he would tell her that he lived mainly off of an inheritance from his parents who had both died young of lung cancer although neither were smokers).

Instead of making her wonder about his work ethic it just made her feel sad for him.

They moved on to childhood tales (he had stories about eating candy floss on autumn days; she had no idea what candy floss was but it sounded wonderful), his days in college (he was a philosophy major who dropped out during his third year because there was nothing more to learn from the professors), his subsequent adventures in London (where he befriended many drug-addicted counterculture artists), and eventually his move to New York (for "the energy"). She briefly told him about how much she loved her career, but mostly she just listened. After a few hours of talking, listening to new wave music that Prilly couldn't believe she had never heard before, and flipping through folders of Pete's work that appeared as totally fragmented bits and pieces of rambling sprinkled with something magical, she realized it was past midnight.

"I should probably go."

"Don't be silly, spend the night. We can go out for breakfast in the morning. There's a wonderful little diner nearby with a fabulous waitress; she has the most unusual face, you have to see it. Do you have plans tomorrow?"

Prilly did have tentative plans with her friend Yvonne, and she wasn't sure if she wanted to sleep with Pete yet, but she just said, "No, no plans."

"Settled. I have only the one bed so you'll have to sleep with me but don't worry, we can just sleep. I'll get you a T-shirt to wear."

Prilly went into the bathroom and put on the oversized Smiths T-shirt he had given her. She looked in the small, toothpaste-splattered mirror above the sink and wondered what the hell she was doing. She also thought about how glad she was that she had brought her toothbrush.

She timidly returned to the bed, and carefully crawled in. Pete smiled at her and said, "Good night," as he flipped off the light switch. She lay awake for hours pretending to sleep.

The next morning, she heard Pete wrestling around in bed. She slowly turned to him, conscious of her morning breath. He looked her in the eyes and softly said, "Good morning." Not wanting to breathe on him she looked down and whispered, "Good morning." She turned around, lying with her back to him. He put his hand on her shoulder and she moved closer to him. He slid his hand under her T-shirt and rubbed her breasts. Then he moved his hands down and gently pulled her panties off. He put his hand on her and started slowly motioning his. He slid into her and they made love, never turning to each other, never kissing.

Commentary by Patricia Leavy

Obviously it is difficult to comment on my own writing. Therefore, I have selected two evaluative criteria and review my intent as a writer as well as some of the feedback I have received from readers.

1. Audience

While I was writing *Low-Fat Love*, I was aiming the book at college students as well as women more generally. It is important to consider design issues in relation to the target audience and I made a concerted effort to do so. For example, I selected the "chick lit" genre because of the emotional capital it carries for many women, especially young women. The book is written in a tone consistent with that genre (including the juxtaposition of serious content with humor) and makes extensive use of interior dialogue to get inside the psyches of the female characters. In an effort to reach women more broadly, I included female characters at various stages in their lives and relationships (a college student, a woman early in her career, a midcareer professional and mother of a teenager, and the elderly mother of two adult women). I also considered how to present the novel to the audience. I included a preface that summarizes the content of the novel, provides context regarding the experiences that informed the book, and states my hopes for how the book will be used. Finally, I have informally gathered quite a bit of feedback from readers. I used the book in several college courses that I taught and I have also given invited book talks at various colleges and universities as well as presentations at conferences. Through my conversations with readers and their comments on various retailers' websites, I am confident that I have reached and engaged my intended audience. I am also confident that my design and content choices have resonated with readers, promoted reflexivity, and cultivated class discussions.

2. Ambiguity

As a feminist writer I was committed to opening the text up to multiple meanings. I attempted to weave together meanings in complex and nuanced ways that could be read and interpreted differently by readers. In this vein I also wrote many scenes that allowed readers an opportunity to watch the action unfold and engage in their own interpretive process. Additionally, there are gaps in the narrative intended to create spaces for the readers' interpretive process. More than anything, I intentionally and repeatedly violated readers' expectations (by employing and subverting master plots and creating and then challenging stereotypical character portrayals). The ending of *Low-Fat Love* was also crafted to contribute to ambiguity. While I indicated that central characters continue on and have been altered by their experiences, I do not provide the kind of closure typically found in women's fiction. My hope was that the ending would force readers to continue to think about the story and characters and their own lives. Despite the fact that many readers have told me they expected a "big ending" and at first were disappointed, they have also told me the book left a deep impression and the ending pushed them to go back and reconsider their previously held assumptions. I view this as a success.

Part III

Conclusion

Chapter 10

Fiction as Pedagogy

> Truth is so hard to tell, it sometimes needs fiction to make it plausible.
>
> —Francis Bacon

Now that you have been introduced to the possibilities of fiction-based research, it is important to consider how fiction and fiction-based research can be used in teaching. In this chapter I consider how fiction can be used as a pedagogical tool across the disciplines (in non-literature courses).

Fiction can be used as a pedagogical tool in order to facilitate a wide range of learning objectives. Critical thinking, consciousness-raising, forging micro–macro connections, and problem solving are widely desired learning outcomes in higher education, all of which can be fostered through the use of fiction as a pedagogical tool. Learning is an interactive process, and fiction can be a wonderful vehicle for engaging students in the issues we think are important. Fiction can also be used to help teach substantive course content across the disciplines. Before getting into specific examples of how fiction can be used across the college curriculum, it is important to situate this discussion within the scholarship on teaching and learning as well as the emerging literature on the relationship between literary reading and cognition.

Teaching and Learning

Teaching strategies should always be linked to learning goals (Leavy 2009b). How something is taught impacts what students learn (Eisner 2008). Historically, the dominant model of teaching has been based on lecturing—"the sage on the stage"— with professors often judging the quality of their teaching based on the quality of their lectures. Research indicates that this model of teaching (involving lecturing, note-taking, and studying) does not produce significant and long-lasting learning (Finkel 2000). Accordingly, those engaged in the scholarship of teaching and learning are reconceptualizing "good teaching." As we consider what "good teaching" might look like, bell hooks (1994) suggests, and I concur, that students must be "active participants" in their learning process. Finkel (2000, 8) reminds us that "good teaching is the creating of those circumstances that lead to significant learning in others. . . . Good teaching must be conceived in terms of learning. . . . [This] formulation reminds us of the primacy of learning, not teaching, in education. Learning is the end, teaching is a means to that end." Similarly, Stephen Brookfield (2006, 17) writes: "Skillful teaching is whatever helps students learn." The alignment of teaching methods with learning goals is a problem-centric approach to teaching (Leavy 2009b, 227).[1] As we start to think about teaching practices in terms of learning outcomes, we need to think beyond the traditional lecture format and find "new shapes" for teaching (Finkel 2000).

There is a growing body of literature on how arts-based approaches to research can be transformed into pedagogical practices in order to reach a range of commonly held learning aspirations. Maxine Greene (2008) advocates "aesthetic education" for two primary reasons: it promotes student engagement, and it fosters imagination, which is vital to consciousness-raising. I would add that *learning should be a joyful experience*. School should be fun. The more pleasure students experience as they learn, the more likely they are to be engaged, to experience lasting learning, and to become lifelong learners. Although there seems to be reticence about discussing the joys of learning in the scholarly literature, just as with research, these are processes that can be, and in my estimation ought to be, pleasurable. Additionally, learning that is relevant to students' lives is more likely to engage them. Colin Irvine (2008) suggests that students are likely to see novels, particularly if selected well, as relevant to their lives. For all of these reasons, fiction as a pedagogical tool is one "new shape" our teaching can take.

Literary Neuroscience

There is a growing body of scholarship on the relationship between neuroscience and literature, often dubbed "literary neuroscience," that has implications for why fiction might be a particularly effective pedagogical tool. Natalie Phillips has recently received considerable attention for her study about how reading affects the brain. Phillips became interested in studying distractibility as a result of her own personal experiences and observations of others. Phillips said: "I love reading, and I am someone who can actually become so absorbed in a novel that I really think the house could possibly burn down around me and I wouldn't notice. And I'm simultaneously someone who loses their keys at least three times a day, and I often can't remember where in the world I parked my car" (quoted in Thompson and Vedantam 2012). She decided to consider how reading affects the brain and turned to the fiction of Jane Austen. Phillips and her team measured brain activity as research participants engaged in close versus casual reading of an Austen novel. The preliminary results have been surprising. They have found that the whole brain appears to be transformed as people engage in close readings of fiction. Moreover, there appear to be global activations across a number of different regions of the brain, including some unexpected areas such as those that are involved in movement and touch. In the experiment, it was as if "readers were physically placing themselves within the story as they analyzed it" (ibid.). Here we can see how important it is to achieve verisimilitude in fiction, so that readers can become fully absorbed in the fictional world.

Phillips findings are less surprising in the context of Mark Turner's renowned book *The Literary Mind: The Origins of Thought and Language* (1996), in which he argues that the common perception that the everyday mind is nonliterary and that the literary mind is optional is untrue. Turner argues that "the literary mind is the fundamental mind," and observes: "Story is a basic principle of mind. Most of our experience, our knowledge, and our thinking is organized as stories. The mental scope of story is magnified by projection—one story helps us make sense of another. The projection of one story onto another is parable" (1996, v).

On a related note, George Lakoff and Mark Johnson (1980) suggest that metaphor is not characteristic of language alone, but it is pervasive in human thought and action. They explain that our conceptual system is fundamentally metaphorical, which implies that "what we experience, and what we do every day is very much a matter of metaphor" (ibid., 3). There are clearly implications for how we best reach and engage students.

It is interesting to note that the history of neuroscience itself is intertwined with fiction. Silas Weir Mitchell (1824–1914) is considered the father of American neurology (Todman 2007). Interestingly, he was also a fiction writer who published an astonishing nineteen novels, seven poetry books, and many short stories. Many of his works of fiction were inextricably bound to patient observations made during his clinical practice and centered on topics dealing with psychological and physiological crises. Given Silas Weir Mitchell's extensive body of fictional work, some suggest that students can learn about the history of neuroscience itself through his fictional writings (De Jong 1982; Todman 2007). Similarly, Charlotte Perkins Gilman's short story "The Yellow Wallpaper" (1892) is used in some neurology and neuroscience programs in order to illustrate concepts in mental illness and doctor-patient relationships with respect to sociohistorical and cultural understandings of gender (Todman 2007).

The more we understand about human cognition, the clearer it becomes that narrative, stories, and fiction can play a major role in the teaching of diverse subject matters.

Fiction as a Pedagogical Tool in College Classrooms

Professors across the disciplines are using fiction in order to teach discipline-specific course content, promote interdisciplinarity, and/or raise critical consciousness and develop critical thinking and problem-solving skills.

The benefits of fiction in teaching extend across the academic landscape. Consider my home discipline of sociology. In 1963 sociology giant Lewis A. Coser published what he deemed an "experimental" text titled *Sociology through Literature: An Introductory Reader*. Coser compiled the volume based on his belief that fiction could be used to teach sociological concepts. He hoped that when used in the classroom fiction would "enrich and enliven" the subject matter (1963, 7). Coser suggested that novelists are unmatched in their ability to describe human experience and therefore sociology had much to gain from literary "untapped sources" (ibid., 3). At the time of publication Coser himself did not know if the book would make any contribution to the teaching of sociology. The publication of this book itself indicates that the borders of fiction as a pedagogical (and research) practice have been explored for quite a while.

Now novels are routinely popping up in social science courses. For example, Kristina B. Wolff (2008) incorporates novels in her Introduction to Sociology course in order to help students forge micro–macro connections, which are particularly challenging for new students. Wolff's students are required to write four papers that analyze one novel using sociological concepts covered over the course of the semester. Similarly, Peter P. Nieckarz Jr. (2008) uses novels in introductory sociology courses, which are a general education requirement at his college and are typically populated with non-majors. The novels offer students with limited life experiences more material to draw on as they build an understanding of the social world they and others inhabit. Illustrative of how fiction can be used to approach students' different learning styles, Nieckarz gives students the option of writing a traditional research paper or writing a "novel analysis" paper.

Psychology professors are also turning to fiction. Grosofsky (2008) has used literature in his Sensation and Perception course for more than a decade. He pairs each novel with an assignment that directly ties the novel's content to course material. Grosofsky has found the student response to be overwhelmingly positive, suggesting that such a method increases students' motivation and also helps them develop empathy and approach course material in a different way.

Many psychology professors use novels in lieu of case studies. For example, Joan Chrisler (1990) asks her students to examine the main character of a novel who is dealing with mental illness; William Tucker (1994) has his students read short stories in order to consider what conducting therapy with the characters would be like; and Dana Dunn (1999) uses fiction to explore a range of topics including the nature of the self, stress and coping, and issues related to aging (Grosofsky 2008, 272–73).

Fiction is also increasingly used in courses across the disciplines that deal with gender. For example, Hillary Lips uses science fiction in her psychology classes in order to explore gender-based assumptions students typically take for granted; Mary Crawford (1994) asks students in her Psychology of Women course to read romance novels in order to investigate gender stereotypes (Grosofsky 2008, 273).

Amy C. Branam (2008) uses novels in a general education course in order to illustrate the idea of women in literature. They read and gather "evidence" from the novel *Maria*, written in 1798 by Mary Wollstonecraft, and use what they have learned over the semester to explore recurrent questions. At the end of the course they reread *Maria* with a different approach, applying what they have learned over the semester. Branam writes that "by teaching the novel in the general education course, these students see the novel as more than a form of entertainment that is a powerful space for negotiating complex contemporary issues" (ibid., 25).

These examples are just a small sampling of how professors are using fiction. There are many documented cases of fiction being used in general education, history, multiculturalism, ethics, political science, and professional courses (see Irvine 2008).

My Use of Fiction-Based Research in College Classrooms

Since fiction-based research is written with broad audiences in mind, including student audiences, and attends to both aesthetics and substantive content, I encourage professors to consider adding these works to their courses. I have used fiction-based research in my sociology and gender studies courses with great success. While students may not be accustomed to reading fiction outside of literature courses, I have found that when they are told a particular work of fiction was informed by teaching and research experiences, and is considered "arts-based research," they are open to valuing and using the work no differently than a traditional form of nonfiction research (although, as one would expect, they ultimately enjoy reading the fiction far more). Using fiction-based research in the classroom is a wonderful way to engage students, jump-start conversations, get students to think concretely about highly conceptual issues, and open-up the interpretive process in ways that promote critical thinking.

I have used my own novel, *Low-Fat Love*, in the following courses: Sociology of Gender; Images and Power: Popular Culture; and a seminar on Love, Intimacy, and Human Sexuality. These are all elective courses that attract students from across the disciplines, making the use of fiction particularly useful because it creates a "shared experience" and a common "social world" for students to discuss. Depending on the particular content of the course, I asked students to read the novel with certain questions or goals in mind.

For example, in my popular culture course I asked students to highlight all mentions of pop culture as they read the novel and to take note of how the pop culture the characters consumed seemed to be impacting them. I also incorporated small group and/or individual writing assignments based on the novel.

In the human sexuality seminar, students were divided into groups and engaged in a four-part problem-based learning exercise over the course of the semester. In the first part students were given the vague assignment to respond to the question: What is an unhealthy relationship? Typically students focused on issues of physical abuse within the context of romantic relationships, although there was nothing requiring them to do so. Next students read *Low-Fat Love*. After we discussed the book in class, groups reconvened and were again asked: What is an unhealthy relationship? At this point students wrote a significantly more complex, researched, and thoughtful paper that covered verbal and emotional abuse in the context of romantic, peer, and family relationships. Many groups also considered the issue of self-esteem and of having a toxic relationship with oneself.

I have also used Diane Conrad's *Athabasca's Going Unmanned: An Ethnodrama about Incarcerated Youth* (2011) in my sociological theories course with great success. This is a required course for sociology majors and minors, and it is often perceived by students as a "dread" course. *Athabasca's Going Unmanned* is based on several years of research that Conrad did with incarcerated youth in Canada. Conrad took insights from her research and incorporated them into a fictional account of inmates planning an escape plot. I used the book as a supplement to our normal course readings on critical race theory, which is a particularly challenging topic for students to discuss. Much like in the United States, there are a disproportionate number of minority youth represented in the prison system in Canada. I believe this aspect is important, because it was easier for students to discuss these issues in relation to fictional characters and characters operating within what they perceived as a different societal and criminal justice system. I can say without hesitation that using the fiction resulted in the most lively and meaningful course discussion I ever had in that class (which I had taught at least twenty times). Students were given the option of writing a short paper exploring the fictional story using theories learned throughout the course, and almost every student in class took advantage of it. They wrote compelling papers that showed a deep grasp of course content as well as an ability to apply that content to the social world presented in the fictional text.

In each instance in which I have employed fiction-based research as a pedagogical tool in my courses, I have found that student engagement and enthusiasm has increased exponentially. I have also found that the use of fiction-based research has led to a much greater understanding of the traditional course content. I have ample anecdotal evidence from other professors who have used books from the Social Fictions series and reported that the same has been true for them.

Original Examples of Professors Using Fiction in Undergraduate Teaching

As I started working on this book, I naturally discussed the project with colleagues at conferences and the like. I was struck by how many professors responded by telling me how much they love using fiction in their sociology, psychology, education, and other non-literature courses. As a result, when I was compiling this book I asked several well-respected professors, who I consider innovators, to share some of the ways they use fiction in their teaching. Their responses serve as rich examples of how we can incorporate fiction into our pedagogical practices and the rewards for doing so.

Dr. Sandra L. Faulkner is an associate professor of communications at Bowling Green State University and shares the following about how she uses fiction in her courses:

> I teach about relationships and relational processes. Understandably, I hear many personal disclosures during the course, both inside and outside of class. I tell students that one way to

> handle the ethics of disclosure is through fiction. I regularly use short stories as a way to teach about relational processes, such as intimacy readiness, relational hurt, and social support. It can be easier to talk about fictional individuals than those we know. At the same time, the distance afforded with fictional characters creates a safe space to explore the "what ifs" of relational processes, which mirror the writing of good fiction that follows the "what ifs." For example, what if I decided to not have children? What if I decided to break up with my boyfriend? What if I lied to a relational partner?
>
> I also allow students to use fiction as a way of representing a major assignment in relational communication. Students interview men and women about friendships and romantic relationships they have begun since college. They ask about environmental, situational, and characteristics that they believe caused the relationship to form. I encourage students to present the findings in a fictional format such as a photo essay or short story.

From this brief example we can clearly see how Faulkner employs fiction as a pedagogical tool in order to achieve two commonly sought after teaching outcomes: engagement and critical thinking. Beginning with engagement, professors who teach sensitive subjects know it can be very challenging to get students to talk openly. Class discussion is vital to lasting learning, and Faulkner demonstrates how using fictional narratives can create a safe space in which students feel more comfortable talking. Faulkner's use of fiction as a way for students to explore "what ifs" is also an effective method for promoting critical thinking. Engaging students and helping them develop their critical thinking skills is fundamental to education in the twenty-first century. It is also important to note that while most professors incorporate fiction into class through reading assignments, Faulkner uses fiction in both reading and writing assignments—maximizing its pedagogical possibilities.

Dr. Mari Dias is an associate professor of counseling psychology and sociology at Johnson and Wales University. Dr. Dias came into the academy with vast experience in the arts as well as community-based research, so perhaps it is not surprising how she has come to creatively employ fiction in her social science classes.

The use of fiction in the social sciences came to me as a delayed epiphany, albeit a prescient one. I had utilized fiction as a conduit for self-directed change at a men's maximum security prison for over six years before it occurred to me that fiction could play an integral role in the study of sociology. It wasn't until I completed a scholarship research project that measured the impact of literature on empathy levels and locus of control that my serendipitous epiphany blossomed. Why not craft assignments involving literature in my undergraduate sociology courses? After all, our life stories are constructed and embedded in the rich detail and complicated relationships that live within fiction. The use of fiction in the social sciences promised to evoke an etiological discussion, provide a learning climate where exploration and engagement are rife, and hermeneutical discussions are endemic.

Fiction is a rich, textured, descriptive story; the author's way of knowing, that serves as a powerful tool for analysis and application of major sociological concepts. As a social constructivist, I believe that fiction allows us to create meaning of our own world, and the world presented in the novel. This is accomplished through an analysis of the novel through the four sociological perspectives: functionalism, conflict theory, feminism, and symbolic interactionism. The macro-sociological views of functionalism, conflict theory, and the paradigm shifts in the waves of feminism invite us to explore the larger view that includes the historical, geographical, social, and political environments that impact the social construction in the novel and increase the student's sociological imagination. The micro-sociological view of symbolic interactionism allows the student the opportunity to examine a series of individual constructs and social interactions (both inter and intrapersonal) as well as the relationship between them and the novel.

The result of my musings is a trimester-long project that employs fiction as a case-study research methodology. Students are given a suggested reading list, which includes novels whose topics are aligned with our text, including but not limited to: culture, gender roles, deviance, socialization, social structure, and social stratification. Once the students make their choice, groups of four/five are created. Group membership is determined by topic, not necessarily their book choice.

Assignment: "Shades of Soc"
Objective 1: Students will be able to analyze the theme of their novel and apply key concepts of the four sociological perspectives to said theme.
Objective 2: Students will be able to evaluate their personal engagement in self-awareness, self-understanding, and perceptions as evidenced by their response to the individual component of assignment 1b.
Objective 3: Students will be able to write and perform a role-play that includes both the major characters and significant social interactions from their novel.
Objective 4: Students will be able to employ all levels of Bloom's taxonomy in the design and implementation of an outcomes assessment within the framework of a game show format.

1. Each group is to analyze their sociological theme (i.e. gender roles, socialization) from the four major sociological perspectives. They may use an arts-based (poster, role-play, photography, video, etc.) or a traditional writing approach to complete this collaborative assignment. The assignment must be very specific in both the understanding of the perspectives and the interpretation of the novel, and the students must cite specific examples to convincingly argue their views. The assignment should clearly answer the question: How do (functionalists, conflict theorists, feminists, symbolic interactionists) view (gender roles, socialization)? Each student is given a bag that contains four sets of sunglasses, each a different color. Each color represents a sociological perspective, and requires students to literally don different colored glasses during both small group discussions and presentations. In this section, students recognize that they are engaged in a visceral role-taking response to the topic.

The second component of assignment 1 is an individual piece. Students remove all "shades of soc" lenses and discuss their novel from their own individual perspective, including a discussion of their interpersonal relationship with and their intrapersonal reaction to the characters, the social interactions, and the story. This component provides a climate rich and replete with stimulating, heuristic discussions from personal, self-disclosing perspectives. The second phase of the project requires groups to choose one of the sociological perspectives, i.e. feminism, and conduct a literature review on the topic that reveals a deeper, personal investigation of the story. Oftentimes students utilize a mind-mapping technique (the Mac app called MindMeister is a good one) to provide a visual, and often reciprocal, connection of the characters to each other and to their historical, geographical, and social environments.

The third phase of the project requires the groups to share the salient points of their novel with the remainder of the class. This task is accomplished through the use of a role-play. Groups are required to write and perform a one-act role-play that summarizes both their novel and their literature review, and are instructed to follow the script format of *W;t* by Margaret Edson as their template. The role-plays may be performed in real time or as pre-taped videos.

The fourth and last phase of this project is an outcomes assessment. Using all levels of Bloom's taxonomy, groups are required to compile questions and present them to their audience in a game-show format. Students have used games such as "Jeopardy", " Family Feud", "Who wants to be a Millionaire," "Are you Smarter than a Fifth Grader," and "Cash Cab". The results of this outcomes assessment are gratifying; competition is fierce as audience members engage in arduous note-taking during the role-play and vie for the win.

Fiction is a work of imagination. In the book *The Big Bang Theory and Philosophy: Rock, Paper, Scissors, Aristotle, Locke* (2012), Littmann reminds of Aristotle's view on art: [fiction] is universal, as it explores "what could happen." Fiction fuels the reader's imagination, assists students in thinking about humanity and the universe, and facilitates learning by allowing them to explore the human condition and simultaneously learn more about themselves.

Dias's use of fiction in sociology courses illustrate the great potential fiction has for improving the teaching of traditional course content.

Dias has developed a detailed course project in relation to her specific learning objectives. In doing so she is able to use novels as case studies in order to better teach traditional sociological content such as the discipline's major theoretical schools of thought. Her approach to teaching and learning mirrors, and thus reinforces, her learning objectives. Through the engagement that comes with reading, discussing, and analyzing novels, students learn how to construct meanings out of cultural texts. Moreover, as any sociology professor knows, helping students to develop a "sociological imagination" (an ability to link micro- and macro-levels), is the best we can hope for. When used as a case study, fiction carries great potential to stimulate students' "sociological imaginations" and as such pass sociology on to the next generation.

Dr. Rachel McCoppin is an associate professor of ethics at the University of Minnesota, where she creatively uses fiction in her courses:

> Fiction can strengthen students' understanding of ethical theories in introductory ethics courses. Without using fiction as an elaborative example in ethics courses, students often have a difficult time connecting to the "other"; abstract ethical scenarios often do not promote commiseration. Fiction offers expanded ethical situations that instructors can use to help gauge students' understanding of ethical theory. Assigning students to read a piece of fiction that presents an expanded ethical scenario, and then asking them to write a paper applying at least two contradictory ethical theories to the same literary scenario, allows for documented assessment of an often illusory learning outcome common to ethics courses—to demonstrate critical thinking and problem-solving skills by applying ethical theory and philosophy to concrete, often sensitive, situations.
>
> A beneficial and productive assignment for achieving evaluation of critical thinking and problem solving in application of theory to situation is to assign a piece of fiction with at least one lengthy ethical dilemma; though not imperative, a novel is ideal, because the ethical scenarios are expanded, but also novels aide students to become more invested in the developed characters. Assigning the fictional text with the students' initial understanding of the components of the theories of choice is essential. Students should also be encouraged before they begin reading the

text to think about how they would apply the theories as they read. Next, open discussion and class dialogue should be an important part of the assignment to ensure that students understand the plot and character development, and more critically the many implications and severity of the ethical situation/s. As students engage in dialogue, it is necessary to continually ask for differing perspectives on the characters' reasoning of ethical decisions; it should also be stressed, through this course dialogue, that the very nature of ethics demands diversity, so each student's voice is needed in illuminating the depth of ethicality in the fictionalized scenario/s. In addition, this assignment benefits from smaller applications of varying theories addressed within the course. Course discussion could be led with one chosen theory being used to either justify or excuse a character's ethical decisions; then discussion should shift to focus on an opposing theory, looking at how the ethics of the same situation can vastly change depending on the chosen theory. There should be continuous discussion of the importance of diversity to ethics, showing that it only takes a differing perspective or theory to totally change the ethicality of the act. After sufficient course discussion, the students should be instructed to write a six to seven page paper highlighting at least one ethical situation within the novel. Then the student should apply at least two opposing ethical theories to the chosen fictional situation, arguing if he/she feels the character's behavior was ethically "right" or "wrong" based on the theory. In applying opposing theories to the same fictional situation, students will find that what is "right" in one theory can be completely "wrong" in another, thus firming the realization that what is "ethical" often depends on the perspective applied.

Some suggestions of novels that have proved successful with this project, because they provide complex ethical dilemmas that can be analyzed through various theories, include: John Steinbeck's *The Grapes of Wrath*, Fyodor Dostoevsky's *Crime and Punishment*, J. M. Coetzee's *Disgrace*, Kurt Vonnegut's *Mother Night*, Nathaniel Hawthorne's *The Scarlett Letter*, Ray Bradbury's *Fahrenheit 451*, George Orwell's *1984*, Mark Twain's *Huckleberry Finn*, and Chinua Achebe's *Things Fall Apart*.

> This assignment helps students to provide evidence to the instructor that he/she has met the outcome of critical thought and application of ethical theory through an expanded written explanation. If students apply various theories to the studied work of fiction, both in class discussions and in written text, they understand the theory better and provide a documentable way to evaluate that understanding. This assignment helps to guide students into seeing that ethics must be analyzed only through a careful consideration of the importance of diversity. Completion of this assignment not only helps students become stronger at critical thinking, but it also helps them achieve a greater sense of ethical compassion and understanding towards others.

McCopin's use of fiction in her ethics course beautifully illustrates how fiction can be exploited to help students understand abstract ideas. By having her students apply opposing theories to fiction, they are better able to learn course content while simultaneously building their critical thinking and problem-solving skills. Moreover, by reading about, relating to, and empathizing with diverse characters who may be dealing with situations they never had to confront personally, students are able to develop ethical compassion, which is an integral part of an ethics curriculum.

Dr. U. Melissa Anyiwo is an associate professor of history and American studies at Curry College. She incorporates fiction into all of her classes and shares the following brief snippet about her experience.

> American Studies is a discipline that marries multiple elements of culture (literature, history, politics) in order to paint a full picture of the past and present. Literature thus becomes one piece of a complex puzzle. It is accepted practice in history that the voices of the past, through primary sources, are an essential learning tool for students. In that sense, literature provides yet one more primary voice to a topic. Good literature offers a source that reflects the moment in which it was written, and the better the tale the more students can glean about that historical era. For example, discussing the experiences of immigrants in the early years of the century can be dry when taught using

statistics and a traditional textbook style narrative. But when I add Yuri Suhl's *One Foot in America*, a coming-of-age novel about a young Jewish boy's first three years as an immigrant in 1920s Brooklyn, the students report a far greater understanding of what it might have been like to live in that period. The richness of the story presented in a narrative form provides a less intimidating vision of the past than a variety of primary sources. Students read literature in a history class in very different ways than they might in a literature course, focusing more on the overall themes and images of the period, and this helps them add richness and meaning to history and create an overall picture of the past.

Anyiwo began using fiction in her history courses because of the interdisciplinary nature of her training. This indicates that as the academy continues to become more interdisciplinary and transdisciplinary, more professors may be drawn to incorporate fiction into their courses. In Anyiwo's case, she is able to help her students develop a greater understanding of history by focusing on the themes brought forth in fictional works, a process that they enjoy. Here we can see how pairing primary sources with related fiction can greatly enhance student learning.

Finally, Dr. Liora Bresler is a professor in the College of Education at the University of Illinois Urbana-Champaign. In the following piece she shares an assignment she has been using successfully in her field research class for two decades. Whereas her assignment focuses on visual artworks, it can be adapted to the use of fiction.

From the syllabus:
Choose two artworks' focal points/spaces, one that appeals to you and one that does not (either one that evokes aversion or one that leaves you neutral). Stay with each for 30–45 minutes. Take field notes to describe in detail what you see, touch, hear, and smell. Identify themes and issues, reflecting on their significance and relevance for you. What are you curious about? Consider what it is that you would like to learn and what perspectives will enhance your understanding of your chosen focus and

> *your issues. Generate a list of questions to 2–3 people of your choice to expand your understanding. Identify relevant bodies of knowledge and contexts that will enhance your understanding for further inquiry.*
>
> This activity targeting the skills of observations, conceptualizations, and generation of further inquiries intends to build a foundation for subsequent class activities and eventually fieldwork research. On a basic level, this activity seeks to support students/researchers in forming an intensified relationship with a case, getting beyond their habitual rapid ways of seeing and hearing, in the same ways they will need to do with their own research projects. The assignment to focus on two artworks (or, as I used on one occasion, spaces in a mansion), one that they find appealing, that is, that they connect with easily, and another one that they don't, is meant to facilitate two types of journeys. This assignment, I explain in class, is not meant to demonstrate knowledge in history, art, or craft, but is rather centered on noticing and getting to know in a connected, exploratory way. Perception is intimately related to the conceptual activities of identifying emerging themes and issues and is required for synthesis (as indicated, for example, in the interpretation of titles).
>
> I have been using this assignment for many (twenty) years and have found this to be effective in helping us go beyond a reductionist "judgment" towards an expanded, intensified perception and meaning-making. It allows the students to make their own choices, identify their inner curiosities and "areas of resonance" and own their voices. These are foundational to all research. In this case, the focus is on fieldwork, where theories and scholarship support their quests and explorations.

We can see how Bresler creatively prepares her students for fieldwork by turning to an arts-based pedagogy. Through this assignment she increases the students' perception and observation skills, which are important aspects of field research. It can be difficult to find ways to cultivate these skills in novices. Bresler's assignment could easily be adapted to use fiction. I think the assignment would work very well with two short stories as the focal point.

Conclusion

One could easily write an entire book on fiction as pedagogy. Therefore, in this chapter I have tried to introduce you to some of the ways in which fiction can be used in accord with teaching goals, and perhaps even to expand on those goals. As noted from the outset, teaching strategies should always be aligned with learning objectives. Therefore, as you develop assignments to incorporate fiction into your courses, begin by detailing your desired learning outcomes, which may be content-based or may center on cultivating critical thinking or problem-solving skills, raising critical consciousness, disrupting stereotypes or dominant ideology, or promoting social reflection or self-awareness. As you adapt some of the assignments you read about in this chapter or as you develop your own, bear in mind that there will be some measure of trial and error, and this is just a part of the process. Above everything else, remember that teaching and learning should be joyful and engaged experiences, and it is here that the potential of fiction is bottomless.

Appendix A
Writing Prompts

> A writing prompt is simply a topic around which you start jotting down ideas. The prompt could be a single word, a short phrase, a complete paragraph or even a picture, with the idea being to give you something to focus upon as you write. You may stick very closely to the original prompt or you may wander off on a tangent.
>
> —Simon Kewin, "Writing Posts 101" (dailywritingtips.com blog)

Writing prompts are commonly used by commercial authors as a means of sparking creativity, getting the creative juices flowing, and exercising the writer's muscle. Academic writers are rarely taught to use writing prompts, but I highly recommend them for both novice and experienced writers, especially if you are new to fiction. There are three primary reasons for researchers writing fiction to work with prompts: 1) sparking creativity; 2) learning to use the tools of fiction; and 3) discipline.

With respect to sparking your creative juices and learning how to employ fictive techniques, it is important to understand that writing prompts are tools to jump-start your writing and do not typically result in a part of your final project. Writing prompts may be based on the topic you wish to write about but need not be, and often are not. Using writing prompts is also an excellent way to get into the habit of writing regularly. Writing fiction takes discipline, and prompts can be used as a way of incorporating writing into your daily schedule even if you aren't ready to work on a large project.

You can use any of the following sources to develop a writing prompt: a headline from a newspaper or magazine; the opening sentence of a book or story; a tweet or a post from Facebook; a photograph or image from a magazine or online source; or an object in your home, office, or somewhere else. Here is how to use the prompts:

- Take a headline from a newspaper or magazine and use it as the title of a story. Just start writing.
- Use the opening sentence of a book or story and keep writing your own story.
- Use a tweet or a post from Facebook as a title for a story and start writing.
- Take a photograph or an image from a magazine or online source and describe it in detail. As an alternative, use the image as the basis for a story. If it is a picture of a person, create a character using the image as your inspiration.
- Take an object in your home, office, or somewhere else and describe it in great detail so that someone who isn't present can envision it. As an alternative, create a story about where the object came from, who uses it, and why.

Again, none of the preceding prompts are meant to be a part of your ultimate writing; however, I recommend saving everything you write in a file, because you never know when a word, phrase, idea, or segment of writing will be applicable to something you are working on.

If you want to use a prompt that more directly relates to your research topic, you can develop opening sentences related to it. For example, if your topic is body image your prompts might be:

- The mirror was her enemy.
- He wanted to be bigger since high school.
- They went to the bathroom together every day after lunch.
- The images in the magazines mocked her.
- No matter what she did, her hair would never look like the models she so admired.

Now create some prompts based on your research topic.
State your research topic as a word or phrase: ____________________.
Next, create five short opening sentences, or "prompts," based on your topic:
1. ____
2. ____
3. ____
4. ____
5. ____
If you are working in class with others or in a writing group, ask a peer for a word or phrase that is significant to his/her research. Write it here: ____

Now write five prompts for your peer and have him/her do the same for you.

1. ____
2. ____
3. ____
4. ____
5. ____

Please note if you are working on your own you can ask a friend to write the prompts for you—they don't need to know anything about your topic. Alternatively Faulkner (2009) suggests using an interview transcript, literature review source or photo from field research as a prompt. To do so, use any of those sources of inspiration as a spark to free write.

Appendix B
Exercises for Transforming Your Research into Fiction

When you are ready to start transforming your research project into a work of fiction, it can be helpful to start with some warm-up exercises (which can be done on your own, in class, or in a writing group). Here are some examples:

- If you're writing a full-length work, such as a novel, try writing the press release for your novel. Consider issues like what the book is about, how it relates to people's lives and interests, and what makes it special. Although your final product may bear little similarity to this faux release, the process of writing it may help you get a better grasp of your focus and major themes.

  If you have conducted research with participants, such as interviews or field research, develop a character profile based on one of your participants. Think about how you would describe the character and his/her major values or motivations, challenges, and family and friendship network. Just sketch your ideas.

  o Once you are warmed up, you may want to complete this activity for all of your characters. To do so you will need to decide if you are creating characters based on each participant or if you are relying on the more common practice of creating composite characters. When you are writing your narrative the characters may change and evolve, but developing these sketches will jump-start your writing and ground you.

- Use a concept or term from your literature review and free write everything that comes to mind when you hear that term. Alternatively, try writing about how that concept or term might impact an individual (even a fictitious individual).

When you are warmed up and ready to start writing your fiction-based research, you will need to consider the research design issues discussed in part I. In particular, you will need to make decisions about where your project sits on the continuum between traditional research methods and writing as research (see chapter 3). The kind of project you are engaged in will help direct your writing efforts. For example, if you have conducted research using a traditional method (such as interviews or field research), you will need to make decisions about how closely you are sticking to the data, how you are using literature, and how you want to represent your voice. Some questions to consider include:

- How will you represent your participants as characters? Will you create composite characters? How will you give them multidimensionality?
- What tense will you be writing in, and why?
- Who is the narrator?
- How will you weave concepts from the literature into the story? For example, will you do this through the voice of the narrator?
- What themes emerged in your research that you want to tap into?

You should have your materials—transcripts, field notes, literature review—nearby as you write. If you are writing your work based on a breadth of experience—research, teaching, and/or personal—you will need to consider issues such as:

- What themes do you want to tap into? What issues do you want to get at?
- Who are the main characters, and what activities are they engaged in? How will you use details and specificity to make the characters come to life and to make them relatable and empathetic? What environments and interactions will we find them in? What is the psychological profile of each character?
- Who is the narrator? What access does the narrator have into the minds of the characters?

Everyone writes differently. For some, once they have decided what kind of project they are writing—once they have made some of the major decisions reviewed above and know what their goals are and what data and/or experiences they are drawing on—the best thing to do is sit and just start writing, either without a plan at all (which is how I wrote *Low-Fat Love*) or with a plot sketch, even if rough (which is how I am writing *American Circumstance*). For others, starting free-form writing is impossible and can lead to staring at a blank computer screen. If you want to use some strategies to start building your project, try some of the following:

- Write a character profile for your protagonist.
- Write a general plotline:
    - How does the story begin?
    - What event or events transpire?
    - What is the central conflict?
    - How does the story end?
- Write a storyline with specific scenes that get you from the beginning to the end of your plot.
- Use your storyline to start writing, beginning with the opening scene. You can always change it later, so just start writing.

Appendix C

Tips for Getting Published

Writing takes practice and patience, and getting your work published does too. Writing fiction-based research is a rigorous act that requires attention to the craft of literary writing as well as to the usefulness of the resulting text. As with any writing endeavor, the best advice is: practice, revise, proof, repeat, and then repeat some more. Work with writing groups and writing buddies, if you find it helpful. As you try to publish your work don't be discouraged by rejections, they are a normal part of the process and simply mean that the particular publisher is not the right fit. As we push on the bounds of art and research there can be resistance, so it is important to remain steadfast, do work that is meaningful to you, and always bet on yourself. Once you have published your work, make peace with it and let it go so you can move on to the next creative project. For now, here are some tips to help you publish your work.

- Before you seek a publisher, think about how you want to package your writing: Who is the intended audience? What are the major contributions of the work? Answering these questions will help lead you to appropriate kinds of publishers. Also, you should be able to describe your work concisely. I recommend writing a one- or two-sentence description, a one-paragraph description, and a one-page description to have on hand as needed. If you are seeking a literary agent (see below) you will also need a query letter and a synopsis of your book that follows the agent's guidelines.
- For shorter pieces like short stories, look at online journals and e-zines—these can be great venues for beginners in particular (often easier to get your work published, to garner feedback from readers, and to develop your portfolio). Several leading qualitative research and art education journals now publish arts-based research.
- For longer works like novels and novellas, you will either need to seek a publisher (with a record of publishing arts-based research or fiction) or

you will need to get a literary agent to do your bidding for you (if you want to publish with a trade press you will probably need an agent, although some now have digital imprints that do accept un-agented author submissions through online submission systems).

- o Publishers: If you are looking for an academic or small press and plan to approach it on your own, there are a few things you can do to increase your chances: do your research so that you are approaching appropriate publishers, spend as much time proofing and revising your proposal as you did on the work itself (it is the first and possibly only thing they will read), try to get face time with publishers at conferences or book shows (and be prepared to answer questions about the market for your work), and then follow up.
- o Literary Agents: There are many books available that can assist you locate potential literary agents and instruct you as to how to write a strong query letter and synopsis. You can also look online, because many agents write blogs with tips for how to attract a good agent. I also suggest perusing your local bookstore—look at the acknowledgments in books that you think are similar to your own. Authors often thank their agents and this can help you make a list of people to approach. It is very tough to get an agent, so be prepared to send out a lot of emails and letters, most of which you will not receive a response to. Don't be discouraged. Finding a good agent is like finding a good life partner, so if the fit isn't right, move on.

- Follow instructions when you contact literary agents or publishers. If an agent asks you to send the first five pages of your manuscript, resist the urge to send more than that. Agents and publishers are bombarded with submissions, and if you can't follow basic instructions they will not consider your work. As an example, as a book series editor I put out a call for fiction-based research that specifically asked for a brief synopsis and the first ten pages only of the text. Someone sent me their entire manuscript with an email that said she felt like sending just ten pages was like cutting a portrait and submitting only the toe. I didn't read her work.
- When you do secure a publisher, share your production and promotion ideas. If you have ideas about cover design, formatting, and back cover content be sure to share this with your publisher. Although they have more experience than you do, which is very valuable, no one has spent more time thinking about your work than you. See your vision through while remaining open to learning from the expertise of others.
- Once your work is published, market it. Many authors miss opportunities to build their audience (and thereby create more publishing opportunities) because they expect publishers to do all of the marketing for

them. You are the person most qualified to sell your work. The more you involve yourself in promotion efforts, the more your work will be read. Some practical things you can do are: ask your publisher for a press release for your book (or create one yourself) and send it to relevant mailing lists, online journals, and e-zines; solicit reviews from readers or colleagues for online retailers; and enter your work in contests or nominate it for relevant awards. You can always enlist the assistance of a publicist too. This isn't difficult like getting an agent but it is costly (some publishers are willing to share these costs with you, and it never hurts to ask and advocate for yourself and your work).

Appendix D
Recommended Resources

Further Reading on Literary Neuroscience

https://www2.bc.edu/~richarad/lcb/home.html
Annotated Bibliography of Literature, Cognition & The Brain maintained by Alan Richardson (Boston College). The site contains book recommendations, links to articles and websites, and conference presentations. Great resource.

Online Sources That Generate Writing Prompts

https://www.CreativeWritingPrompts.com
https://www.SundayScribblings.blogspot.com
https:// www.OneMinuteWriter.blogspot.com
twitter.com/writingprompt
twitter.com/NoTelling
twitter.com/writingink

Journals That Publish Arts-Based Research

CTheory (http://www.CTheory.net): This free online journal publishes cutting edge research on the borders of pop culture, technology, politics, theory, and methodology. They typically publish work in alternative writing genres, including fiction-based work.

International Journal of Education through Art (Intellect): Focuses on arts in education.

International Review of Qualitative Research (University of California Press): This journal focuses on experimental forms of qualitative research including arts-based research.

Journal of Curriculum and Pedagogy (Educators International Press): This journal publishes one short essay on arts-based educational research (ABER) in each issue.

Qualitative Inquiry (Sage): A qualitative research journal that publishes articles and essays about arts-based research, including the products of arts-based research.

The International Journal of Education & the Arts (free email journal): Focuses on arts in education.

The Qualitative Report (http://www.nova.edu/sss//QR/index.html): A free online journal that publishes articles and essays about arts-based research, including the products of arts-based research. There is also a free weekly version that can be received by signing up on their website. The weekly version contains notices about publishing opportunities (journals and book editors seeking submissions).

Reed Magazine: A Journal of Poetry and Prose (San Jose State University): This literary magazine publishes poetry and short stories from around the United States.

Small Presses That Publish Fiction-Based Research

Backalong Books (Big Tancook Island, Nova Scotia, Canada) publishes alternative-genre books with commercial and academic audiences in mind, including arts-based research and fiction.

Sense Publishers (Rotterdam, The Netherlands) publishes the Social Fictions series, which features exclusively fiction-based research intended for use in college classrooms.

Notes

Chapter 1

1. Kip Jones (2006, 12) suggests that "novelty always makes people uncomfortable."
2. It is important to note that in the early history of scholarship, the arts were not artificially severed from the sciences, as evidenced for example by the earlier link between mathematics and poetry.
3. There are different terms that appear in the literature to describe arts-based research or related practices—for example, arts-based educational research (ABER), A/R/tography (A/R/T), and arts-informed inquiry.
4. For a full discussion of the emergence of arts-based research, please see my book *Method Meets Art: Arts-Based Research Practice* (2009a).
5. Other genres one might review include literary nonfiction and memoir.
6. "Nonfiction novel" appears to be a similar term to "historical novel"—both of which could be viewed oxymoronically, but more accurately, as the inevitable blurring of fiction and nonfiction.
7. In this regard fiction is a way of tapping into the "sociological imagination" (Wright Mills 1959) that exists at the intersection of personal biography (micro-level) and sociohistorical forces (macro-level).
8. Lee Gutkind was termed, to his dismay, "the godfather of creative nonfiction" in *Vanity Fair* magazine in 1997. Gutkind suggests that although he used the term "creative nonfiction" in the 1970s, he has only been able to trace the official use of the term to 1983, when it was used at a meeting held by the National Endowment for the Arts.

Chapter 2

1. I have talked about the idea of conceiving research in "new shapes" in previous work (see Leavy 2009a, 2011a) and in conference presentations (for example at the 2012 International Congress of Qualitative Inquiry).
2. It is worth noting that for some there is no middle ground between fiction and nonfiction (Abbott 2008). For example, Dorrit Cohn (2000) suggests

that while both forms involve story and discourse, only nonfiction explicitly references the empirical world.
3. Banks and Banks borrow the term "possible worlds" from Ruth Ronen (1994).
4. The issue of how to label or present fiction as research is discussed in the next two chapters. This is an important issue when considering fiction as a research practice.
5. This section is influenced by Ketelle (2004), who draws heavily on Wittgenstein.
6. Second-person narration involves a narrator who is also clearly a character in the text; however, this is by far the least common way of writing fiction and I believe the least likely to suit the needs of qualitative researchers, so I will not specifically review this style.
7. How much information a writer discloses about the generation of the work is linked to the work's purpose and the way it is published and disseminated. This is discussed in later chapters.

Chapter 3

1. I am influenced by Porter Abbott (2008), who uses the term "the architecture of narrative."
2. Elizabeth de Freitas (2004, 267) insightfully suggests that narrative is a form of open argument.
3. Johnny Saldana (2003) distinguishes between plot and storyline in his writing about ethnodrama. I am influenced by his explanation of these terms.
4. Please note that the term archetype also frequently appears in the literature. Renowned psychologist Carl Jung posited that archetypes are born out of the collective unconscious.

Chapter 4

1. See Leavy (2010) for an earlier discussion of usefulness as a key evaluative criterion in ABR.
2. An alternative way to present this list of criteria would be to distinguish audience and disclosure as two separate criteria. I have decided to discuss audience and disclosure together because when we talk about the presentation of the text we are talking about presenting it to an audience. Therefore, I see audience and disclosure as linked, though they could certainly be conceptualized as distinct criteria.

Chapter 10

1. A problem-centric approach to teaching parallels a problem-centered approach to research. Indeed, as Finkel (2000) writes about teaching in new shapes, I have suggested that we need to conceive of our research in new shapes (Leavy 2009b, 2011a, 2012).

References

Abbott, H. P. 2008. *The Cambridge Introduction to Narrative*. 2nd ed. Cambridge, UK: Cambridge University Press.

Banks, S. P. 2008. Writing as Theory: In Defense of Fiction. In J. G. Knowles and A. L. Cole (eds.), *Handbook of the Arts in Qualitative Research*, 155–64. Thousand Oaks, CA: Sage.

Banks, S. P. and A. Banks. 1998. The Struggle Over Facts and Fictions. In A. Banks and S. P. Banks (eds.), *Fiction and Social Research: By Fire or Ice*, 11–29. Walnut Creek, CA: AltaMira Press.

Barone, T. and E. W. Eisner. 1997. Arts-Based Educational Research. In M. Jaeger (ed.) *Complimentary Methods for Research in Education*, 73–116. 2nd ed. Washington, DC: American Educational Research Association.

———. 2012. *Arts-Based Research*. Thousand Oaks, CA: Sage.

Behar, R. 1995. Introduction: Out of Exile. In R. Behar and D. A. Gordon (eds.), *Women Writing Culture*, 1–29. Berkeley, CA: University of California Press.

Berger, M. 1977. *Real and Imagined Worlds: The Novel and Social Science*. Cambridge, MA: Harvard University Press.

Bochner, A. 2000. "Criteria against Ourselves." *Qualitative Inquiry* 6(2), 266–72.

Bochner, A. and C. Ellis. 1998. Series Editors' Introduction. In A. Banks and S. P. Banks (eds.), *Fiction and Social Research: By Fire or Ice*, 7–8. Walnut Creek, CA: AltaMira Press.

Booth, W. C. 1961. *The Rhetoric of Fiction*. Chicago, IL: University of Chicago Press.

Bowles, S. and H. Gintis. 1976. *Schooling in Capitalist America: Educational Reform and the Contradictions of Economic Life*. New York, NY: Basic Books.

Boyne, J. 2006. *The Boy in the Striped Pajamas*. Denver, CO: Ember.

Branam, A. C. 2008. Reading Wollstonecraft's Maria from Cover to Cover and Back Again: The Novel in the General Education Course. In C. C. Irvine (ed.), *Teaching the Novel across the Curriculum: A Handbook for Educators*, 13–27. Westport, CT: Greenwood Press.

Brookfield, S. 2006. *The Skillful Teacher: On Technique, Trust, and Responsiveness in the Classroom*. San Francisco, CA: Jossey-Bass.
Cahnmann-Taylor, M. and Siegesmund, R. 2008. *Arts-Based Research in Education: Foundations for Practice*. New York, NY: Taylor & Francis.
Capote, T. 1965. *In Cold Blood: A True Account of Multiple Murder and Its Consequences*. New York, NY: Random House.
Caulley, D. N. 2008. "Making Qualitative Research Reports Less Boring: The Techniques of Writing Creative Nonfiction." *Qualitative Inquiry* 4(3), 424–49.
Cheney, T. A. R. 2001. *Writing Creative Nonfiction: Fiction Techniques for Crafting Great Nonfiction*. Berkeley, CA: Ten Speed Press.
Chrisler, J. C. 1990. "Novels as Case Study Materials for Psychology Students." *Teaching of Psychology* 17(1), 55–57.
Clough, P. 2002. *Narratives and Fictions in Educational Research*. Buckingham, UK: Open University Press.
Coffey, A. 1999. *The Ethnographic Self: Fieldwork and the Representation of Identity*. Thousand Oaks, CA: Sage.
Cohn, D. 2000. *The Distinction of Fiction*. Baltimore, MD: The Johns Hopkins University Press.
Cole, A. L. and J. G. Knowles. 2001. Qualities of Inquiry: Process, Form, and "Goodness." In L. Nielsen, A. L. Cole, and J. G. Knowles (eds.), *The Art of Writing Inquiry*, 211–29. Halifax, Nova Scotia, Canada: Backalong Books.
Cole, A. L., L. Neilsen, J. G. Knowles, and T. C. Luciani. 2004. Introduction. In A. L. Cole, L. Neilsen, J. G. Knowles, and T. C. Luciani (eds.), *Provoked by Art: Theorizing Arts-Informed Research*, vi–vii. Halifax, Nova Scotia, Canada: Backalong Books.
Colebrook, C. 2002. *Gilles Deleuze*. New York, NY: Routledge.
Conrad, D. 2011. *Athabasca's Going Unmanned: An Ethnodrama about Incarcerated Youth*. Rotterdam, The Netherlands: Sense Publishers.
Coser, L. A. 1963. *Sociology through Literature: An Introductory Text*. Engelwood Cliffs, NJ: Prentice Hall.
Crawford, M. 1994. "Rethinking the Romance: Teaching the Content and Function of Gender Stereotypes in the Psychology of Women Course." *Teaching of Psychology* 21(3), 151–53.
Dellasega, C. 2001a. *Surviving Ophelia: Mothers Share Their Wisdom in Navigating the Tumultuous Teen Years*. New York, NY: Ballantine Books.
________. 2001b. *The Starving Family: Caregiving Mothers and Fathers Share Their Eating Disorder*. Fredonia, WI: Wisdom Champion Press.
________. (forthcoming). *Waiting Room*. Rotterdam, The Netherlands: Sense Publishers.

De Freitas, E. 2003. "Contested Positions: How Fiction Informs Empathetic Research." *International Journal of Education & The Arts* 4(7). http://www.ijea.org/v4n7/.

———. 2004. Reclaiming Rigour as Trust: The Playful Process of Writing Fiction. In A. L. Cole, L. Neilsen, J. G. Knowles, and T. C. Luciani (eds.), *Provoked by Art: Theorizing Arts-Informed Research*. Halifax, Nova Scotia, Canada: Backalong Books.

———. 2007. "Compos(t)ing Presence in the Poetry of Carl Leggo: Writing Practices That Disperse the Presence of the Author." *Language & Literacy* 9(1). http://www.langandlit.ualberta.ca/Spring2007/deFreitas.htm.

———. 2008. "Bad Intentions: Using Fiction to Interrogate Research Intentions." *Educational Insights* 12(1). http://www/ccfi.educ.ubc.ca/publication/insights/v12n01/articles/defreitas/index.html.

De Jong, R. N. 1982. *A History of American Neurology*. New York, NY: Raven Press.

DeMarrais, K. B. and M. D. LeCompte. 1995. *The Way Schools Work: A Sociological Analysis of Education*. White Plains, NY: Longman.

Dillard, A. 1982. *Living by Fiction*. New York, NY: Harper & Row.

Dunlop, R. 2001. Excerpts from Boundary Bay: A Novel as Educational Research. In L. Neilsen, A. L. Cole, and J. G. (eds.), *The Art of Writing Inquiry*, 11–25. Halifax, Nova Scotia, Canada: Backalong Books.

Dunn, D. S. 1999. Interpreting the Self through Literature: Psychology and the Novels of Wallace Stegner. In L. T. Benjamin, B. F. Nodine, R. M. Ernst, and C. B. Broeker (eds.), *Activities Handbook for the Teaching of Psychology*, 362–65. Washington, DC: American Psychological Association.

Eisner, E. 2002. *The Arts and the Creation of Mind*. New Haven, CT: Yale University Press.

———. 2008. "Commentary: What Education Can Learn from the Arts." *LEARNing Landscapes* 2(1), 23–30.

Faulkner, S. 2009. *Poetry as Method: Reporting Research through Verse*. Walnut Creek, CA: Left Coast Press.

Finkel, D. 2000. *Teaching with Your Mouth Shut*. Portsmouth, NH: Boynton/Cook.

Finley, S. and J. G. Knowles. 1995. "Researchers as Artist/Artist as Researcher." *Qualitative Inquiry* 1(1), 110–42.

Fitchen, J. M. 1981. *Poverty in Rural America: A Case Study*. Boulder, CO: Westview Press.

Franklin, R. 2011. *A Thousand Darknesses: Lies and Truth in Holocaust Fiction*. New York, NY: Oxford University Press.

Freire, P. 1998. *Pedagogy of Freedom: Ethics, Democracy, and Civic Courage*. Trans. by Patrick Clarke. Boulder, CO: Roman & Littlefield

Geertz, C. 1973. *The Interpretation of Cultures*. New York, NY: Basic Books.

Glesne, C. and A. Peshkin. 1992. *Becoming Qualitative Researchers: An Introduction*. White Plains, NY: Longman Press.

Goodall, H. L. 2000. *Writing the New Ethnography*. Walnut Creek, CA: AltaMira Press.

________. 2008. *Writing Qualitative Inquiry: Self, Stories, and Academic Life*. Walnut Creek, CA: Left Coast Press.

Gosse, D. 2005. *Jackytar: A Novel*. St. Johns, Canada: Jesperson Publishing.

________. 2008. Queering Identity(ies) and Fiction Writing in Qualitative Research. In M. Cahnmann-Taylor and R. Siegsmund (eds.), *Arts-Based Research in Education: Foundations for Practice*, 182–93. New York, NY: Taylor & Francis.

Grealy, L. 2003. *Autobiography of a Face*. New York, NY: Harper Perennial.

Greene, M. 2008. "Commentary. Education and the Arts: The Windows of Imagination." *LEARNing Landscapes* 2(1), 17–21.

Grosofsky, A. 2008. Stories in Psychology: Sensation and Perception. In C. C. Irvine (ed.), *Teaching the Novel across the Curriculum: A Handbook for Educators*, 272–77. Westport, CT: Greenwood Press.

Gutkind, L. 1997. *The Art of Creative Nonfiction: Writing and Selling the Literature of Reality*. New York, NY: Wiley.

________. 2012. *You Can't Make This Stuff Up: The Complete Guide to Writing Creative Nonfiction—From Memoir to Literary Journalism and Everything In Between*. Boston, MA: Da Capo/Lifelong Books.

Harrison, F. V. 1995. Writing Against the Grain: Cultural Politics of Difference in the Work of Alice Walker. In R. Behar and D. A. Gordon (eds.), *Women Writing Culture*, 233–45. Berkeley, CA: University of California Press.

Hesse-Biber, S. and P. Leavy. 2005. *The Practice of Qualitative Research*. Thousand Oaks, CA: Sage.

________. 2011. *The Practice of Qualitative Research*. 2nd ed. Thousand Oaks, CA: Sage.

Hoffer, C. R. 1973. *Teaching Music in the Secondary Schools*. 2nd ed. Belmont, CA: Wadsworth Publishing.

hooks, b. 1994. *Teaching to Transgress: Education as the Practice of Freedom*. New York, NY: Routledge.

Hunsaker-Hawkins, A. 1999. *Reconstructing illness: Studies in Pathography*. West Lafayette, IN: Purdue University Press.

Irvine, C. C. 2008. Introduction. In C. C. Irvine (ed.), *Teaching the Novel across the Curriculum: A Handbook for Educators*, 1–11. Westport, CT: Greenwood Press.

Iser, W. 1980. *The Act of Reading: A Theory of Aesthetic Response*. Baltimore, MD: The Johns Hopkins University Press.

———. 1997. "The Significance of Fictionalizing." *Anthropoetics* III(2), 1–9. http://www.anthropoetics.ucla.edu/ap0302/iser_fiction.htm.

Jones, K. 2006. "A Biographic Researcher in Pursuit of an Aesthetic: The Use of Arts-Based (Re)Presentations in "Performative" Dissemination of Life Stories." *Qualitative Sociology Review* 2(1). www.qualitativesociologyreview.org/ENG/index_eng.php.

Kamen, P. 2006. *All in My Head: An epic Quest to Cure an Unrelenting, Totally Unreasonable, and Only Slightly Enlightening Headache*. Cambridge, MA: Da Capo Press.

Keneally, T. 1982. *Schindler's List*. New York: Simon & Schuster.

Ketelle, D. 2004. "Writing Truth as Fiction: Administrators Think About Their Work Through a Different Lens." *The Qualitative Report* 9(3), 449–62.

Lakoff, G. and M. Johnson. 1980. *Metaphors We Live By*. Chicago, IL: University of Chicago Press.

Langer, L. 1977. *The Holocaust and the Literary Imagination*. New Haven, CT: Yale University Press.

Leavy, P. 2009a. *Method Meets Art: Arts-Based Research Practice*. New York, NY: Guilford Press.

———. 2009b. "Arts-Based Research as a Pedagogical Tool for Teaching Media Literacy: Reflections from an Undergraduate Classroom." *LEARNing Landscapes* 3(1), 225–41.

———. 2010. "Poetic Bodies: Female Body Image, Sexual Identity and Arts-Based Research." *LEARNing Landscapes* 4(1), 175–88.

———. 2011a. *Essentials of Transdisciplinary Research: Using Problem-Centered Methodologies*. Walnut Creek, CA: Left Coast Press.

———. 2011b. *Low-Fat Love*. Rotterdam, The Netherlands: Sense Publishers.

———. (forthcoming). *American Circumstance*. Rotterdam, The Netherlands: Sense Publishers.

Leggo, C. 2012. *Sailing in a Concrete Boat: A Teacher's Journey*. Rotterdam, The Netherlands: Sense Publishers.

Lennon, J. 2008. Novel Truths: The Things They Carried and Student Narratives about History. In C. C. Irvine (ed.), *Teaching the Novel across the Curriculum: A Handbook for Educators*, 169–78. Westport, CT: Greenwood Press.

Littmann, G. 2012. Aristotle on Sheldon Cooper: Ancient Greek Meets Modern Greek. In D. Kowalski and W. Irvin (eds.), *The Big Bang Theory and Philosophy: Rock, Paper, Scissors, Aristotle, Locke*, 7–20. Hoboken, NJ: John Wiley & Sons.

Mauss, M. 1947. *Manuel d'ethnographie*. Edited by D. Pauline. Paris, France: Payot.

McCoppin, R. 2008. Questioning Ethics: Incorporating the Novel into Ethics Courses. In C. C. Irvine (ed.), *Teaching the Novel across the Curriculum: A Handbook for Educators*, 179–93. Westport, CT: Greenwood Press.

McIntyre, M. 2001. The Artfulness of the Everyday: Researcher Identities and Arts-Informed Research. In A. L. Cole, L. Neilsen, J. G. Knowles, and T. C. Luciani (eds.), *Provoked by Art: Theorizing Arts-Informed Research*, 220–27. Halifax, Nova Scotia, Canada: Backalong Books.

Nieckarz, P. P. Jr. 2008. Science Fiction as Social Fact: Review and Evaluation of the Use of Fiction in an Introductory Sociology Class. In C. C. Irvine (ed.), *Teaching the Novel across the Curriculum: A Handbook for Educators*, 231–47. Westport, CT: Greenwood Press.

Norris, J. 2009. *Playbuilding as Qualitative Research: A Participatory Arts-Based Approach*. Walnut Creek, CA: Left Coast Press.

Oates, J. C. 1997. *We Were the Mulvaneys*. New York, NY: Plume Publishers.

Pennebaker, J. 1997. *Opening Up: The Healing Power of Expressing Emotions*. New York, NY: Guilford Press.

Richardson, L. 1990. *Writing Strategies: Reaching Diverse Audiences*. Newbury Park, CA: Sage.

________. 2001. Alternative Ethnographies, Alternative Criteria. In L. Nelson, A. L. Cole, and J. G. Knowles (eds.), *The Art of Writing Inquiry*, 250–52. Halifax, Nova Scotia, Canada: Backalong Books.

________. 2004. Creative Analytical Practice (CAP) Ethnography. In M. S. Lewis-Back, A. Bryman, and T. Futing Liao (eds.), *The Sage Encyclopedia of Social Science Research Methods*. http://srmo.sagepub.com/view/the-sage-encyclopedia-of-social-science-research-methods/n188.xml.

Ronen, R. 1994. *Possible Worlds in Literary Theory*. Cambridge, UK: Cambridge: Cambridge University Press.

Roney, L. 2000. *Sweet Invisible Body: Reflections on Life with Diabetes*. New York, NY: Owl Books.

Rosenblatt, L. M. 1978. *The Reader, the Text, the Poem: The Transactional Theory of the Literary Work*. Carbondale, IL: Southern Illinois University Press.

Ryan, M. 1991. *Possible Worlds, Artificial Intelligence, and Narrative Theory*. Bloomington, IN: Indiana University Press.

Saldana, J. 2003. Dramatizing Data: A Primer. *Qualitative Inquiry* 9(2), 218–36.

________. 2011. *The Fundamentals of Qualitative Research: Understanding Qualitative Research*. New York, NY: Oxford University Press.

Schroeder, G.F. 2008. Novels in History Classes: Teaching the Historical Context. In C. C. Irvine (ed.), *Teaching the Novel across the Curriculum: A Handbook for Educators*, 204–18. Westport, CT: Greenwood Press.

Semprun, J. 1998. *Literature or Life*. Trans. by L. Coverdale. New York, NY: Penguin Books.

Simeone, D. P. 2008. Usefulness of Lord of the Flies in the Social Psychology Classroom. In C. C. Irvine (ed.), *Teaching the Novel across the Curriculum: A Handbook for Educators*, 278–85. Westport, CT: Greenwood Press.

Sinner, A., C. Leggo, R. Irwin, P. Gouzouasis, and K. Grauer. 2006. "Arts-Based Education Research Dissertations: Reviewing the Practices of New Scholars." *Canadian Journal of Education* 29(4), 1223–70.

St. Pierre, E.A. 2004. Circling the Text: Nomadic Writing Practices. In N. K. Denzin and Y. S. Lincoln (eds.), *The Qualitative Inquiry Reader*, 51–69. Thousand Oaks, CA: Sage Publications.

Stronach, I. and M. Maclure. 1997. *Educational Research Undone: The Postmodern Embrace*. Buckingham, UK: Open University Press.

Thomas, S. 2001. Reimagining Inquiry, Envisioning Form. In L. Nielsen, A. L. Cole, and J. G. Knowles (eds.), *The Art of Writing Inquiry*, 273–82. Halifax, Nova Scotia, Canada: Backalong Books.

Thompson, H. and S. Vedantam. 2012. "A Lively Mind: Your Brain on Jane Austen." NPR Health Blog. http://www.npr.org/blogs/health/2012/10/09/162401053/a-lively-mind-your-brain-on-jane-austen.html.

Todman, D. 2007. "Letter to the Editor. More on Literature and the History of Neuroscience: Using the Writings of Silas Wier Mitchell (1829–1914) in Teaching the History of Neuroscience." *The Journal of Undergraduate Neuroscience Education* 6(1), L1.

Tucker, W. 1994. "Teaching Psychiatry through Literature: The Short Story as Case History." *Academic Psychiatry* 18, 211–19.

Turner, M. 1996. *The Literary Mind: The Origins of Thought and Language*. New York, NY: Oxford University Press.

Van Maanen, J. 1988. *Tales of the Field*. Chicago, IL: University of Chicago Press.

Visweswaran, K. 1994. *Fictions of Feminist Ethnography*. Minneapolis, MN: University of Minnesota Press.

Wilentz, A. 2002. *Martyrs' Crossing*. New York, NY: Ballantine Books.

Wittgenstein, L. 1953. *Philosophical Investigations*. Oxford, UK: Blackwell.

Wolff, K. B. 2008. Reading our Social Worlds: Utilizing Novels in Introduction to Sociology Courses. In C. C. Irvine (ed.), *Teaching the Novel across the Curriculum: A Handbook for Educators*, 219–30. Westport, CT: Greenwood Press.

Wright Mills, C. 1959. *The Sociological Imagination*. New York, NY: Oxford University Press.

Wurtzel, E. 2002. *Prozac Nation*. New York, NY: Riverhead Trade Books.

Yagoda, B. 2010. *Memoir: A History*. New York, NY: Riverhead Trade/Penguin Group.

Young, J. E. 1988. *Writing and Rewriting the Holocaust: Narrative and the Consequences of Interpretation*. Bloomington, IN: Indiana University Press.

———. 1994. *The Texture of Memory: Holocaust Memorials and Meaning*. New Haven, CT: Yale University Press.

Index

Notes: This index covers the content in Parts I and III of this book, but not Part II. Fictional names are indexed under the first name of the character. When the same note number occurs more than once on a page, the chapter that it is from is indicated in parentheses.

About the Authors

Patricia Leavy is an independent scholar, formerly associate professor and chairperson of the Sociology & Criminology Department and the founding director of the Gender Studies Program at Stonehill College in Easton, MA. She is the author of *Iconic Events: Media, Politics, and Power in Retelling History* (2007), *Method Meets Art: Arts-Based Research Practice* (2009), *Essentials of Transdisciplinary Research: Using Problem-Centered Methodologies* (2011), *Oral History: Understanding Qualitative Research* (2011), and the novels *Low-Fat Love* (2011) and *American Circumstance* (forthcoming 2013). She is coauthor of *Feminist Research Practice: A Primer* (2007) and *The Practice of Qualitative Research* (2010, 2nd ed.), and coeditor of *Hybrid Identities: Theoretical and Empirical Examinations* (2008), *Handbook of Emergent Methods* (2008), *Emergent Methods in Social Research* (2006), and *Approaches to Qualitative Research: A Reader on Theory and Practice* (2004). Patricia is also the editor of the Oxford University Press book series Understanding Qualitative Research and of the Sense Publishers book series Social Fictions and Teaching Gender. Leavy was named the New England Sociologist of the Year 2010 by the New England Sociological Association. She also publishes op-eds and is frequently quoted by the media for her expertise on gender and popular culture. For more information please visit www.patricialeavy.com.

Elizabeth Bloom is an associate professor of education at Hartwick College in Oneonta, where she specializes in the social and philosophical foundations of education, pre-service teacher education, and social studies. In addition to writing ethnofiction, her current research interests involve the cultivation of positive character dispositions in pre-service teachers.

Elizabeth de Freitas is an associate professor at Adelphi University. Her research interests include philosophy and cultural studies applied to studies of education. She focuses especially on experiences of mathematics teaching and learning. She is author of the novel *Keel Kissing Bottom* (1997) and coeditor of the book *Opening the Research Text: Critical Insights and In(ter)ventions into Mathematics Education* (2007).

Cheryl Dellasega is a professor of humanities in the College of Medicine and professor of women's studies at Pennsylvania State University, an expert on relational aggression, and the author of many books on issues affecting women: *When Nurses Hurt Nurses* (2011), *Forced to Be Family* (2007), *Mean Girls Grown Up* (2007), *Girl Wars* (2003), *Surviving Ophelia* (2002), and *The Starving Family* (2001). Dr. Dellasega's writing and teaching offer essential insights into the different conflicts that arise in female-to-female relationships.

John L. Vitale is currently an associate professor in the Schulich School of Education at Nipissing University in Brantford, Ontario. As a music education scholar, Dr. Vitale has numerous international publications and conference presentations to his credit. As a professional bass player, Dr. Vitale has performed at over one thousand national and international venues with four different Juno Award-winning artists.